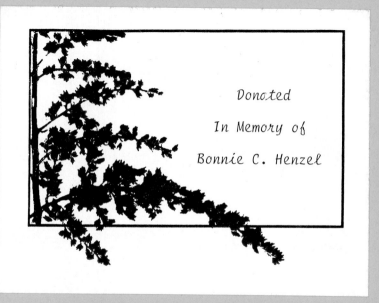

RUNNING SCARED

RUNNING SCARED

How Athletics Lost Its Innocence

STEVEN DOWNES and DUNCAN MACKAY

MAINSTREAM
PUBLISHING PROJECTS

EDINBURGH AND LONDON

ILLUSTRATION CREDIT

All the photographs reproduced in this book are by Mark Shearman and
the authors and publishers are grateful to him for his permission to
reproduce them

Copyright © 1996, Steven Downes and Duncan Mackay

First published in Great Britain in 1996 by
MAINSTREAM PUBLISHING PROJECTS LTD
7 Albany Street
Edinburgh EH1 3UG

ISBN 1 85158 855 8

A catalogue record for this book is available from the British Library

Typeset in Times
Printed and bound in Great Britain by Butler and Tanner Ltd, Frome

CONTENTS

Prologue   7

Chapter One: The Summer of Strife   11

Chapter Two: Dr Linford and Mr Christie   27

Chapter Three: The World-Weary Championships   47

Chapter Four: Death on the Track   58

Chapter Five: Over the Edge   67

Chapter Six: Take the Money and Run   79

Chapter Seven: A King's Ransom   87

Chapter Eight: The Beginning of the End   99

Chapter Nine: The Never-Ending Money-go-Round   113

Chapter Ten: Primo's Plaything   130

Chapter Eleven: From Hero to Zero   144

Chapter Twelve: Guilty Until Proven Innocent   160

Chapter Thirteen: Totalitarian Commitment   173

Chapter Fourteen: Out of Africa   186

Chapter Fifteen: That's Shoe Business   196

Chapter Sixteen: The World's Up and Running   203

Chapter Seventeen: The Rings of Gold   215

PROLOGUE

DALEY THOMPSON was sitting on the wooden bleachers which ran the length of one side of the college athletics track. From his position there, high above the rubberised orange oval, he could look down on the training efforts of the groups of athletes as they sprinted one way and then slowly walked back to their starting point under the fiercely hot mid-morning sun.

The sun was the reason why around a dozen nomadic British sportsmen and women had arrived in southern California just a week earlier that April. It was Olympic year, 1992, and in four months' time, they would be expected to produce the greatest efforts of their short lives. They all intended to be ready, and training in the warmth of California, with the use of the extensive facilities which the University of California at Irvine had to offer, would help them to be ready.

The British athletes at Irvine that year came from three distinct groups: the sprinters and hurdlers from John Isaacs' training group based at Haringey, north London; another group, smaller in number but bigger in terms of the 'names' of the athletes, training under the supervision of Mike Whittingham; and then there was Thompson.

Thompson, possibly the most talented all-round athlete that Britain has ever produced, had the air of a man who had seen it all before. That was probably because he had. The winner of two Olympic decathlon gold medals, three times champion of the Commonwealth, twice European champion and the world champion in 1983, in his pomp Thompson had claimed, with some justification, the title of the world's greatest athlete. But now things were different. It was four years since he had last completed a decathlon, the gruelling two-day combination event where ten disciplines are contested, and this was to be Thompson's last hurrah. Injuries and time had taken their toll: now a 33-year-old husband and father, the fiery temper which had made Thompson notoriously difficult to deal with in his younger years had mellowed into a razor-sharp wit which the athlete made good use of as a television pundit.

It also seemed that perhaps Thompson's desire to compete, and win, had lost its edge. Separated from his wife, Trish, and their daughter for around two months so that he could train for the Games, he was showing willing by being in the modern, sporting form of monastic seclusion at Irvine. But the fact that he was sitting on the sidelines, watching his British team-mates training, rather than being out there working on his own strength and fitness, was perhaps an indicator of his waning desire.

For this was the man who used to break into his locked local athletics track on Christmas Day, theorising that if his rivals were not training, then by putting in another eight-hour day 'at the office', he would gain an extra advantage over them when it came to the championship showdown the following summer. Now, Thompson just watched as down below him, John Regis was harnessed to what looked like a 20-foot elastic band, which Marcus Adam held as if he was about to use his fellow 200-metre sprinter to plough up the track. Regis sprinted hard, the elastic grew taut, and then Adam pitter-pattered after him until the two big men nearly collided at the far end of the track, eventually collapsing in laughter rather than pain. Then they dusted themselves down, picked themselves up and walked back to the other end of the straight to try all over again.

Thompson shared the amusement at this spectacle with a couple of journalists who had been waiting on his every word for more than an hour, yet who had not taken a single note. Both of those details were unusual. In the past, Thompson had barely given *any* journalists the time of day. Here, he was being garrulous, frank and open. Yet he gave away very little. The reason for the lack of notebooks was that this was, Thompson insisted, totally off the record, for information only, totally unattributable.

The journalists were working for a BBC television programme investigating the career of a man whom one of the journalists insisted as tagging 'the Mr Big of athletics': Andy Norman. Their research had taken them to Canada, the Low Countries and now California. Very often, the people approached by the journalists would agree to meet, and then at the last moment cancel. They would agree to send notes of remembered details, letters or copies of contracts, and then decide not to. And when they did talk, they always did so with one proviso: *don't quote me on this, I don't want my name getting back to Andy.*

Thompson, though, was different. No provisos, no pull-out. He met as agreed, ultimately insisting on holding the meeting in the open, where he would be seen talking. This meeting, Thompson insisted earlier, was a preliminary. He wanted to get to know the journalists, to see what they had to say for themselves, before he would agree to be interviewed on camera.

For the journalists, as Thompson probably guessed, this could be the making of the programme. Around the corner, out of sight from the track, was a film crew waiting in their car, ready at short notice to set up and conduct an interview with Thompson. Fortunately for them in the stifling heat, the film crew's car was air conditioned.

Thompson gave nothing away. An anecdote here, an aside there, but he never agreed to be filmed. He acknowledged that he had little to fear: as a decathlete, he was relatively untouched by Norman's seemingly all-pervasive influence on the world of athletics; financially, Thompson was already made for life; and as a competitor at the end of his career, he was hardly at risk.

Eventually, after nearly two hours' discussion in the broiling sun, Thompson said that he had nothing to say. The obvious contradiction seemed lost on him. An appeal to his nobler instincts failed. He felt no 'duty' to the wider interests of the sport or his fellow athletes, he said. Thompson, the arch individualist, restated that in his sport, the only individual to matter was yourself.

He took one final look down at the track, where the athletes' training sessions were coming to an end, where they were warming down, easing away the pain of their earlier efforts, the main part of their day's work done. Norman's power and influence, Thompson said, stretched far and wide, even to the west coast of the United States.

'It's Olympic year,' Thompson said, 'one word out of place and you're out . . . it's too big a risk. They won't speak to you, no one will speak to you,' he said, his hand sweeping across the breadth of the track as if to embrace the whole world of athletics. *'They're all running scared.'*

One

The Summer of Strife

ATHLETICS is in trouble. Scan the sports page headlines during the summer track season and, often, the 'big stories' seem to have little to do with what goes on within the arena or what an athlete accomplishes. Often, the sport seems relegated to a sub-plot for an on-going orgy of celebrity and greed. There have been times when the sport of *Chariots of Fire* has been made to seem more like Chariots of Fear.

It was not always like that. There was a time when athletics had heroes who, despite aspiring to Olympian achievements, still somehow managed to retain their humanity. Their talent helped them to win medals, but it also took sheer hard work and dedication. Nearly 50 years ago, in what seems now another age, Emil Zatopek was one of athletics' greatest human heroes.

Zatopek was an officer in the Czech army who won four Olympic distance running gold medals, including a unique treble of 5,000 and 10,000 metres and marathon golds at the Helsinki Games of 1952. His head-rolling, grimacing style while churning out lap after lap in the lead of his races made him popular wherever he raced, the crowds usually responding by chanting his name, 'Zat-o-pek, Zat-o-pek', rhythmically throughout his races. For six years, from 1948, Zatopek proved he was unbeatable by remaining unbeaten over 10,000 metres.

Zatopek's achievements were based on simple, hard work. At a time when many athletes still believed that they should conserve their precious energies, like delicate, highly strung greyhounds, only going out for a few gentle strides as 'training' twice a week, Zatopek instead went out in army boots for long yomps through the forests outside Prague, often with the snow knee-deep. He would run up to 100 miles in training each week. Even at the Helsinki Olympics, where he ran and won three track races in four days, Zatopek still went for a training run on the rest day.

'Emil Zatopek isn't human in his achievements,' said Roger Bannister, the British 1,500-metre runner in Helsinki who two years later was to ensure his own athletics immortality by becoming the first to run a mile in less than four minutes. 'While he goes out for a 20-mile run on his only free day, we lie here panting and moaning that the gods are unkind to us.' And on the last day of the Games, Zatopek, running in his first marathon, won gold again. But Zatopek's greatness was also founded in his humanity. In 1968, during the Prague uprising against the Soviet troops who had occupied Czechoslovakia, Zatopek – nearly a decade after he had retired from the track and despite his position within the army – came out on to the streets to try to stop the tanks mowing down protesting students.

Some time later, Ron Clarke, the great Australian distance runner, was in Prague to compete at a track meeting. Despite Clarke's record-breaking exploits, the Australian had never won an Olympic gold medal, principally because at the Mexico City Games in 1968 he had had little chance of a 'fair' race in the thin air of Mexico's high altitude against runners who had been born and brought up in mountainous regions. Clarke, the world record-holder, finished the 10,000 metres tailed off. He had to be carried from the track on a stretcher, an oxygen mask clasped to his face, his team doctor in tears because he thought that Clarke was dying, that he had literally run himself into the ground.

Fortunately, Clarke did recover, but years later, when Clarke required open heart surgery, the consultant attributed the ex-runner's condition to the effort and strain of hard running in that race staged at 7,000 feet above sea level. Clarke's quest for Olympic gold had, according to his surgeon, broken his heart.

It was not the first time Clarke had been burnt by coming too close to the Olympic flame. Twelve years before Mexico, when the Games had been staged in Melbourne, Clarke, as a promising young miler, was selected to carry the Olympic torch into the Melbourne Cricket Ground for the opening ceremony of the 1956 Games. While proudly holding the torch aloft, a mischievous breeze caught the flame and it lapped at the runner's arm, burning his skin. Clarke grimaced, but continued on his way. Metaphorically, at least, it would not be the last time Clarke was scarred by the Olympic experience.

In later years, Clarke and Zatopek became firm friends, each with mutual admiration for the other runner's achievements, and the audacious, unrestrained manner in which they were accomplished. When Clarke visited Czechoslovakia for the first time after the uprising, he was concerned about his old friend's state of health. The Soviets had withdrawn all the Czechoslovakian hero's privileges. Sweden offered Zatopek a way out, with a $10,000 a year coaching post, but he proudly declined. 'Why should

I leave? This is my home, Czechoslovakia is my country. Why should I go anywhere else?'

After Clarke had raced in Prague and was making his way to the next venue in his annual summer tour of the tracks of Europe, Zatopek accompanied the big Australian to the airport. Surrounded by guards armed with machine-guns, the atmosphere in the terminal was one of fear and suspicion. Zatopek, in all probability, was being watched. Nonetheless, he managed to slip a small packet into Clarke's jacket pocket. 'I want you to take this to remember me, because you deserve it,' Zatopek told Clarke, asking him not to open the package until he was safely out of the country. Clarke was bemused: what could it be? Why the secrecy? Was Zatopek getting him to smuggle something out of the country? Once the plane was safely airborne, Clarke reached into his pocket, pulled out the package and opened it. Inside was an Olympic gold medal, the medal Zatopek had won for the 10,000 metres at the 1952 Helsinki Games. The inscription read: 'To Ron Clarke, from Emil Zatopek'.

Emil Zatopek is one of those rare people who transcend the sporting condition, to become a hero, perhaps even a 'legend', yet retain their basic humanity. Being a good person was more important to Emil Zatopek than being a good runner. Athletics, after all, was his sport.

Even in today's often cynical times, athletics still offers a beautiful simplicity. It is the sport based on the most basic human activities, which everyone can readily understand. In athletics, the winner was the person who could run fastest, who could throw furthest, who could jump highest or longest. Simple.

It was the sport which produced so many fine champions, so many great deeds, so many memorable sporting moments which would become part of sporting legend. Among the first was Dorando Pietri, whose collapse at the end of the Olympic Marathon in London in 1908 did so much to capture the public's imagination that it effectively institutionalised the marathon's distance at the oddly chosen 26 miles 385 yards, which was used for that race from Windsor to London for no better reason than to give the Royal Family a better view of the finish in the White City stadium.

In the 1920s, the world was to be equally amazed by the feats Paavo Nurmi and the other 'Flying Finns' who dominated distance running events for a decade, and then the watching public was in utter awe as the sprinter Jesse Owens won four gold medals to defy the Nazis at Hitler's Olympics of 1936.

Fanny Blankers-Koen, Roger Bannister and John Landy, Jim Peters and his version of a desperate Dorando in the heat of Vancouver in 1954, the unbeatable Herb Elliott, Lynn Davies, Mary Rand and Ann Packer, David Hemery and Bob Beamon: through the 1940s, 1950s and 1960s, all were to join sport's pantheon of athletics heroes. Then things began to change.

It is perhaps the most telling of contrasts that, in 1956, despite having had a hernia operation shortly before the Games, Emil Zatopek nonetheless went to the Melbourne Olympics, to try to defend at least one of his Olympic titles, and was placed sixth in the marathon. For Zatopek, the Olympic ideal still held true: 'The most important thing in the Olympic Games is not to win but to take part, just as the most important thing in life is not the triumph but the struggle. The essential thing is not to have conquered but to have fought well'.

This epigram was warmly adopted by the founder of the modern Olympics, Baron Pierre de Coubertin, when he was at the London Games in 1908. Yet before the century was over, such noble sentiments seemed to be cast aside by a more cynical, calculating sporting society. 'As far as I'm concerned, the man who said "It's not the winning that matters but the taking part", was a loser,' said none other than Linford Christie.

During the 1980s and 1990s, track and field athletics at international level, such as the Olympic Games and Grand Prix spectacular meetings which millions of people watch on television, has undergone more fundamental changes to the way it is operated than had occurred in the entire first century of its history as an organised sport. The essential simplicity of the sport has been undermined by official incompetence and complicity, by greed and venality. There has been chicanery and cheating, and the end result has been a sport riddled with doubt. No longer is the fastest runner necessarily the winner of the race, nor is the longest jump guaranteed to win a medal. Too often, the best throw in a competition may be discounted, disqualified some months later.

No longer is the sport simply an extension of the running race every child tries when in their school playground. Now it is a multi-national, multi-million dollar business, and the first thing for sale is the sport's morality. For athletics is the sport that disqualified the winner of its Blue Riband event at the 1988 Olympics, but let him back in time to compete at the 1992 Games. It is the sport where officials at the 1987 World Championships in Rome were ordered to 'lengthen' the measurement of a long jump to make sure an Italian got a bronze medal. It is the sport which, at the World Championships in Tokyo in 1991, deliberately ignored its own rules on the construction and composition of tracks in order to allow a super-fast surface which helped to ensure world records in both the men's 100 metres and the long jump.

Athletics is also the sport which at the 1990 European Championships chose to 'reinstate' one British runner in the final of the 1,500 metres, even though he had failed to finish his heat, just because he was one of the favourites for gold. It is the sport where officials in Britain 'arranged' drug tests to make sure no one got caught, and when they did, it covered up the test results so that no one found out.

It is the sport where at some meetings athletes were deliberately excluded, or where races were 'fixed' with bribes, to guarantee the 'required' outcome. And it is the sport where one man became so convinced of his own power and importance that, according to an official coroner's enquiry, he felt able to threaten and terrorise another to the point of suicide.

Athletics is the sport which, after a century of Olympics, has lost its innocence.

In the past, athletics had at least *appeared* to be a bastion of amateurism and Olympism. From the first Games in Athens in 1896, which had used the Games of ancient Greece as its model, athletics was the principal sport at the Olympics. There was nothing simpler in sport, purer in its ideal, than the running, jumping and throwing contests. *Citius, Altius, Fortius* is still the Olympic motto.

Not that track and field athletics had always expressed such ideals so nobly. In the early 19th century, when athletics in England was an increasingly popular pastime but the rules had yet to be properly formulated, there were instances of athletes taking bribes to throw races on which there had been heavy gambling coups, of promoters who 'fixed' the handicap systems, and of other competitors taking 'secret potions' to get an added edge over their rivals. Only by the end of the 20th century, when similarly extravagant amounts of money were once again at stake, would a similar degree of corruption be rediscovered within the sport.

In Georgian and Victorian England, athletics was spectacularly popular. In 1809, more than 10,000 spectators flocked to Newmarket Heath in Cambridgeshire to see Captain Barclay Allardice attempt to cover 1,000 miles in 1,000 hours. They were hardly there for the excitement or spectacle: betting was the draw. For Captain Barclay, who succeeded in his feat, the reward was handsome indeed, £16,000 (at least £1 million at 1996 values).

It was the formation of the Amateur Athletic Association in 1880 that was to turn athletics into a sport that was 'respectable' by the standards of the time. Much of what is universal in athletics today was initiated by the Victorian gentlemen who founded the AAA. Class conscious, they shunned the artisans and labourers who would only compete for money; by making the sport for amateurs only, they made it impossible for the working class to compete, simply because they could not afford to. The AAA codified the basic track and field programme, and when the modern Olympics were staged for the first time in 1896, they used the AAA Laws for Competition. Such impressive acceptance of the AAA Laws ensured that betting was outlawed and payments to athletes would be forbidden throughout the world for nearly a century.

For many thousands of athletes over that first 100 years of organised athletics, the sport was their pastime, their hobby. For a few of those, it was their all-consuming passion. They might never make the Olympics but, for them, beating their previous best performance was satisfying enough. Sometimes that might have meant moving on to greater things, such as selection to compete for their country, and that was more than welcome.

But for the majority of athletes, the sense of perspective was always maintained: it was just a sport.

These athletes might train at the track every Tuesday and Thursday, come rain or shine, hail or snow, and compete each weekend. After their time as competitors, some of them might have stayed with their club as a coach, or become an official judge or timekeeper, perhaps helped to organise the club's affairs. Like most sports at a grass roots level, no one did these sort of things with any reward in mind. They did it because they enjoyed doing it. But through the 1980s and 1990s, athletics at the élite level steadily became part of the entertainment industry, just like any other professional sport. International athletes became highly paid performers, some of them becoming millionaires. Yet this new professional sport continued to exist within an amateur structure. By 1995, it was this dichotomy which was threatening to tear British athletics apart.

Whatever way you look at it, 15p per mile travel allowance is not in the Linford Christie league for earnings from athletics. Yet that was all Gordon Dixon, one of Christie's predecessors as a sprinter for Thames Valley Harriers, got for his hours of effort as an official at the London Grand Prix extravaganza at Crystal Palace one hot night in July 1995.

It was in 1985 that international athletics introduced a set of new eligibility rules which at last permitted athletes to be paid openly for competing, although only a handful of international, 'star' athletes would benefit. At first, there was not much money available, and even among the top performers many kept their 'proper' jobs, and continued to train and compete in their spare time. Only a very few were able to become what was euphemistically called 'full-time athletes'. The sport still shied away from the word 'professional'. But sure enough, athletics during the 1980s finally went pro.

Not only could athletes legitimately earn money from 'endorsements' by lending their name to a product for advertising without fear of the ultimate sanction, of being banned from the next Olympic Games, but they could even be paid a fee for competing at certain top invitation meetings. With television and sponsors eager to invest in track and field athletics during the 1980s, meetings such as Zurich, Oslo and Cologne were soon openly offering tens of thousands of dollars to the big name draw cards such as Steve Cram, Carl Lewis and Edwin Moses. So much so that, by the summer of 1995, the organisers of the top 15 meetings on the international Grand Prix circuit paid a total of £10 million in appearance fees for athletes. The London Grand Prix, staged at Crystal Palace that July, had one of the smaller overall budgets that year, about £650,000 in total. Of that sum, the majority was spent on the athletes. Although there could be no meeting without the officials, timekeepers and track judges, it meant that there was little left over to be paid to the likes of Gordon Dixon.

Dixon is typical of the legion of unsung heroes in athletics who, just for the love of the sport, give up their time and energy to organise track and field meetings. At the very highest levels of the sport, such officials do at least get their out-of-pocket expenses reimbursed, plus a small food allowance or a cardboard box of sandwiches, and sometimes, if they are very lucky, perhaps a waterproof, nylon jacket in the garish colour-scheme of the event sponsors.

Then, from the in-field at these élite events, officials like Dixon can watch as top stars race past them on the track, sometimes earning five-figure sums by the second. The division between the haves and have nots in athletics has yet to be reconciled. In the main, the sport is still administered by enthusiastic amateurs in their spare time. Every day, they confront mundane, seemingly trivial problems in the running of their area association, their county, or their club, and rarely do they command the means with which to deal with them.

While the Linford Christies of this world may demand £50,000 per meeting, much of the rest of the sport is struggling just to make ends meet. In 1995, the British Athletic Federation – BAF, the governing body for the whole sport in Britain – decided to make a stand against the ever-rising fees demanded by a few star athletes. The result was a summer-long feud between the BAF and the Olympic sprint champion Christie and his business partner, Colin Jackson, the sprint hurdles world record-holder. By the end of the summer, Christie and Jackson had raced in only two of BAF's programme of televised meetings, their 'strike' at British events splitting the sport right down the middle, with Jackson vowing never again to race at a BAF meeting as long as Peter Radford remained executive chairman of the federation.

But it was not only in Britain that meeting promoters, feeling the pinch between the spiralling demands of athletes and a decline in television and sponsor revenues, had begun to cut back in their spending. In Oslo, since the early 1970s, the climax of the Bislett Games had always been the Dream Mile. Coe, Ovett, Cram, Elliott, Walker, Wessinghage had all taken part in the Dream Mile, the world record always seeming to be in danger of revision in Oslo. In many years, that one race had been the highlight of the entire season. Yet in 1995 there was no Dream Mile at Oslo.

By 1995, the greatest middle distance runner of the moment, Noureddine Morceli, held six world records, including the mile, and was so far ahead of all of his rivals that it seemed that no one else could threaten the Algerian's world marks. Morceli, though, does not come cheap, demanding up to £50,000, plus bonuses for records, to race. Sven-Arne Hansen, the Oslo meeting promoter, was unable to afford such an amount for just one athlete. He decided that no Dream Mile would be better than a Dream Mile without Morceli.

Yet there are still huge sums being paid at some meetings. Res Brügger, the former banker who now organises the Zurich Weltklasse, the richest meeting of the year – dubbed 'the three-hour Olympics', and not without reason – had £3 million to spend on athletes' appearance fees, by far the biggest meeting budget in 1995. Zurich's huge budget is a factor which forced other meeting promoters to compete for the top athletes.

Thus the promoter of the Paris meeting, despite the indifferent form of Carl Lewis, the world's most be-medalled athlete, decided that $100,000, ten per cent of his entire athletes' budget, was not too much to pay for the American to race in the 100 metres against Christie, the man who had succeeded Lewis as world and Olympic champion. In the event, Lewis finished the race struggling in fifth place, behind Christie, and three other sprinters, none of whom was paid one-fifth of the American's fee. With the stands of the new Stade Charlety nonetheless half empty, Paris's $100,000 gamble had failed to pay off.

Unlike Paris, the organisers of the biggest meetings in Britain opted not to 'up the ante' on athletes' fees. But the stand taken in Britain during the long hot summer of 1995 was more than just an argument over athletes' wages. In many respects, it represented the latest stage in the battle for the sport's integrity.

In athletics' first ten years of professionalism, a strange, arcane system of 'subventions' had grown up, mainly as a result of the sport's continuing coyness about paying large sums of money to its leading performers. Under this subvention system, star quality was rewarded, but not actual performance. The meeting promoters would decide on an athlete's worth, and agree a fee with the competitor or their agent in advance of the meeting. Athletes were being paid to appear, not to compete. The sport's values soon began to warp.

It was the subventions system, of paying for reputation, which saw Zola Budd race in a £150,000 mismatch against Mary Decker-Slaney at Crystal Palace in 1985. Budd, the gangling, South African-born teenager, had brought down the American Slaney, the world champion, in the Olympic 3,000 metres final in Los Angeles the year before. The American's supporters in the LA Coliseum's stands were outraged and afterwards Budd was pilloried. The re-match at Crystal Palace was sold to television (in Britain, the United States and South Africa) as Slaney's chance for revenge. The meeting was even extended to a second day, with the Budd-Slaney race staged late on the Saturday night to suit American TV. 'This is the re-match the world has been waiting for,' the meeting promoter, Andy Norman, announced confidently. When Norman had phoned Budd to arrange the race, he asked her how much it would take for her to run against Mary. 'I just said £90,000,' Zola recalled, 'because I thought it was such an outrageous amount they would never pay it. I didn't want the race.' Norman agreed immediately. 'I wished I'd asked for more,' Zola said. It was soon discovered that Slaney was to be paid £60,000.

In the event, it was never really a contest. Budd was woefully out of form and struggled to finish fourth, while Slaney was never really challenged. Even that was engineered to get the right ending for TV, too. Maricica Puica, the Romanian who had actually finished and won the infamous race in Los Angeles, desperately wanted to race against Slaney. Because of the American's tumble, she felt she had been denied the acclaim she was due for winning the gold medal. Yet the Olympic champion was offered just $2,000 to take part in 'the re-match the world has been waiting for'. It was an offer the Romanian federation refused to accept.

Rewarding notoriety and reputation, rather than performance, is anathema to the essence of athletics, in which the stopwatch or the tape measure used to be the only things to determine who is the winner. As Mel Watman reported on the Budd-Slaney race for *Athletics Weekly*, 'The Peugeot Talbot Games, Britain's first Grand Prix meeting, was to provide a glimpse of the shape of international athletics spectaculars of the future. It did . . . and gave cause for deep concern. For all the publicity hype and astronomical sums of money involved, the end result fell far below what the public had the right to expect.'

This system of subventions had another effect, too. It invested power and influence not in the athletes themselves, but in a small band of promoters and agents. These promoters and agents were able to dictate their own terms to athletes, and wield supreme power and influence. As Lord Acton suggested, such power corrupts.

When in 1995 BAF's Peter Radford and his new team came along with a set of fresh ideas, they did not receive an overwhelming welcome. There were some within the sport who had too many vested interests in maintaining the *status quo*. There were those who, perhaps, wanted those in charge at BAF to fail, and to be seen to fail. Over the previous 20 years, there were some who had built up a profitable little empire within athletics, and they had too much to lose.

So it was that 1995 became British athletics' 'Summer of Strife'. By the middle of 1995, Professor Peter Radford had been in post as executive chairman of the British Athletic Federation at their Birmingham headquarters for 18 months. It was a period characterised by crisis management.

On his desk waiting for him when the former head of Glasgow University's physical education department moved into his new office in February 1994 was a report about his promotions director, Andy Norman, and allegations that Norman had issued threats against journalist Cliff Temple which led to Temple's suicide in January 1994. Eventually, Norman – the promotions officer who had staged the notorious Budd-Slaney re-match and who was to become known as the most powerful man in British athletics – was dismissed.

After barely a month in office, Radford then had a show-down with Frank Dick, British athletics' chief coach for 15 years. Dick publicly objected to cutbacks in his coaching budget. In the past, Dick had often spoken openly of resignation. Whether he was bluffing on this occasion can only be guessed. But this time he had his notice to quit accepted. It was clear that Radford was determined to stamp his own authority on the running of athletics in Britain, a sport which had always been resistant to change and modernisation.

Until 1990, British athletics was organised by 16 different governing bodies in a confusing miasma of administration, full of duplication, as well as conflicting and contradicting interests. The AAA, the oldest athletics body in the world, which still governed the affairs of men's athletics in clubs throughout England, was the richest and most powerful, and was not alone in its reluctance to cede its independence and authority to a new group. But after 30 years of debate, wrangling, consultation reports and more discussion, the sport finally, if somewhat reluctantly, came together under the umbrella of a single federation, the BAF, in 1991.

Yet the new federation was not immune from disaster and internal strife. Malcolm Jones, the first appointment as chief executive, seemed unable to control the two big characters within his organisation, Norman and Dick. Nor was Jones, despite his accountancy background, able to turn around the sport's suddenly dwindling finances. A high-profile campaign saw the election of a group of new officers, with Radford voted in as the honorary chairman. Within a year, Jones had been ousted and Radford offered the £60,000 per year new post of executive chairman, ahead of all other candidates.

Superficially, it seemed to be a dream job, heading up what, after the golden successes of the Barcelona Olympics in 1992 and the 1993 World Championships in Stuttgart, was Britain's most successful sport. But Radford knew that there were underlying problems. 'You can't hide behind the top athletes doing well on the international stage and say that because of that, everything must be all right,' he said. Having faced down Norman and Dick in his first year, Radford chose his second summer in the post to draw a line in the sand over athletes' payments.

The London Grand Prix meeting in July 1995 was the first in which the executive chairman and his new promotions manager, Ian Stewart, used a revolutionary new system of payments linked directly to performance. Instead of deals being made in dark corners of smoky rooms, with a brown envelope stuffed full of used notes being passed over to the athlete at the end of the night, the new system used a complex chart and table setting out exactly what times or distances were worth in pounds and pence. The payments chart was even distributed to the press and public.

It was perhaps the first stage towards a fully open and public system of prize money. With many Grand Prix meetings becoming staid and formulaic, and with attendances down, prize money was seen by Radford and Stewart as possibly the thing to rekindle the public's excitement once more. Above all, it would mean that performance, not reputation, would be the deciding factor in athletes' payments, giving the new kids in their starting blocks the same chance of boosting their earnings as the other, more established athletes. BAF also wanted to link the performance-related pay scheme in with two other documents, one a code of conduct, the other an athlete's contract.

Not all the athletes welcomed the new, formalised approach to negotiations. Colin Jackson, unable, because of illness, to race at the London Grand Prix, felt that some of the contract was too demanding. 'The conditions presented to me were far too restrictive when it came to my racing programme. The BAF wanted to tie me down completely for their five meetings this season with no leeway at all,' said the then 110 metres hurdles world champion. His comment perhaps belied a lack of understanding of the concept of a contract, even though a year earlier he had willingly been 'tied down' to racing in, and winning at, all the Golden Four series of meetings on the continent in order to collect his share of the £160,000 special bullion bonus on offer to winners of the 'grand slam of athletics'. There was no leeway on offer then if he did not compete in the full series.

One of the biggest losers in Radford's shake-up of athletes' payments was John Regis. The former European 200 metres champion had been badly affected by injury in 1994 and spent the summer of 1995 struggling, in vain, to return to form. Regis is a close friend of Christie and Jackson, and a client of their Nuff Respect agency. If his payments for 1995 were to be determined by performance, rather than reputation, he could be hit hard in the pocket.

Negotiations between BAF and Nuff Respect, on behalf of Regis, Christie and Jackson, failed to be resolved until July, too late for any of them to race at the Grand Prix meeting at Crystal Palace. Regis was furious. 'The deal was struck too late. It should have been sorted out ages ago. We have world and Olympic medals and we don't expect to be treated unprofessionally. We shouldn't have children at the highest points of the sport,' he said. 'They tried to treat us like children. They wanted us to run before they would tell us how much they would pay us. It's ridiculous.' Under the published new performance criteria, by the end of the season Regis stood to take a drop from £12,000 per race in Britain in 1995 to just £800 in 1996.

Such drastic rationalisation may be too late. The Golden Decade for British athletics was the 1980s, from the time Coe, Ovett, Wells and Thompson enjoyed Olympic successes in Moscow, through to the Great Britain team dominating the European Championships in Split in 1990. Such success brought vast riches to the sport, with an estimated £35 million pouring into British athletics' coffers from 1985 to 1995. Yet while Christie & Co have become millionaires from the sport – Christie's personal wealth by 1995 was estimated by *Business Age* magazine at £3.1 million – little had made its way down to the grass roots of the sport, the clubs.

The excuse often provided was that the 'shop window' of the sport – that is, the televised spectacular meetings – had to be kept attractive in order to keep television content and in turn bring in more sponsors and more money. In time, it was argued in a sporting version of 'trickledown economics', that even the lowliest parts of British athletics would see the cash benefits. But after ten years, the theory was widely discredited, as British athletics had very little to show from the £20 million investment from television and the estimated £15 million in sponsorship revenue generated in that time.

An amateur sport which professionalises both its competitions and administration obviously creates tensions. Even so, track officials such as Gordon Dixon tend not to be envious. 'We got £5 a day for refreshments, a track suit and a pair of trainers. Normally we don't get anything,' Dixon said, with surprise, of the modest treatment he received when officiating at an earlier international event staged at Crystal Palace, the World Cup of September 1994.

One of the biggest problems for British athletics, in fact, is that there are not enough Gordon Dixons to go around.

The weekend before the 1995 London Grand Prix, there were another 120 athletics meetings going on around the country, involving thousands of athletes, at national championship level, in schools events, in inter-club leagues, in road races and fell runs. It was the same the following weekend, and continued every summer weekend until October. And then the cross-country season started. All such meetings require volunteers, to time the races, to measure jumps and throws, to make the teas, or to drive the club mini-bus. Without them, British athletics would grind to a halt. Committee meetings at most of the country's 1,700 affiliated clubs have familiar themes: Where are we to find new members? Who is to coach them? Where are we to find officials? And where are we to get the cash to pay for transport to next weekend's league match?

British athletics allowed the marathon boom of the early 1980s, which might have brought vast numbers of new people into organised athletics, to pass it by, almost unnoticed. Sometimes there was even a sense that some clubs deliberately ignored the running boom, not wanting to get involved in any way with 'mere joggers'. 'This is an *athletics* association, we're not here for joggers,' one senior official announced to a Southern Counties AAA committee meeting in 1985. A rich source of new blood, and funding, was lost to athletics forever.

The sport was also guilty of doing too little too late to recruit youngsters inspired by the deeds of Seb Coe, Steve Backley or Sally Gunnell. With school PE teachers no longer willing to act as unpaid recruitment officers for athletics clubs, new members became harder than ever to come by. One indicator was the all-time low for entries at the annual county championships, staged in May 1995.

Yorkshire, the county which had produced Mick Hill, the 1993 World Championships bronze medallist, had only two entries for its junior men's javelin championship in 1995. In Surrey, the total number of women's entries in all events was half that of 1985. Yet Surrey had been one of a number of counties in the south of England which for three years had had a full-time, professional development officer working within its borders in an attempt to halt such decline.

'The parlous state of Britain's field events', in the words of Malcolm Arnold, the man who succeeded Frank Dick as Britain's chief coach, is another way of measuring the sport's (poor) health. When BAF announced its selections for the 1995 European Junior Championships, only six field event athletes were among the 29 who had achieved the qualifying standards, hardly strength in depth among the up-and-coming generation of those likely to be representing Britain at the Olympic Games in 2000.

Yet superficially, things seem fine. On the same weekend as the London Grand Prix was staged there was also the biggest annual athletics meeting in the country, the English Schools' Championships. Over the two days, Nottingham's Harvey Hadden stadium probably did not appear any different for the guest of honour, Steve Cram, from the time when, as a gangling teenager 16 years before, he had run down the home straight of the same track, to set a championship best and collect one of his first gold medals.

Also a medallist at Nottingham in 1979 was Linford Christie, second to Phil Brown in the 200 metres. Yet there have been many changes behind the scenes at the English Schools' since Linford was a lad. Phrases which may have become familiar to Christie during the summer of 1995 – about not spending more than can be afforded – were also being heard at the Schools'. For the first time, the rising cost of billeting athletes (competitors from outside the organising area lodging for two or three nights with local parents) meant that some counties had their team allocations cut so that the overall number of competitors was kept to a 'more manageable' 1,500.

That is 1,500 youngsters, aged between 12 and 19, who are already mustard keen athletes, and often very talented. If you take a look below that élite level, though, and the sport is slowly suffocating for a lack of new athletes, coaches and officials. David Littlewood is an official with a vast depth and breadth of experience. As well as serving as the secretary of the English Schools' Athletic Association, in 1994 he was the chief technical official at the European Championships in Helsinki. At a more mundane level, he has been treasurer of his south London club, Hercules Wimbledon, for 35 years. 'Without doubt, the number of youngsters that become committed athletes is definitely going down,' Littlewood says. Thus, a week before his busiest time of the year, Littlewood was bemused when he received a copy of *Athletics 21*, sent by Peter Radford to all clubs. The 16-page document, BAF's strategic plan for the 21st century, was full of worthy sounding phrases and theories. Yet, as a 'discussion document', it was lacking in concrete proposals. David Littlewood was unimpressed. 'We were very disappointed at the lack of references to school athletics and to how it can function as part of the continuum in athletics,' he says.

A few miles across south London from Littlewood's home, at Crystal Palace's National Sports Centre, on the evening before the Grand Prix meeting was staged there, and Blackheath Harriers were having their weekly training night. There, the disenchantment with the sport's leadership was more pronounced. On the Friday night, with all the paraphernalia and razzmatazz of the Grand Prix, all may have appeared to be fine on television. But just 24 hours before the glitz and glamour of the televised spectacular, when the same Crystal Palace track was being used for an ordinary club training night, athletics' national stadium of the past 25 years looked tired and weary.

The facilities at what passes for a National Sports Centre are, by European standards, poor. There is a shed, about 100 metres long, which is used as an indoor sprints and jumps training area. In the winter months, it is always cramped and overcrowded: high jumpers darting here, hurdlers breezing past them, pole vaulters trying not to knock themselves out on the low ceiling. Yet it is the only indoor facility of its kind for winter indoor athletics training in Britain's capital city. However, even that may not be available within five years. Maintenance costs for Crystal Palace – which has one of the country's few Olympic-size swimming pools as well as the sports stadium to run – are so high that one of the local councils that border on to the sports centre has even proposed that, once the Sports Council's lease expires at the end of the century, the whole complex should be bulldozed.

Despite such problems, Blackheath's die-hards stoically get on with their training. They pay for the privilege, and use the track up to three times a week during the summer. That's on top of their £40 annual membership fee, plus kit costs (£20 a vest), spikes (£50 per pair), training shoes (at least another £50 per pair), and travel and accommodation charges for away fixtures.

Blackheath, as one of the country's oldest clubs, is also one of its most successful. Tradition has not been allowed to get in the way of achievement. In 1995, Blackheath's senior men's teams won the coveted National Cross-country Championship and 12-stage Road Relay title, a rare and distinguished 'double'. In the summer, their track team competed in Division One of the National League, while their young athletes' squad won the national title for a record seventh consecutive time. Yet Blackheath are on the verge of bankruptcy.

The cost of travelling to and entering team competitions is crippling, the problems of recruiting new members and unearthing officials worsening. 'It's the price of success,' one club official admits.

Blackheath faced a five-figure deficit by the end of 1995. 'We'll find a way of funding it,' Steve Cluney, a past president and coach, says, 'we always do. We'll economise, we'll do fund raisers. But it's never easy.'

Cluney works in the City of London with an asset finance group. Despite two years' efforts, he was unable to find a sponsor for the club. The club's coaching scheme was saved when a keen parent of one of the members put up £1,500 from his own firm, the amount doubled with money from SportsMatch, a government scheme designed to encourage more commercial involvement in sport. But that still left around £8,000 for the club to find.

'Money is hard to come by for all businesses, and you have to think in terms of what any company backing the club would get from an amateur sport,' Cluney says. Thames Valley Harriers, one of Blackheath's National League rivals, wear a sponsors' name on their club vests in return for a five-year deal worth £40,000. But then, one of their members, Linford Christie, sometimes wears Thames Valley's vest when appearing on television. The commercial return is there for all to see.

Blackheath, therefore, must hope that their Julian Golding, the 20-year-old who raced instead of Christie in the 200 metres at Crystal Palace's Grand Prix meeting, starts to enjoy a similarly high profile. And soon. 'We don't begrudge Linford his money,' Cluney says, 'but when you hear them discussing the difference between £35,000 and £50,000 for one race, it does make you wonder . . .'

Golding is a product of Blackheath's all-conquering youth programme. It is here, though, that Blackheath find they have the biggest drain on their finances. In the summer of 1995, Blackheath's 25-strong junior team faced away fixtures as far away as Middlesbrough, Telford and Birmingham. 'With matches starting at 10 a.m.,' Cluney says, 'overnight stays are necessary. We don't stop at the Ritz, but each trip still costs about £1,000. And then, as champions, we represent Britain in Europe. In 1994, we had to go to Poland. That cost £5,000. It's the price of success, I suppose.'

BAF pitched in with half of Blackheath's cost to go to Poland but as champions again, Blackheath faced similar costs in 1995 and 1996, and while BAF might again pay half, it still left the club members having to scrimp and save, organising whist drives and tombolas, to find up to £3,000 to be able to send a team abroad to represent the nation.

Therein is the dilemma for any go-ahead club. To find new talent, they need to run a developed coaching scheme and have a high percentage of teenaged and student members, many of whom may never graduate to senior ranks. 'And they are exactly the ones who can least afford to pay their way,' says Cluney.

Yet it is only by sending club coaches into schools, looking for talent, that the next generation of British athletics champions are likely to be unearthed. There is rarely any funding for such schemes. There was not even any money available to send personal coaches with their athletes to the European Junior Championships, staged in Hungary in 1995. Staged for athletes aged under 20, Britain has an unrivalled medal-winning record at these championships, but very little seems to be learnt from those successes.

Other nations at the European Junior Championships have schemes to assist financially personal coaches to travel with their younger athletes. Not only does it help the athletes through what may be a nerve-wracking ordeal at their first international championship, it also helps the coaches to learn about what it takes to succeed internationally. Britain in 1995, as it had been for nearly 30 years, was reliant on Sir Eddie Kulukundis, a millionaire athletics fan who helped to pay for the travel costs for two young coaches to see their charges win medals at the European Juniors.

Against such personal generosity, BAF's total coaching budget for 1995 was £700,000, not even ten per cent of the sport's £7.2 million turnover. It is a similar pattern in all declining British industries, which find themselves struggling to compete internationally through lack of investment for the future.

Even junior success is no guarantee against senior disillusionment. When Matt Simson was 19, he won the bronze medal in the shot putt at the European Juniors. Five years later, he had progressed to become champion of the Commonwealth. Another 12 months on, though, and he had quit the sport altogether, finally defeated by despair, a young man who knows he is being cheated at every turn.

'I knew that if I wanted to be the best in the world, to win a medal at the Atlanta Olympics, I had to start taking anabolic steroids,' Simson says. 'I had to make a difficult choice, and in the end I decided I could not live with myself as a drugs cheat, so I turned my back on the sport I love.

'At the end of 1994, I could say to myself, "I'm probably in the top six clean athletes in the shot putt this year", but who cares? It did not mean anything to anybody because I might be ranked fortieth in the world.

'Most people look at athletics and think it is a glamorous sport. In reality it is very mercenary. I only ever really got involved in sport because it was fun. But all that has gone. Athletics has created a monster that is out of control. Club athletics is still wholesome and enjoyable, but at international level the sport is very different. The need for sensation and new records to maintain the flow of money comes first, the health of the athletes a poor second.'

Simson's is a depressing but increasingly common viewpoint. Despite their own complaints, it is probable that officials and coaches such as Gordon Dixon, Dave Littlewood and Steve Cluney will carry on working in athletics long after Linford Christie has retired. It is, after all, their *sport*. The problem which remains to be answered is whether they can continue to keep British athletics running on just 15p per mile.

Two

Dr Linford and Mr Christie

LINFORD CHRISTIE is unarguably the greatest sprinter Britain has ever produced. It is possible that history might eventually adjudge him to be the greatest British athlete of all time. For Christie has a massive haul of honours, including an Olympic gold and two silver medals, a world championship, three European titles, and three Commonwealth Games gold medals. Certainly, Christie's medal collection – 27 international championship and cup golds by the end of 1995, accumulated during an unusually long international career that lasted for nearly a decade – looks unlikely ever to be bettered. Yet it might have all been so different had an official hearing into his conduct at the Seoul Olympics in 1988 not gone in Christie's favour by just one vote.

Christie has never made any secret of the fact that the trauma of being accused of using a performance enhancing drug after a doping control test following the 200 metres in Seoul was the worst day of his life. It was bad enough just being accused.

Had the decision of the International Olympic Committee's medical commission gone the other way Christie might have been stripped of the Olympic silver medal he had been awarded after the infamous 100 metres final at those Games; he would have been barred from racing for Britain in the 4x100 metres relay the following day, when he won his second silver and he would have been banned for three months. Such a set-back may have stopped him ever becoming British team captain, and it might have even seen him prevented from competing for Britain at another Olympic Games, including Barcelona, where he won the 100 metres gold medal. The course of Christie's career would have been radically altered by that vote.

The 100 metres final at the 1988 Olympics in Seoul had provided the most famous drugs bust in world sport. Ben Johnson was sent home to Canada in disgrace when he was caught using steroids after he had taken the gold medal in the Blue Riband of the Olympics. As a friend of Johnson, Christie's resulting promotion from third place in the race to silver medal position in the record books was bittersweet: 'I cried that day,' Christie said.

That was Tuesday 27 September. Just two days later, Christie was to go through the gamut of emotions for himself. It was the evening of Thursday 29 September when a small white envelope was delivered by hand to Dick Palmer, the British head of delegation. The envelope from the International Olympic Committee contained news of two positive drug test findings, one for diuretics by judo player Kerrith Brown, who had won a bronze medal earlier in the week, the other of pseudoephedrine, a banned stimulant, in Christie's drugs sample following the 200 metres final, in which the Briton had placed fourth.

The resulting inquiry in the British camp saw Christie grilled by the team management. The investigation quickly discovered that Christie had been using some ginseng. Ginseng is a traditional oriental herbal remedy for fatigue, believed to have aphrodisiac qualities, and is extremely popular in the Far East. The Koreans claim that their blend of the powder, derived from crushed plant roots, is pure. Ginseng from China and Japan, though, can contain impurities. While the British team was at a pre-Games training camp in Nihon, Japan, Dr Roy Axon, the British Olympic Association's chief medical officer, was consulted about the properties of ginseng, and he was concerned enough to send out a warning to competitors to totally avoid any form of the herbal remedy. Christie, apparently, never received the warning. He had been using Chinese ginseng. Impurities in the blending may have seen the addition of some pseudoephedrine to the ginseng Christie was using. The drug is a common ingredient in cold remedies, but is banned from sports use because its stimulant effect is proved to improve performances in competition.

The day after he had been told the dreaded news, Christie was summoned to the IOC's headquarters hotel to present his case. The British entourage included Dr Mike Turner, the Cambridge don who was the athletics team manager, Arthur Mapp, his counterpart with the judo team, Dick Palmer, Dr Malcolm Read, the athletics team doctor, Brown and Christie. When they arrived at the plush, five-star Hotel Shilla, they were ushered up to the 21st floor and the suite where the IOC's medical commission would sit in judgement. It was also the same floor on which Princess Anne, the president of the BOA and a member of the IOC, had her rooms. The Royal security staff soon became very concerned because of the large number of people who were gathering in the hotel corridors.

The rumour factory in the Olympic Village had been working overtime:

in the same week that Ben Johnson had been uncovered as a drugs cheat, the news of another big name drugs positive spread through Seoul like a bush fire. By the time the British party arrived for the hearings, the press had gathered to report the outcome across the world.

It was 9.10 p.m. before Kerrith Brown was summoned to present his case. Brown's hearing lasted about two hours. Just before midnight, behind closed doors, the trial of Linford Christie began.

Christie was to be represented by Robert Watson, the honorary treasurer of the British Olympic Association and a barrister by profession. The following day, the last Saturday of the Games, would see the last athletics events contested in the Olympic stadium, including the finals of the relays. As Christie entered the room to begin his hearing, there was some suggestion that because it was already so late the panel should hear some of the evidence and then adjourn until later the following day to conclude the hearing.

'I was going to have none of that,' Watson recalls. 'We wanted to have Linford in the relay the following day, and I was going to stay there all night to get a decision.'

Watson's persistence would pay off. In the large room, there were 23 members of the medical commission, with five languages spoken. 'I felt like I was in the United Nations,' Christie recalled. Tables were arranged in a large horseshoe shape, with the accused, Christie, in the middle, and Watson and Dr Turner alongside. Everything said in evidence needed to be translated. It was late, at the end of a long day, towards the finish of a long two-week Olympics for many of the panel. The proceedings moved slowly. Watson presented what Christie described as 'a very impressive case', producing examples of ginseng, talking about the quantities of the drug involved in the case.

'Why did you use so much ginseng?' one of the committee members asked Christie.

'Because the 200 metres is twice as far as the 100,' the sprinter said.

After about an hour's evidence, Christie was allowed to return to the Athletes' Village, being smuggled out by the hotel's back door to avoid the waiting reporters. The hearing continued, Watson refusing to allow an adjournment.

It was past 3 a.m. when finally a vote was taken to decide the fate of Linford Christie. 'Eleven voted for Christie, ten against, and two were asleep,' Watson says. By just one vote, Christie was cleared. Fired by the frustrations of the previous 48 hours, when he returned to the Olympic stadium later that day to race in the final of the relay, he sprinted like never before to lift the British squad from fourth to second place down the home straight.

Though Christie was completely exonerated by the IOC hearing, the ordeal had been almost too much to bear. 'I've been to hell and back,'

Christie said that afternoon after collecting his second Olympic silver medal. 'I was so close to suicide, I really was.'

It was by no means the end of the matter, though. Shortly after returning to Britain after the Games, Christie reacted angrily because the chairman of the IOC's medical commission, Prince Alexandre de Merode, had said that Christie had been given 'the benefit of the doubt'.

'The IOC should apologise for the way it allowed my name to be released to the press, and what that put me through,' Christie demanded.

'The benefit of the doubt': the phrase would still rankle Christie seven years later, when in his book he said that de Merode's 'English wasn't very good which is why, I think, he used a phrase like that'. In fact, Prince Alexandre, a Belgian with degrees in philosophy, literature and law, who had been a member of the IOC for nearly 30 years, had chosen his words most carefully. And it was not just because a single vote had saved Christie's career. For according to Professor Arnold Beckett, the British member of that IOC medical commission, 'Christie was lucky to be given the benefit of the doubt and not stripped of his medal. After the 200 metres sample had shown traces of the banned substance, I went back and re-tested his 100 metres sample, which was negative, and found that there were traces there too.'

It seems, though, that Christie did not learn the lessons of that sorry episode. In fact, had he studied the press coverage of the Seoul affair carefully, he would have discovered a reference to a Chinese plant, Ma Huang, which might have saved himself and his friends a good deal of anguish six years later.

In October 1994, at the formal hearing which confirmed that another British sprinter, Solomon Wariso, was to serve a three-month suspension for a stimulant violation, Christie was named, along with high jumper Dalton Grant, in connection with the 'Up Your Gas' pep pills which had caused the unwitting Wariso to miss both the European Championships and Commonwealth Games that summer. The confidential report of the official hearing says that Wariso 'said he was assured by Mr Grant that the tablets had been obtained by Mr Grant whilst Mr Grant and Mr Linford Christie were in Florida and that the supplier had assured them that they contained nothing that would be prohibited by the International Olympic Committee'. Before giving evidence to the hearing, Wariso had also said that his 'friends' – whom he did not name publicly – had used the Up Your Gas pills, had been drug tested, and had never given a positive test. At his hearing, Wariso elaborated. The report says Wariso 'relied on the statements made to him by Mr Grant and the fact that Mr Grant and Mr Christie were using it and had apparently not been tested positive during its use'.

What Wariso probably overlooked, somewhat unfortunately for him, was that stimulant drugs are not tested for during out-of-competition doping controls. A stimulant has only a brief, pick-me-up effect. A stimulant used during warm weather training in March, for example, would have little, if any, effect on competitive performance in July. But take the pills just before a race in the middle of the season, as Wariso did, and the in-competition test will find the stimulant.

Christie's version of his involvement with the Up Your Gas pills is somewhat more remote. In his book, he says that he was aware of Up Your Gas because of a full-page advertisement for the pills that he had seen while in the United States. According to Christie: 'I can remember being in a health shop in the States when the assistant . . .' said to an unnamed athlete " . . . It's all legal".'

Of course, that was never quite the case. The 'magic' ingredient in Up Your Gas, the potion that claimed to be 'the wildest and craziest product around', was Ma Huang. Wariso made much of the fact that he and the British athletics team doctor, Dr Malcolm Brown, had been unable to find any reference to Ma Huang in any medical or scientific reference books. Yet in the aftermath of Christie's dope case hearing in Seoul, Thomson Prentice, medical correspondent of *The Times*, had reported that Ma Huang was the Chinese name for ephedra, the plant which provides the raw material for the drug ephedrine.

In Britain, apart from being found in very small amounts in some cough mixtures, ephedrine is usually only available with a doctor's prescription. Six years on from what Christie called 'the worst day of my life', Wariso, at the start of his international career, was banned for three months when caught using a similar drug. According to one account at least, the similarities were not lost on Christie.

At his hearing, Wariso gave a version of a conversation he had with Christie after he had been told by officials that he had tested positive. At the time, there had been some dispute as to whether Wariso ought to travel to Helsinki for the European Championships – technically he was not suspended until the confirmatory 'B' sample test had been carried out, but were he to race in Finland and the 'B' test were to confirm a suspension, as seemed likely, the complications would be enormous. Wariso turned to his team captain for advice.

According to the secret hearing report, 'Mr Wariso said that he discussed the matter with Mr Christie who advised him to go and participate fully and that the outcome would be the same as that which had happened to Mr Christie at Seoul in 1988 when he had been accused of using ephedrine and had been acquitted because the ephedrine had been shown to be added to some ginseng that Mr Christie had taken. The chairman of the panel . . .' namely Sir Arthur Gold, a long-time campaigner against drug use in sport ' . . . indicated that this version of what happened at Seoul was not wholly accurate'.

Nor was Christie's advice wholly helpful. Wariso did go to Helsinki, only for news of his positive test to be discovered on the opening day of the championships. Flanked by British team officials, Wariso boldly gave a press conference, just as the first round of Christie's 100 metres was getting under way. Straight after he had safely qualified, Christie went over to the press centre. When the conference finished, Christie helped to usher Wariso away from the press. 'Don't even come near me,' Christie muttered menacingly to one journalist who approached to ask his thoughts on the affair.

It was a scene that was almost repeated later in the week. After the high jump, Dalton Grant became the only British finalist at the championships who was unavailable to give an interview following his event. It was his team captain, with his arm around Grant's shoulders, who led him away from the arena before he could speak to any pressmen.

Perhaps the ultimate irony of the sad case of Solomon Wariso was that, in 1988, when Christie was given 'the benefit of the doubt', his test for pseudoephedrine found more than ten milligrams per litre of the drug in his sample. By 1994, the scientists who administer the doping control rules had reduced the minimum for a positive test for such stimulants to just eight milligrams per litre. Solomon Wariso, therefore, was banned for having a smaller quantity of the drug in his system in 1994 than Christie had been caught with in 1988. This time, there was no benefit of the doubt for Wariso, though.

Controversy and confrontation with the doping control system seem to have dogged Christie's career ever since Seoul. It was the aftermath of the Johnson affair which saw a radical overhaul of drug testing around the world. Out-of-competition tests, taken when athletes are in training and therefore most likely to use body-building anabolic steroids and other banned drugs, became far more common. Testing as a whole became more frequent and more stringent.

Christie was vociferous in his public support for such moves. Over the years, Christie – with 'Pure Talent' written across his T-shirt – had frequently stated his total opposition to the use of drugs in athletics. He even went so far as to suggest that sport's doping offenders ought to serve time in prison. 'If you're going to keep the sport clean,' he said, 'money shouldn't be a problem. They can test me all the time. I have no problem. It shows that I am clean.' Indeed, in 1994, the last full calendar year for which figures have been made available, Christie was tested a total of 17 times by a combination of in- and out-of-competition tests by either the Sports Council (on behalf of the British Athletic Federation) or the IAAF. All results were negative.

But Christie was not always as available for drug testing as stipulated by the protocols by which most other athletes have to abide. In 1993, in a secret paper for the BAF from the Sports Council's Doping Control Unit, Christie was reported as not being at his notified address for a drugs test. Since all international athletes are supposed to be on a register so that they are available for drug testing at any time, technically this was an offence which could have resulted in a hearing with the sport's governing body. If the hearing had found against Christie, the maximum penalty for his missed test might have been a four-year suspension.

There have been investigations in other cases when champions have been unavailable for tests, even when they have been away from their home. In March 1992, when Sally Gunnell was 'missing' from an address in Phoenix, Arizona, which received a surprise visit from the testers, she was summoned to a BAF disciplinary hearing on her return from America. The hearing accepted Gunnell's explanation – she had moved from the hotel she was using during warm weather training because the accommodation was inadequate – and she was allowed to continue her track career. Later that year, Gunnell won Olympic gold in Barcelona.

But a year after the Gunnell episode, the federation chose to take no further action when the testers reported that they had no record of Christie's home address. More than two years were to pass before the Sports Council was finally, officially informed of Christie's address. In the intervening period, Christie never received a no-notice knock on the door of his home from the drug testers. Though the Sports Council aspires to a system of no-notice testing, approaches to test him out-of-competition from 1993 to mid-1995 had first to go through the offices of Nuff Respect, Christie's management company.

This saw the testing procedures sometimes descend into farce. Early in 1995, the drug testers were forced to intercept Christie at Heathrow airport as he was about to leave the country for some warm weather training. He delivered the required sample in a mother and baby room. 'It was difficult,' said Steffan Sahlstrom, a Swedish member of the international testing team, 'we were missing the home address so we had to notify him with short notice instead of conducting the test unannounced.'

As far as Christie was concerned, BAF had always had his home address details, and it was therefore the Federation's fault for not providing this information to the Sports Council. But the athlete was also lax in fulfilling his own responsibilities in returning official forms. In December 1994, BAF official Chris Carter took over as the sport's out-of-competition drug testing co-ordinator, and, within a couple of months of being in the post, he sent a letter to all international athletes to outline the requirements of doping control. The letter made the athlete's responsibilities under the rules quite clear.

'As you will see,' Carter's letter read, 'Rule 24 para (4) specifies that the athlete on the register must *always* update the Federation of any changes of address. . . It is the athlete's own personal responsibility that they may not pass onto anyone else, parent, coach, agent etc. . .' Enclosed with Carter's letter was an address form to be filled in and returned. This form reiterated the rules that any changes in address – even if the athlete is away from home for just five days – must be notified.

Some of the letters were sent to athletes' agents. According to Carter, 'I didn't deliberately ask if there was an address for Linford Christie. I did know that there were certain athletes only available through agents.' Asked if Christie was one of these athletes, Carter said, 'As far as I was aware, he was.'

It was not only at out-of-competition tests that Christie presented problems for the testers. At the Barcelona Olympics in 1992, Christie might even have lost his cherished gold medal over a row in doping control. Apparently annoyed that he had been selected for testing yet again, the British team captain refused to co-operate for the officials. It was only after he was threatened by a senior official with being recorded as 'a refusal to be tested' that Christie co-operated. Christie realised that had he been registered as a 'refusal' in Barcelona, it might have seen him not only banned from future competitions for four years, but also subjected to the ultimate sanction and stripped of the Olympic gold medal he had battled so hard to win in the 100 metres. Because Christie complied, no further action was taken. In fact, Christie's row in the Olympic drug testing centre never came to light until the end of 1994, when Christie was reported to the IAAF's governing council for another display of ill temper in doping control at that September's World Cup meeting in London.

Routinely in championship competition, the first three in each final, plus one at random, are called into doping control. Because of Christie's continued and consistent success, he does therefore tend to be selected for drug testing more often than most. The sheer embarrassment of being watched while urinating, and the hassle of having to wait around in doping control at the end of a meeting, unable to get away for a warm down, a meal or rest, must be very tiresome. At the three-day World Cup at the end of the 1994 season, Christie was summoned to doping control after winning the 100 metres on the cool, damp first evening, and then, the following day, he was called upon for another drug test after the 4 x100 metres relay.

That summer had already seen seven positive drug tests announced in British athletics, including the controversial case of Diane Modahl, which was vigorously defended by the athlete and her family, as well as questioned by many of the country's top internationals, including Christie. For many athletes, there was something about the Modahl case which just did not make sense. Thus it was against this background of fear and suspicion that Christie was called in for his second test at Crystal Palace in the space of less than 24 hours. 'It has reached the stage,' Christie later wrote, 'where I feel like the more I compete and take part in tests, the better chance there is of being set up.'

According to a confidential report from the IAAF's senior doping control official who oversaw the testing arrangements during the World Cup, 'Christie's arrival on day one was noisy and there were accusations that he had been targeted . . . '

On the second day, prior to Christie's arrival at the control, I was approached by Dr Malcolm Brown, the British team doctor, who asked that Christie be given preference over waiting athletes and moved straight through the system. I refused on the grounds that all athletes have equal status in the doping control, but told the doctor that if he could obtain approval from each of the waiting athletes I would give the matter further consideration.

'When Christie arrived, the two sampling rooms were occupied. Christie, loudly and rudely, demanded to be processed immediately, saying that, if we did not have facilities available, we should release him and that we would be responsible if he developed cystitis.'

An embarrassed junior sampling officer ushered Christie to a toilet in the adjoining physio's room, to the annoyance of at least one of the other athletes patiently waiting their turn to be tested. According to the senior official, this 'gave a signal to Christie that by being abusive he can gain an advantage . . . Having learnt that Christie regularly acts in this manner I made an informal complaint to Professor Peter Radford, chief executive of BAF, and suggested that both Christie and Dr Brown should be warned as to their actions'. Christie's outburst was referred to the IAAF medical committee, where the official who had warned Christie in Barcelona two years earlier remarked on the similarity of the circumstances. As a result, the IAAF sent a formal letter to the British federation, leaving it to BAF to deal with their athlete. According to Christie, he has never been reprimanded for his outbursts at Crystal Palace or Barcelona.

Such anomalies of treatment for Christie and his fits of pique in doping control rooms around the world have often led to him being linked to rumours of other positive drug tests, despite his long record of negative results. In an interview given in Tampa, Florida, in early 1995, Christie himself told of his dismay that even after he had won the world title in Stuttgart two years earlier, he was still not immune from such damaging rumours. According to Christie, an Uzbekistan javelin thrower, Dimitri Polyunin, who had tested positive for drugs in Stuttgart, had been saying that he had been told by a technician at the laboratory that Christie had also tested positive. Nothing ever came of the allegation. 'They say, "Well everybody uses them, so a champion has to, too",' Christie told his interviewer. 'Bull. That's sour grapes.'

Christie's anger and rage is not reserved for the doping control system. Kenneth Williams, the cult comedy actor who starred in numerous 'Carry On . . .' films, was fond of saying that theatre critics 'were like eunuchs at an ancient court. They were there every night, they watched every night. But they couldn't do it themselves.' Linford Christie undoubtedly feels that way about those who review his performances, the press.

By 1995, Linford Christie's status had long ago transcended that of mere sports star. His legion of achievements had transformed him into something of a cultural icon, his name becoming acknowledged short-hand for speed and power, he was revered by the public as a national treasure. As such, in newspapers, Christie attracted front-page as well as back-page headlines for his deeds, on and off the track, plus double-page spreads in the features sections.

Christie is by no means new or unique in attracting both public adulation and ridicule simultaneously. Babe Ruth, the hard-hitting, hard-living base-ball player of the 1920s and '30s was probably the first professional sportsman to become as famous for his off-the-field antics as his sporting achievements. In Britain more recently, footballers such as George Best, Paul Gascoigne and Eric Cantona, England rugby player Will Carling and cricketer Ian Botham have all been propelled to the fore of the nation's affections by their on-the-field deeds and to the forefront of an even wider national consciousness with their extra-curricular notoriety. Observing Christie's dual, Jekyll-and-Hyde public and private personae, the French daily sports paper, *L'Equipe*, headlined a profile of the 1992 Olympic 100 metres champion 'Dr Linford and Mr Christie'.

It could be that Christie's dual nature owed much to the paradox of being a professional in an amateur sport, for the sprinter was part of the first generation of athletes who openly admitted that running was their job. Christie was therefore also among the first professional athletes to discover that fame has a price.

Linford Eceiro Christie was born in Jamaica in 1960, one of seven children. Two years later, his parents emigrated to England where his father, James, found work in a factory making baths, and tried to save enough money from his £3-a-week wage packet to be able to bring the rest of his family over to join him and his wife, Mabel. Young Linford grew up with his grandmother until he was seven years old, when his parents sent for him to join them in a house barely a free kick away from Queens Park Rangers football ground in west London.

Linford was in for a culture shock in many ways, from the moment he was introduced to his long-forgotten mother, through the time he burned his fingers with the cold of his first snowfall, to his first encounter with racism. The latter episode has often been described as a defining moment in Christie's life. Playing a game of tag in the playground of his primary school, Linford, speedy even as a child, caught and touched a white girl, who protested because, 'My Mummy said I shouldn't play with blackies'. Quick enough to win races, in later years Christie still felt he struggled to win acclaim. Often, he would blame an inherent racism in British society for the lack of the respect which he demanded.

It could be possible to sympathise with Christie's complaints against prejudice. The way Christie was repeatedly stopped by police simply because he happened to be a young black driving an expensive car had all the hallmarks of racially motivated harassment. On one day in 1988, when he was at the wheel of a new hire car, on loan through the British Olympic Association, Christie was stopped *four* times, which ultimately cost the police £30,000 in legal damages.

Some might have been able to perceive hints of racism, too, in newspaper headlines such as 'Linford's heart of darkness', and *The Sun*'s famous 'lunchbox' jibes after his Olympic victory in 1992. It has also been suggested that press criticism of Christie was because he was considered to be an 'uppity' black.

Yet when Christie's running style was described by one of his Great Britain team-mates as being 'perfectly balanced because he's got a chip on both shoulders', the opinion came not from a middle-class, middle-aged white journalist, but from Derek Redmond, the former British record-holder at 400 metres, who happens to be black.

In the summer of 1995, the black newspaper, *The Voice*, asked on its front page: 'Is Linford Just A Big Girl's Blouse?' as inside, columnist Tony Sewell railed against Christie's constant outbursts, suggesting that black Britons need not portray themselves as victims, something which Sewell said was 'encouraged by celebrities who are stinking rich and go on as if they were the first Black man on the slave ship'. Sewell continued: 'Linford Christie is no Martin Luther King. Perhaps he needs to get a grip on the real meaning of his contribution. Sprinters are important but none feature in my top ten of great Black Brits.'

Yet for all that, surely, in the midst of Christie's finest moment, after he had won the Olympic 100 metres gold medal in Barcelona in 1992, he was entitled to more respect than to have newspaper features devoted to the contents of his shorts? 'I felt very humiliated,' Christie recalled of the time he first read *The Sun*'s 'lunchbox' article. 'My first instinct was that it was racist. There we are, stereotyping a black man . . .

'If I'd been a different type of person, I could have capitalised on it, because we've had offers – "Can we make lunchboxes for Linford, use his name to sell it?" But I don't want to make money out of something that I just don't think is right. I don't want to go through life being known for what I've got in my shorts. I'm a serious person when it comes to the track.' But two years before Christie made those outraged remarks, he had already managed to turn the cause of his complaints to his profit. In the year following his Barcelona triumph, Christie lent his name to an advertising campaign for bananas which suggested that we should all eat more of what Linford kept in his 'powerpack'. Despite all his later protests about being referred to as a 'legend in his own lunchbox' – 'They don't talk about Sally Gunnell's tits' – Christie gave his personal approval to the banana campaign, and was paid an undisclosed sum.

Nor was Christie above making his own jokes about the size of his genitalia. In June 1995, Christie appeared on *Sport In Question*, the television programme he was to make famous when he broke down and tearfully announced his retirement. Yet before the recording began, one member of the audience jokingly asked, 'Linford, just how big *is* your manhood?' Christie's light-hearted reply belied the anger of the protests he was to make once the cameras were rolling. 'If your girlfriend knew how big it was,' Christie bragged, 'then she'd leave you.'

It was Christie's appearance on *Sport In Question* which was to throw British athletics into turmoil even before the season had begun. The first hints that 1995 might be fraught came towards the end of the indoor season. As the only man ever to have held the world, Olympic, European and Commonwealth 100 metres titles simultaneously, the only global title which continued to elude Christie was the world indoor 60 metres.

Throughout the 1994-95 winter season, Christie refused to say whether he would compete for Britain at the World Indoor Championships, to be staged in the Palau Sant Jordi, just a warm-up jog away from Barcelona's Olympic stadium where three years before Christie had enjoyed his finest moments. Christie gave the occasional heavy hint or suggestion about his participation in the World Indoors, but never an outright 'yes' or 'no'. His first ever individual world record, an indoor 200 metres of 20.25 seconds at Lievin, northern France, in February 1995, perhaps gave him another option of an event to consider for Barcelona.

Barely two weeks before the championships were due to start, Christie announced to a press conference at Birmingham's National Indoor Arena, 'It's all right fellas, you can book your tickets for Barcelona now. I'm definitely going.' Yet a week later, just hours after running one of his fastest ever 60-metre races at Sindelfingen, Germany, Christie said he was too tired to run in Barcelona. Appearing on a late-night German chat show, Christie announced that he had changed his mind, and would not be racing. The news was greeted with dismay, not only by the British federation and media who had looked upon Christie as a certain medal success, but also by Primo Nebiolo, the head of the International Amateur Athletic Federation, the governing body which invests so much prestige in its world championships.

The IAAF has in recent years made a problem for itself by creating too many championships. As well as World Cups, an annual Grand Prix, and various world championships for road races and cross-country, during the outdoor season world titles are now contested every two years. The relatively new World Indoor Championships, too, comes round once every 24 months. For top-flight international athletes, trying to fit in all such events together with the Olympic Games and continental championships has two effects: tiredness and injury. As a result, some athletes have begun to avoid some of the less important meetings, preferring instead to train and prepare for the events which offer the greater prestige or financial rewards.

Commercially, for the athletes, an indoor world title is worth very little. The shoe companies, which often have athletes signed to endorsement contracts, rarely offer big bonuses for medals won at the World Indoors. The higher profile outdoor World Championships – which were to be staged later in 1995 in Gothenburg – or the 1996 Olympic Games offered the prospect of far more lucrative rewards. Thus it was that the World Indoors in Barcelona in March 1995 looked as if it might be bereft of the big name stars who satisfy television moguls and sponsors. 'An event whose title is incompatible with its status', was the description of the championships given by Britain's chief coach, Malcolm Arnold.

For Nebiolo's IAAF, Christie's presence in Barcelona offered a lifeline of credibility. Nebiolo personally appealed to the sprinter to change his mind, and the IAAF even approached the British federation to try to persuade it to alter its selections for the 60 metres, who were named after Christie's withdrawal, in order to make way for the main man.

On 7 March, two days after the German chat show had been transmitted and three days before the championships were due to begin, on hearing that Nebiolo had made an appeal to Christie to compete, Sue Barrett, Christie's agent, sent a one-page faxed letter saying that he would 'indeed honour your request providing that the two British athletes (Darren Braithwaite and Michael Rosswess) are not affected by his inclusion in the 60 metres'. Effectively, this was a request for Christie to be given special treatment and to be granted an extra, 'wild card' lane at the championships.

The IAAF's reply the following day, from chief of staff Robert Fasulo, welcomed Christie's offer: 'Linford's participation, both as a distinguished champion and as a fine example for the youth of the world, would certainly be one of the highlights of these championships.' But it stopped short of creating any precedent: 'the IAAF president's hope was and remains with the understanding that Linford would be one of the two athletes representing Great Britain in the 60 metres and/or 200 metres at the championships'. The whole exchange left Tony Ward, the official spokesman for the BAF and the collaborator on Christie's first autobiography, unimpressed. 'It's beginning to make us look slightly ridiculous.'

This latest *volte face* over his participation also made Christie's withdrawal from the championships seem all the more inexplicable. Appearance fees are not supposed to be paid at world championships – the athletes compete for the honour of representing their country. But before the outdoor World Championships in Stuttgart two years before, it had been established that some top athletes had done deals with the IAAF to *promote* the event. By getting the athletes to appear in official pre-publicity, a fee could be paid without it becoming payment to *compete* at the championships. There were suggestions of similar deals being done before Barcelona. Even Christie had featured in some official publicity for the World Indoors in a local newspaper months before the event, when the athlete had yet to announce any intention to compete there. But both Christie and the IAAF firmly denied that any deals had been done.

The whole saga left one IAAF official, press chief Christopher Winner, completely bemused. An urbane, charming American journalist who is fluent in Italian and French, Winner was a relative newcomer to the ways of the IAAF. He had a habit of wearing an FDR lapel badge on his jacket and his heart on his sleeve, not a style which necessarily suited Nebiolo. Indeed, Winner, who had worked for an international news agency during the Lebanon civil war, did remark that the crossfire in Beirut was never as ferocious as that he encountered working for the IAAF in Monte Carlo. When confronted by Christie's withdrawal, Winner said, 'He has damaged the quality of the competition and the credibility of the sport. It is disappointing and disheartening and not befitting of a champion.'

Christie was furious. When his complaint reached Nebiolo, the patrician head of the IAAF ordered Winner to make a public apology or resign. Believing his comments had been made with the authority of the IAAF president himself, the press chief refused to do either.

Christie went to Barcelona as a spectator and after the first evening of the championships, he was eating in the restaurant of the official IAAF hotel. Winner was at another table and, in an attempt to pour oil on the troubled waters, approached the athlete. Christie rounded on him, calling Winner 'a worm', and humiliating him publicly. In an interview in a Barcelona newspaper the day after the championships ended, Christie described Winner as 'an idiot'.

It was probably just a coincidence, but during the weekend of the World Indoors – and therefore much more quickly than is usual – Christie had the formal ratification of his 200 metres indoor world record announced by the IAAF. And within four months of the Barcelona episode, Winner had resigned his post in Monte Carlo to take up another job. But Winner never did retract his comments about Christie as Nebiolo had ordered.

As 1995's summer track season approached, it became increasingly obvious that no deal had been agreed between the British Athletic Federation and Christie's management company, Nuff Respect, for him and his colleagues to race at BAF promotions. All the scorn which Christie had targeted at Christopher Winner while in Barcelona was as nothing to the anger he was to express that summer against BAF's executive chairman, Professor Peter Radford.

Christie's 200 metres indoor world best at Lievin that February was the first sprint world record by a Briton since Radford, the Rome Olympics 100 metres bronze medal-winner, had broken the 220 yards world best in 1960. By the end of the 1995 season, there was a gulf between Christie and Radford which seemed far wider than those 35 years.

Through all his rows with the federation, though, Christie's greatest contempt was always reserved for the press. 'Slugs', 'fat slobs', 'drunk as skunks' were Christie's descriptions of the dozen-or-so British journalists who regularly followed the athletics circuit. 'Often I don't recognise the man called Linford Christie who I read about in the papers. Maybe those writers think that because I'm big and strong, I must be aggressive too, but that isn't the me that I know.' Perhaps Christie had forgotten those occasions when his assaults on pressmen have gone beyond the verbal. There is a sense from his continuing complaints that Christie's objections about his press coverage arise because he does not like what he sees of himself in what he reads. Often, he says, it lacks respect.

Respect is an important word for Christie. After the Olympics in 1992, he and hurdler Colin Jackson formed their own management company and called it Nuff Respect, taking the company's name from the street argot of young blacks. To help to run the new company, Christie and Jackson recruited two young account executives, Sue Barrett and Alison Morgan, whom they had worked with and grown to trust through their dealings with one of the sponsors of British athletics, the Milk Marketing Board.

The first anyone knew of this move in his business was when Christie, as the new Olympic 100 metres champion, was asked at a meeting in Belfast of his plans for the next summer. 'Speak to my manager,' said Christie, pointing to a corner of the interview room where Barrett was standing quietly. The journalists paused for a moment, as if there was some mistake. 'At first we didn't believe him,' said one. 'We thought he was having a joke.' Barrett's appointment was not a joke. The woman whose previous job had duties which included handing out milk cartons to children at the English Schools' Cross-country Championships was thus propelled into managing the business affairs of one of the world's biggest sports stars.

It was Nuff Respect who handled the business deals which saw Christie produce a book in the autumn of 1995, entitled *To Be Honest With You*. 'Well, ummm,' wrote Sir Clement Freud, reviewing the book for *The Times*. 'According to the publishers, the book is by a ghost writer called Maurice Hamilton who manages to get a mention in the sixth and final verse of a poem called *Acknowledgements*.'

For his second ghosted 'autobiography' in half a dozen years, Christie would not counsel having an athletics specialist write up his recollections for him. By the end of the summer of 1995, Christie had reached a point where virtually only one British athletics specialist was deemed suitable to be granted an audience. Part of the breakdown in Christie's relationship with the press might be put down to the management of Nuff Respect. Barrett and Morgan became notorious for failing to return calls or delays in passing on requests for interviews, as if they were trying to protect their employer from being bothered by irrelevancies, or too busy arranging his hectic and lucrative schedule. Christie, after such humble beginnings in Jamaica and west London, had reached the pinnacle in the world of professional athletics. Few other athletes could command appearance fees to match Christie's: his personal wealth was estimated in 1994 at more than £3 million.

As a well-paid professional athlete, it is important that he maintains a highly visible presence on the track, and while many of Britain's other athletes sometimes have to rely on the NHS when they get injured, Christie is able to afford the advice and treatment of one of the world's leading sports medicine practitioners. Christie regularly consults Dr Hans-Wilhelm Müller-Wohlfahrt, who for 18 years was the team doctor for Bayern Munich football club. Now, he serves on the medical staff of the German national soccer team.

At his private Bavarian clinic, Dr Müller-Wohlfahrt has also treated such sporting luminaries as Boris Becker, Katarina Witt, Stephen Roche, Jimmy Connors, Daley Thompson and Diego Maradona. Christie first went to Munich for treatment of a hamstring strain. In the middle of the track seasons of 1994 and 1995, Christie again flew to Germany for treatment from Müller-Wohlfahrt after suffering injury, and quickly made winning returns to racing. Müller-Wohlfahrt's unorthodox therapy for sports injuries involves an injection of cell parts from the foetuses of calves, amino acids, enzymes, honey extract, traces of zinc and other elements. Sometimes, the patient may be injected six times a day, three times a week.

The treatment is supposed to reduce inflammation and to speed up the healing process. Christie first went to Müller-Wohlfahrt's clinic on the recommendation of Britain's then chief coach, Frank Dick. 'He's one of the best in the world in terms of evaluation, treatment and getting the athlete back into the firing line,' Dick said of the doctor. Other opinions of Müller-Wohlfahrt's treatment are less effusive. Professor Arne Ljungqvist, the chairman of the IAAF's medical commission, has said that he has never found any scientific reports on the clinical benefit of such therapeutic practices. But as far as athletes such as Christie are concerned, the important thing is that Müller-Wohlfahrt's treatments get them back to winning ways.

Throughout the early summer of 1995, the Granada television programme *World In Action* was pursuing aspects of the Christie story. To complete their programme, they needed to interview Christie himself. Philip Clothier, the programme researcher, wrote to Nuff Respect twice, on both occasions avoiding any specifics about the programme. The second letter went as far as to suggest that the programme makers were prepared to go anywhere in the world to fit in the interview with Christie's busy diary.

From her mobile phone, Sue Barrett eventually called Clothier to arrange an interview. It was a Friday night in July, just as Christie was settling into his starting blocks to race in the Bislett Games in Oslo when she called. 'Just a moment,' Barrett said to Clothier. There was a pause on the line for barely ten seconds, then she came back on the line. 'It's all right. He's won again. He's still the Number One,' she said. Clothier was amazed: Barrett was calling him from the stands of the Bislett stadium.

Barrett and Clothier arranged for Christie to be interviewed in Sheffield, where he was due to race two days after his Oslo victory. It may have been merely a coincidence, but it was around this time that the Sports Council was finally contacted with official notification of Christie's home address. At last, after a two-year wait, they could contact him directly to arrange random doping tests.

When he arrived in Sheffield with Colin Jackson and Barrett, Christie refused to shake Clothier's hand. 'I don't want to be nice to you. Let's get on with it,' Christie said. At this point, Clothier was convinced that, had Christie known the full nature of the interview, he would never have agreed to do it. During the early questions, Christie seemed nervous, his answers terse, but as the interview developed, he gained confidence and began addressing the camera directly, rather than his interviewer. Christie assured the nation that he would demand an explanation from the BAF as to why they had failed to pass on his home address to the Sports Council so that they could test him (though not before he claimed, and had to be corrected, that he had been tested at his home). As the interview ended, Christie insisted: 'I want to answer more questions'.

Yet it was the many questions he left unanswered during an appearance on television earlier in the year which created some of the biggest sporting headlines. Christie had broken down in tears on *Sport In Question* as he announced he would quit the sport and definitely not compete at the Atlanta Olympic Games in 1996. 'At the end of the season, that's it, I'm finished. I'll never wear a running vest again. I've had enough. I can't take any more. The federation are not supporting me. They say I should take a pay cut. When I go out there on the track, I am not just fighting the other athletes, I'm fighting my own camp. The federation and the media are not on my side. I love athletics dearly. But when you love something, it's supposed to be fun. And I just don't want to feel any more pressure in my life.'

The following morning, Christie was greeted by front page stories about his impending retirement, *The Sun* leading the way with the inevitable, 'Linford's hanging up his lunchbox'. Two days later, when on his way to a competition in Germany, Christie turned on photographers at Heathrow airport: 'Do you want some? Do you want some, eh?' he threatened. 'If you lot want some today you'll have something different to write about. I don't want to see blood shed on this airport, but if you want some . . . ' Christie had apparently cracked under the sort of pressure which he had always seemed able to cope with during his decade as a top international track star. The probable reason for his outbursts lay in a bed in an intensive care ward at Hammersmith Hospital. His mother, Mabel, was dying.

'You don't become world and Olympic champion without being very, very strong. And I'm strong where it really matters,' Christie once said, tapping the side of his head. But no amount of mental toughness can prepare someone for the grief that goes with the loss of a parent.

Two days after his mother's death, Christie was back racing at a low-key meeting. Following the funeral a week later, he made a late decision to take an early morning Channel Tunnel train the next day to join the British team in Lille for the European Cup. As has come to be expected of the team captain, that afternoon he won his 100 metres and anchored the relay squad to victory, too. They were the 11th and 12th Europa Cup victories for Christie, another record.

Because of the trying and confusing circumstances which surrounded Christie at that time, it is difficult to know if he was truly beleaguered, or whether he had chosen to recast himself as an underdog again, so that he could once more be lauded for overcoming all the odds. In the past, he used to have Carl Lewis to chase, but by 1993, Christie's dominance of the 100 metres was so complete that he seemed to have psyched out an entire generation of American sprinters, for whom the 100 metres used to be their sole preserve. Leroy Burrell, the holder of the 100 metres world record but a notorious under-performer in championships, is probably among the biggest losers to Linford Christie's ability to rise to the occasion. A training partner and friend of Carl Lewis, Burrell has said of Christie: 'He runs on hate.'

In July 1993, Britain's Olympic champion had beaten Lewis in the famed 'Dash for Cash' at Gateshead, where both men received £100,000 for their efforts. Then Christie went on to lift the world championship in Stuttgart. Scientists estimated that when he came out of his starting blocks in the final, Christie generated enough power to drive a small family car from 0-60mph in 10.4 seconds.

But by 1995, into his 36th year, Christie's days of big pay days at British meetings were coming to an end. Christie, from his earliest days as an international, had had his racing appearances organised for him by Andy Norman, who was also the British federation's meeting promoter. Indeed, it was Norman who had fiercely chastised Christie for wasting his talent: the rebuke transformed the sprinter's attitude, and his life.

Christie's appearances in British meetings organised by Norman had been well rewarded. In 1994, he reportedly had a deal worth £200,000 for appearances at six British track meets. With lucrative off-the-track endorsement deals with firms including Lucozade, Mercedes-Benz and Puma, by 1995 Christie's total income was suggested to be more than £1 million per year. Christie has claimed that 'money has ruined athletics'. However, in 1995, perhaps with a view to his retirement, Christie was asking for a £250,000 package deal to compete in Britain (with one less meeting than in his 1994 package). This worked out at nearly £5,000 per second of his races. As the world's leading sprinter of the previous three years, Christie could name his price. They played *Land of Hope and Glory* on the public address system in Oslo when he won there, while the crowd in Zurich greeted another Christie victory with a football chant of his name. The value of Christie's appearance for British meetings would surely be greater still. Yet other economic factors were in force by the summer of 1995: the recession had hit athletics.

The BAF, already in a bind through less TV and sponsorship income, was looking to negotiate new deals. Such astronomical demands, even for someone of Christie's stature, could not be met. In negotiations with Peter Radford and Ian Stewart, BAF's promotions manager, Christie also took up the cause of one of his Nuff Respect clients, John Regis, the former European 200 metres champion whose appearance fees were beginning to reflect two lean years hit by injury.

Christie related the disappointing attendance at the London Grand Prix meeting to his own absence from the competitors' list. 'I just have to walk on the track and everybody cheers. It's a shame that Peter Radford and Ian Stewart cannot see that.' But when Christie did eventually race on a British track, in the AAA Championships 100 metres at Birmingham, his appearance for the final was greeted by some jeers from the crowd. Christie had failed to qualify from his heat into the semi-finals earlier in the day, because of an injury. But in a startling development, BAF's meeting organisers allowed him to run in a 'spare' lane in the final. Running as a 'guest', Christie won, while Darren Braithwaite finished second but was officially the national champion. Not that anyone noticed. BAF explained that by letting Christie run, they were giving the spectators and television what they wanted to see. In so doing, it was a bit like giving Manchester United a bye into the FA Cup Final after they had been knocked out by a bunch of non-Leaguers in an early round, simply because the crowd would prefer to see them play at Wembley.

Despite concerns over Christie's injury, his performance in Birmingham was enough to confirm his selection for the British team for the highlight of the season. This was the World Championships in Gothenburg, Sweden. After everything that he had said in the two months beforehand, Gothenburg seemed likely to be Christie's championship swansong.

As if the big man had not made enough news during the summer, the week before the championships saw him grab more headlines when it was revealed that Merric Osborne, at 16 the eldest of Christie's three illegitimate children from two broken relationships, had himself become an unmarried father.

Earlier comments made by Christie, critical of single mothers for not taking enough responsibility for their children, now came back to haunt him. It was discovered that, apart from making maintenance payments (and only after he had insisted on DNA tests to prove that he was indeed the father of the twins born to another ex-girlfriend), the multi-millionaire's extended family was receiving state benefits.

The birth also raised again another of Christie's taboo subjects: his age. As he arrived in Gothenburg for what he maintained would be his last international championships, Christie was dubbed 'the world's fastest grand-father'. 'People have said I was too old since I was 26,' said Christie. 'Then I won in Barcelona at 32. I am a winner.' But at 35, was his time as a winner running out?

Three

The World-Weary Championships

WHEN history recalls the World Championships of 1995, staged in Gothenburg, Sweden, they will probably be remembered for Michael Johnson's historic 200 and 400 metres double, for Jonathan Edwards twice breaking the triple jump world record, for Sergei Bubka being as peerless as ever in winning his fifth pole vault world title, and for the 800 metres victory by Ana Quirot, who had been close to death barely two years before.

But Gothenburg might also be remembered for the way Spanish marathon runner Martin Fiz reached down to pull his sunglasses from his shorts as he left the glare of the city streets and entered the shaded finishing straight in the stadium, in order to fulfil an obligation to his sponsors. Or perhaps the abiding memory will be of Moses Kiptanui, the Kenyan winner of the 3,000 metres steeplechase, who slowed down on his final lap to ensure that he *did not* break the world record. He saved that for five days later in Zurich, the most lucrative Grand Prix meeting on the circuit, where huge bonuses are available for record-breaking performances.

Kiptanui and Fiz were just two illustrations of the way money had come to dominate even championship events for athletes in the new professional era. And it was confirmation of the fears widely expressed five years earlier when the International Amateur Athletic Federation made the decision to hold its World Championships every two years rather than four. Devaluation had set in.

It was all too much, too soon. In the space of four years, Gothenburg was the third city to stage the athletics World Championships.There had been an Olympic Games slotted into that period, too. To make matters worse at Gothenburg, the event was stretched thinly over nine days. When the World Championships was first staged in 1983, the meeting had taken just seven days of competition. There was too little outstanding talent spread across the programme in Gothenburg: each passing day's final session always seemed, in some way, incomplete, like a restaurant meal when the main course has never been served.

Sally Gunnell, who had won gold for the 400 metres hurdles at the previous World Championships in Stuttgart two years earlier, summed it up when she said, 'I don't know what it is, it just feels flat. It hasn't got that *specialness* that you expect.' For too much of the time, Gothenburg felt as if it was a world-weary championships.

By being staged every two years, the World Championships had lost its rarity value. Michael Johnson and Noureddine Morceli have between them now won nine World Championship gold medals. But neither has an individual Olympic gold medal, a treasure both will be straining every sinew to acquire at the Atlanta Olympic Games. For without Olympic gold, their status as all-time great athletes might still be questioned. 'The World Championships have status,' said the American sprinter, Darnell Hall, seemingly unconcerned by his performance after trailing in sixth behind Johnson in the 400 metres final, 'but only for winners.'

Together with the winners' status at the World Championships went a Mercedes-Benz car, a prize introduced at the 1993 World Championships to stave off a threatened boycott by leading competitors such as Johnson and Mike Powell. In Athens in 1997, at the next World Championships, the IAAF president, Dr Primo Nebiolo, will at last bow to the inevitable and make up in cash what his championships lack in status, when prize-money – $100,000 for gold medallists, and smaller cheques for athletes placing in the top eight – will be awarded for the first time. Will cash prizes make up for the secret ingredient that was missing in Gothenburg?

Carl Lewis did not seem to think so. Before flying home to tend the hamstring injury that forced him to withdraw from the long jump, the only individual event for which the world's most be-medalled athlete managed to qualify, Lewis joined the critics of the Gothenburg championships. 'This World Championships, it's boring. The electricity is not there. There's no buzz, no passionate missions. There's something missing.' The missing element, according to Lewis, was Lewis. 'The one American they're trying to build up, Michael Johnson, he doesn't have it. He's not doing anything for them.'

Had Lewis stayed in Sweden a little longer, even he might have been touched by a spark of excitement on the Friday evening, the seventh day of the championships. For that was when the championships belatedly came to life. In the women's 400 metres hurdles final, the Americans Kim Batten and Tonja Buford seemed closely matched. From the gun, they seemed locked together in a symmetry of strides and leaps, all the way through to the final barrier, when Batten touched down a shade earlier. Yet Buford has often been the stronger finisher. 'If she'd won, I couldn't have been disappointed,' Batten said. 'I leaned as best I could lean,' said Buford.

Batten leaned the better. The contest carried both of them across the line, oblivious to the 40,000 screaming voices in the bowl of the Ullevi stadium. And the crowd, too, immersed in this extraordinary struggle down the home straight, had failed to spot the time on the clock just beside the finishing line. There was a moment's stillness, of realisation, then a thunder of applause as the spectators recognised the significance of the figures: 52.61. Batten was the first to sense what it might mean. 'Tonja,' shrieked Batten, 'we broke the world record!'

Michael Johnson did not break any world records that week, but his sprinting was nonetheless awesome. Exceptionally for a 400-metre sprint, Johnson seemed to accelerate from halfway, into the final bend of the race to leave his rivals looking flat-footed. In the stands, Robert Pariente, a correspondent with the French sports paper *L'Equipe*, was timing each section of Johnson's race. The big Texan had barely crossed the finishing line when Pariente leapt in the air. '*Mon Dieu*, 10.45 seconds for the third 100! On the bend!' he said. '*C'est impossible.*'

When Johnson stood on the podium after the 200 metres on the seventh day of the championships to collect the second of his three gold medals (he was later to take gold in the American 4x400 metres relay team), the tension was gone from his face for the first time in a week. The normally poker-faced Johnson beamed, and though they were playing the *Star Spangled Banner*, his anthem could have been written by Vangelis. The American's uniquely golden 200-400 double had just succeeded the feat of Eric Liddell, the Scottish sprinter with a similarly upright running style who won 400 gold and 200 bronze at the Paris Olympics in 1924, as featured in the film *Chariots of Fire*.

Johnson's unprecedented feat also drew comparisons with Jesse Owens, the great champion who even managed to embarrass Hitler at the 1936 Berlin Olympics. 'But I don't think you can compare any athlete today with what Jesse Owens did,' Johnson said, 'because we never have to put up with the things he did, we're treated properly as athletes and as human beings.'

This was a display of humility and, unusually, an appreciation of the wider world beyond the athletics track, rarely found in a modern athlete. But then Johnson is something special in other regards, too. There can rarely be athletes for whom the entire schedule of a championships is changed to facilitate their own, personal ambitions. Yet this is what happened for Johnson, with a shifting of heats times of the 200 metres to avoid too harsh a clash with the final rounds of the 400 metres. No one seemed to remark that the very reason the 200-400 double had not been accomplished before was because of the lack of rest in the schedule of the championships – by making it easier for Johnson to achieve, the comparison with feats of the past were rendered irrelevant. But there were other factors involved, such as the need to establish a new superstar for American track and field. Thus it was that, within six months of his Gothenburg triumphs, Johnson's calls to have similar special treatment to enable him to double up at 200 and 400 metres at the Atlanta Olympics were also granted.

For Britain, everything at the championships seemed to depend on a moment's hop, step and jump one azure blue Monday evening. With all three of Britain's world champions from 1993 injured – Sally Gunnell and Colin Jackson so badly that they were not even able to compete – there was an obligation, an expectation, on the second rank of often unheralded competitors to reach the heights in Gothenburg. Triple jumper Jonathan Edwards rose to the task magnificently.

There was another packed house in the Ullevi stadium that afternoon for the second full finals session. Unusually, their attention, full of expectancy, was focused on an unprepossessing Briton in the first round of the triple jump, an arcane field event which rarely merits even a paragraph in even the most detailed of reports on the sport. But in Jonathan Edwards, the sport had suddenly discovered a superstar, something which British athletics, in particular, needed with desperate urgency after a wretched summer of rows and rancour for the sport, which had yet to recover from the internal strife, the drugs exposures and scandals which the previous year had scarred what had been regarded previously as a squeaky clean activity to which you could take the family.

Edwards, clean cut son of an Anglican vicar from Devon, was just the tonic British athletics might have been praying for, and with his very first leap on that sunlit afternoon in Gothenburg, every prayer must have been answered. The light-framed athlete pattered down the long runway, hit the white, wooden take-off board as perfectly as could be hoped for, and soared; he bounced off the track again, exploded with one final effort, and splashed down into the flattened sand, his heels well clear of the 18-metre mark. The delay while the officials measured the jump seemed to last forever: 18.16 metres made Edwards the first to leap beyond 18 metres without the help of a strong tailwind, and improved the world record by more than six inches over the 17.98-metre effort he had registered in Salamanca, Spain, just three weeks earlier.

With 12 athletes in the final, there was a long delay before Edwards's next turn to jump. After an hour of sitting at the trackside, constantly stretching, trying to keep the muscles supple and warm, he was called to jump again. Just as before, in a routine honed by months and years of practice, he seemed to hover above the red rubber surface of the runway before eventually landing in the pit. The jump was even longer, at 18.29 metres it was officially the first jump beyond 60 feet.

Jonathan Edwards buried his head in his hands when the distance was announced in a combination of shock and joy. No one was more shocked than Edwards himself. He called the experience, 'a quite humbling thing'.

Away from the track, wearing his thin, round glasses, Edwards looks more like a scholar than a world-beating athlete. His degree in physics and his record-shattering year in the triple jump testify that he is both. But like *Chariots of Fire* sprinter Eric Liddell, what really defines Jonathan Edwards is his faith.

Until 1993, Edwards had refused to compete on Sundays. Sunday was a special day, the Lord's day, he maintained. His decision roused memories of the 1924 Olympics when Liddell, a devout Christian, had declined to race in the 100 metres because the heats were staged on a Sunday, thus leaving the way clear for his rival, Harold Abrahams, to take the gold for Britain.

Edwards eventually changed his mind about competing on Sundays, and he says that he believes that his talent and abilities, his failures and successes are all an expression of God's will. 'Man makes plans, but God directs their path,' said Edwards. Soft-spoken and without a trace of self-consciousness, Edwards talks more like a missionary than an athlete whose whole being depends on what they achieve in one burst of effort lasting less than ten seconds.

'I'm not remarkable. I don't think I'm special,' he says. 'In a sense, it's the way God has done it. My overall perspective is, "It's God's providence. He's arranged it." There are many talented athletes, but things don't come together for them.'

Despite new-found wealth, a champion's Mercedes-Benz with the personalised number plate 'J18 JDE', and the prestige that winning the BBC Sports Personality of the Year award carries, Edwards's achievements do not seem to have changed him. He remains a homebody, a reader of theology and philosophy. He continues to strum religious tunes on his guitar, play golf, snooker and chess, enjoy the occasional Chinese takeaway, and dote on his two young sons.

When reflecting upon his season, Edwards was frank enough to admit that 'if anyone else had achieved what I did, I would probably think they were on drugs'. Edwards's leap towards athletics immortality had begun in February 1995, when he visited Tallahassee. There, he received unexpected technical and psychological assistance and a spiritual boost from Dennis Nobles, the jumps coach at Florida State University.

Edwards had gone to Florida to begin rebuilding his training after being laid low during the previous season by the debilitating Epstein-Barr virus. Edwards was introduced to Nobles on his first day in Tallahassee. But their most fateful meeting took place at the end of that week when, by chance, Edwards went to Grace Church in the city and saw the coach again. 'I tend to think there was a divine influence in Jonathan coming here and our meeting at the church,' Nobles said. Especially so, since there were more than 200 churches for Edwards to choose from in Tallahassee. 'God blessed me to meet him, and I'm just happy I was in the right place at the right time,' Nobles said.

'Our relationship goes a lot deeper than talking about training and technique. Our relationship is more friendship. We share a basic value system. I believe that God created the universe and takes a personal interest in His creations. I believe Jonathan is an instrument in God's will.'

Nobles and Edwards agreed to meet on the FSU track once a week. They worked on lifting Edwards's torso on take-off, holding the hop and skip for as long as possible, improving the pumping action of the athlete's arms, and extending his feet forwards as he lands on the final jump. Using a shorter approach run than he would in competition, by the time he had finished working with Nobles, Edwards was jumping four inches further than he had ever managed when competing. Short of growing wings, Edwards had learnt to fly.

The highlight of Edwards's career up to that point had been the bronze medal at the 1993 World Championships. Now Nobles calculated that, off his full run-up Edwards would break the world record which Willie Banks had held unchallenged for a decade. Once Edwards had returned to his home in Newcastle, Nobles wrote to him telling him just that. 'It's scary to write to somebody a letter saying "You can break the world record" when he was half-a-metre away before the season,' Nobles said.

Edwards was the bright new star, but, as often as not, the starter's pistol in Gothenburg signalled the crashing fall of other athletics giants. First Christie, then Joyner-Kersee, then Drechsler and Sotomayor all lost crowns which had been theirs, some for nearly a decade.

After Christie collapsed on the track following his sixth place in the 100 metres final, having failed in his attempt to recover from hamstring and cartilage injuries, John Smith, the American who had coached Ato Bolden to the bronze medal, remarked of the newly deposed champion: 'That's the most courageous thing he's ever done on an athletics track.'

It was ironic that in the end, it was not Christie's 35 years, or his squabbles with the British Athletic Federation and the media, which led to his downfall, but his own body. The hamstring injury flared up during the semi-final and only frantic physiotherapy and Christie's own determination enabled him to line up for the final three hours later.

Hindered by injury, Christie, for once, was lacking power in the decisive phase of the race, as Canadian team-mates Bruny Surin and the yelling Donovan Bailey raced away to silver and gold. Christie ended up face down on the track with an ice pack applied to the back of his damaged knee. 'If you are going to go down, you should go down fighting,' Christie said. The pain of defeat hurt more than the pain of injury, as Christie the next day publicly restated bitterly that he would never again compete in the big time; laughing and talking with friends and team-mates just hours later, he admitted that the only thing he would not be doing in the coming year would be defending his Olympic title in Atlanta. Christie knew there was still good money to be made on the Grand Prix circuit.

The often pallid Gothenburg championships emphasised that a new world order was establishing itself. To follow events, you needed an atlas as often as a stats book. Never before had so many athletes from so many different nations been so successful. Athletes from a record 43 countries won medals in Gothenburg, usually at the expense of the established powers such as Britain and Germany, who both saw their medal counts from Stuttgart halved. Among the nations who emerged on the world scene for the first time were Syria, Saudi Arabia and Madagascar.

'The little guys have proved that we can compete with the rest of the world,' declared Troy Kemp, the high jump world champion, of the Bahamas. 'Track and field is the most global sport in the world. Everyone understands it. Anyone can do it.'

Helmut Digel, the head of the German federation, predicted that if this pace of change was maintained, in a few years, 'European nations could end up being the developing countries'.

The re-drawing of the world athletics map could be traced back to the day in 1989 when the Berlin Wall came down. When the Soviet Union and East Germany broke up, the sporting structure – including state-sponsored drugs programmes – that had nurtured a constant stream of world-beaters, was broken up with them. 'Now it is more difficult to be an athlete in Russia because there is no money to prepare properly,' said Evgeni Kuznetov, his country's senior coach.

At the same time, other countries had been investing heavily in sports development. Even previously minor athletics countries, such as Saudi Arabia, were spending huge amounts of state money on their athletes. 'If we are to maintain our status in future,' warned Malcolm Arnold, Britain's chief coach, 'a radical change in attitude is needed in the funding of athletics by the government.'

Arnold was appealing for a change in the policy of allocating all the sports funding from the National Lottery to capital projects – new buildings and facilities. He wanted the option of having lottery funds for revenue spending, to offer training grants to promising athletes, a system which is used successfully to finance sport in many other countries. 'Four million pounds a year would allow a model for coaching and development to be put in place which would ensure success into the next century.' In fact, Arnold's annual coaching budget, funded completely out of the BAF's own resources, was nearer £700,000. And in the autumn following Gothenburg, it became plain that the Sports Council, the government agency which grant aids most of British sport, was in fact facing a three per cent budget cut for 1996-97 – amounting to about £1.5 million – despite previous government assurances that the advent of the lottery would not affect public funding of sport.

Had the level of funding Arnold desired been in place after the 1993 World Championships, Britain might have doubled its gold haul in Gothenburg. The achievement of the Slough-born Fiona May in winning the women's long jump gold medal was only marred, in British eyes, because she was competing in the azure blue vest of Italy. In a way, Fiona May was proof of Arnold's point.

May had switched nationality because she felt she was getting too little cash back-up from Britain to help her translate her promise as a junior – she was world junior champion in 1988 – into senior success. In 1993, May was offered a grant of £500 by the British federation. She was so disgusted that, since she had married an Italian international pole vaulter and was based in Italy, she took the opportunity to switch national allegiance. The decision soon brought dividends. In 1995, the Italian federation paid her £62,000. That comprised a £20,000 grant as top-ranked international, a £2,000 bonus for breaking the Italian record, and £40,000 for becoming world champion. In addition, under the wealthy Italian system, her Milan club, SnamGaz, also paid May £11,000 in grants and bonuses. Add the £16,000 she receives from her shoe company, and probably a similar amount in bonuses from them for winning the world title, throw in the £20,000 Mercedes-Benz, and you are talking about a woman who in one jump leapt out of the paupers' and into the princesses' league.

The link between athletic investment and performance is not automatic. Germany, with an annual coaching budget of £3 million – four times the British level – produced a level of performance far from four times better than Britain. One of the most surprising of Britain's high achievers in Gothenburg, marathon runner Peter Whitehead, who finished fourth, showed that grit and determination are also necessary qualities for success. He went to the World Championships having trained at altitude for nine months in New Mexico, an expensive excursion which, since he had quit his job to pursue his athletics ambitions, was initially funded by his wife, Sandra, who works in a Leeds bank, and his mother, Dorothy.

Having become successful by winning cash prizes on the road race circuit in the United States, Whitehead is now self-financing his long-term training at Albuquerque, but his chances of winning an Olympic medal at Atlanta would be greatly enhanced were he to receive the sort of state assistance which his marathon rivals from Spain and Portugal get. It was no coincidence that these two countries provided the winners of the men's and women's marathons in Gothenburg: Martin Fiz for Spain, and Manuela Machado for Portugal.

Part of the globalisation of the 1995 World Championships was the success of Caribbean athletes. Jamaica has always been a sprinting power-house, from the days of Arthur Wint and E. Macdonald Baily, through to Don Quarrie and Merlene Ottey, and including those born on the island, such as Linford Christie and Donovan Bailey, who emigrated with their families to make new lives elsewhere but who also never forgot their roots. But with medallists such as Dominica's triple jumper Jerome Romain and Trinidad sprinter Ato Bolden, the calypso beat was heard loud and clear in Gothenburg.

All the islands' top athletes have links with American universities, where they have studied and trained while on scholarships. 'There were always good athletes in the Caribbean, now they have the chance to train at our colleges,' said John Smith, whose training group based at the UCLA track in Los Angeles includes 400 metres world champion Marie-Jose Perec, who was born and brought up on the French Caribbean island of Guadaloupe. Troy Kemp has said that the US college system has been crucial to the islanders' success. 'In America, you have the chance to fully develop your talent. It's no coincidence that when you combine Caribbean athletes who have the talent, with American coaches, who have the knowledge, they should be outstandingly successful. They just need that opportunity.'

Talent scouts from American colleges have always recruited aggressively. In the mid-1980s, the University of Nebraska – whose former students include Merlene Ottey – had an annual budget of £27,000 for telephone calls to recruit athletes from abroad. In July 1995, at the European Junior Championships staged in the remote Hungarian town of Nyiregyhaza, there were half a dozen American college coaches prowling around the edges of the track, ready to sign up the cream of Europe's young athletes. With scholarship packages sometimes worth as much as £30,000 per year – including food, accommodation, tuition and extensive training facilities – plus a degree education, it is an offer which can make an athlete's life on a student loan in Britain seem eminently resistible.

The sole aim of these American universities is success for their track and field team in National Collegiate Athletic Association competition. Pete Cava, the spokesman for USA Track and Field, the national governing body, explained the logic behind the system. 'We are training the cream of the world's athletes and the reasons why lie with college coaches fighting for success in the NCAA leagues. Success means bigger budgets for the university and more kudos for the campus.

'The trouble with the NCAA is that it has no rules and it's a law unto itself. It did have to impose an age restriction a few years ago because too many top internationals were beating American kids who were still developing. But by and large, anyone can come and compete.' And they do. Results from the 1995 NCAA Championships show that most track events were won by non-Americans.

As Carl Lewis observed, 'American athletes are being short-changed. The United States is training foreigners to beat its own.' At Gothenburg, America's sprinters had their worst championships since the Munich Olympics of 1972. The Americans were in a dire situation. Lewis flew home, injured; 100 metres world record-holder Leroy Burrell never even got as far as Sweden; Olympic bronze medallist Dennis Mitchell pulled up lame in his 100 metres heat; and 1993 world silver medalist Andre Cason did not make the team. By the end of the week in Gothenburg, the nation which has always produced the world's greatest sprinters, was scratching around to find four men fit enough to run in the sprint relay. 'After Jeff Williams,' said Mike Marsh, 'our next fastest is Gwen Torrence.'

With the Olympic Games being staged in Atlanta in 1996, it was imperative for the sport in the United States that its team performed up to standard in Gothenburg. Track and field in America had plummed an all-time low in popularity. The San Jose Grand Prix meeting was saved only after an infusion of European money, and the New York Games was attended by fewer than 5,000 paying spectators. With Sunkist pulling out of their long-term association with its Los Angeles winter meeting, indoor track moved one step closer to extinction in the United States.

As he surveyed the empty stands at the US Championships in Sacramento in June, Harrison Dillard sighed. 'Track in this country seems to have fallen on hard times,' said the man who won four Olympic gold medals, two in 1948 and two in 1952. 'Baseball, football, basketball, golf and tennis have become very lucrative for athletes in the US. This country's got the world's greatest track and field stars, but no one here seems to care. They've all got to go to Europe to get the recognition that they deserve.'

'I've never seen the sport lower,' said Carl Lewis. Michael Johnson shared the despair. 'I'm ready to throw up my arms and say "This is the nature of the sport in this country, and that's it". People have just got too many other things to watch,' Johnson said. But in Johnson, athletics in America still has some hope. By winning three golds in Gothenburg, Johnson helped his team to a total of 12. No other country won more than two gold medals in Gothenburg. If Johnson can repeat his achievement in Atlanta, then maybe America will start to take athletics seriously again.

'It is so important for us to have a good meet in Atlanta, to make the sport attractive to sponsors and television and, most important, to America's young people,' said Pete Cava as he watched the Gothenburg closing ceremony from high in the stands of the Ullevi. 'Pro sports are down in a big way . . . there is a chance for us to move in. Michael Johnson can be a god to a generation of kids.'

Whether Jonathan Edwards could equally inspire a generation of British youngsters is a moot point. As the future careers of crowd-pullers Linford Christie, Sally Gunnell and Colin Jackson were left uncertain by the absences and defeats in 1995, the need for someone to replace them among Britain's sporting heroes became more urgent.

Yet in other respects, Edwards represented not the ending of an era, but the revival of one. For in financial terms, one of the most successful people at the Gothenburg championships had been Andy Norman, the same Andy

Norman who 16 months earlier had been kicked out of his promotions job with the British Athletic Federation after he was shown to have made threats against *The Sunday Times* journalist Cliff Temple which contributed to his suicide.

The BAF seemed powerless to prevent Norman working as an athletes' agent. On an official IAAF list of athletes' managers, distributed at the World Championships, it was suggested that Norman's only client was Edwards – a rich enough jewel in himself. But in fact, Norman also represented Britain's three other medallists in Gothenburg: middle distance runner Kelly Holmes, 110-metre hurdler Tony Jarrett, and javelin thrower Steve Backley.

Norman's departure from BAF headquarters seemed to have been followed by the sport descending into a tailspin of chaos and confusion. It was only much later that it transpired that Norman had still assisted the BAF in the organisation of some of its meetings during the summer of 1994, and was recruiting athletes in America to compete in British meetings the following summer. Add to those roles Norman's involvement in the organisation of meetings in Helsinki and Moscow, of a series of events in South Africa, and his continuing position on the IAAF's influential Grand Prix Commission, and by the end of the championships in Gothenburg, it seemed as if Norman, the most powerful figure in British athletics for two decades, had never gone away.

Four

Death on the Track

IT WAS cold and overcast, an ordinary grey Saturday morning in January. A group of railway engineers were working their way along the railway track, carrying out preparatory work for the line which was to form part of the Channel Tunnel route into Folkestone later that year.

The workmen were laughing and joking as they made their way past Sandling Station, an unexceptional, rural halt with a large, empty space flattened into a hill beside the main road to serve as a car park to accommodate the vehicles of the commuters who travel by train into London during the week. At the weekend, though, things were a good deal quieter, on the roads as well as the rails, and this allowed the engineering work to be carried out.

Although it was still early, with no one about on the platform, none of the engineers noticed anything odd about the ageing Rover car which was parked in the station car park. From the heavy dew resting on its paintwork, it looked as if the car may have been parked there all night.

Another hundred yards or so further on down the railway line, and the first of the workmen made his way into the dark of Sandling Tunnel. Not very much further along the track, he made a gruesome discovery. There, lying beside the rails, was the badly disfigured body of a middle-aged man. The train which had obviously hit him had broken every bone in his body.

The police were called to the scene straightaway, but once there they could not identify the man because he carried nothing – no wallet, credit cards, old letters – in his lightweight sports jacket. So they tried to retrace the man's likely last steps and that led the police to the car park, and the old Rover. It was registered in the name of a local man at an address a short distance away, at Hythe.

A call at the address brought no immediate answer. The police tried the neighbours and so managed to get inside the house, where they discovered five letters, neatly put to one side in such a way that ensured they would be found. The notes confirmed the police's suspicions: the man found on the railway line had indeed intended to take his own life. His name was Cliff Temple.

Cliff Temple was 46 when he died, and at the peak of his profession. He had been athletics correspondent of *The Sunday Times* since 1969: 1994 was to have been his twenty-fifth anniversary at the paper, where he had won awards for his journalism and had been widely acknowledged, by his colleagues as well as those in athletics, as one of the most perceptive and sensitive of sports writers, a group of people not usually known for those qualities.

Temple's unique insights into athletics were often aided by another of his skills, that of coach to some of Britain's leading distance runners. He was widely known in athletics circles as a friendly, very approachable man, usually smiling, always helpful with some advice or a suggestion. So what was it that caused him to die in such an agonising, lonely manner, a deeply troubled man? On the evening before his body was discovered, he had given no hint of what was to happen.

Regularly, Temple would visit his widowed mother's flat in Folkestone for dinner. This Friday was no different. Until, that is, he came to leave. This time, he left earlier than usual, around nine o'clock, for the ten-minute drive home. He had to be up early next morning, Temple told his mother, because he had a flight to catch from Heathrow so that he could cover an international cross-country event in Belfast for his newspaper.

Earlier in the week, Temple had told colleagues that he was particularly keen to make the trip to Northern Ireland. The highlight of the meeting at Mallusk, just outside Belfast, was to be the race between Paula Radcliffe – the British 20-year-old whose progress had excited Temple since he had watched her win the junior title at the 1992 World Cross-country Championships in Boston – and Ireland's Catherina McKiernan, senior silver medallist at the World Cross for the previous two years and who Temple had also had good cause to write about regularly in *The Sunday Times*'s new Irish editions.

'When he left, he seemed fine,' Joan, his mother, recalled. 'I asked him whether he had a ticket and he told me that he was going to buy one on his credit card at the airport. I told him to drive safely and to give me a call. Then he kissed me goodnight and I waved him away. I thought everything was normal.'

Temple's absence from Mallusk the following morning was noted. In the small band of athletics writers, Temple was soon missed. But there seemed to be a perfectly reasonable explanation. As his colleagues sat down to lunch in the Chimney Corner Hotel a couple of hours before the race was due to start, they wondered aloud where Temple had got to. They guessed that nothing was seriously wrong and that *The Sunday Times* had probably decided that he should cover instead the first important indoor meeting of the winter, which was being staged at the National Indoor Arena in Birmingham that same afternoon. Perhaps Temple was on to a better story; he usually was. 'Lucky bugger,' one of the lunch party said. 'I'd much rather be in Birmingham than be standing here, knee-deep in mud and freezing my bollocks off.'

But *The Sunday Times* had made no such decision. At their offices in a refurbished wine warehouse by the Thames at Wapping, just to the east of the Tower of London, one of the staff had been routinely ticking off the names of various correspondents as they made their usual morning call, to check on their lineage – the number of words they had for their report – and their deadline times. Temple's name remained unticked. But because Temple was totally dependable – in the words of his sports editor, Chris Nawrat, 'Temple was the model pro, always on time, always to length' – his colleagues in the office gave this omission hardly a second thought. Perhaps there was a problem with the flight? Maybe Temple had had difficulties getting through to the sports desk when the office telephone was busy?

However, come five o'clock that evening, with the first edition deadlines barely an hour away, and the realisation dawned that not only had Temple not made his preliminary call, but that he had not filed any copy at all.

Greg Struthers, that day's chief sub-editor, rushed through from his open plan office to the sports desk 'back bench', where Nawrat and other senior staff members were working, reading edited reports, checking and revising them. 'Cliff's still not called,' Struthers said, *sotto voce* to Nawrat. 'I never even thought about it when he didn't ring this morning, but he hasn't filed at all. What are we to do?'

According to Nawrat, 'In my mind, at that point, I had a deep suspicion of what may have happened.' In 25 years of working on the paper, Temple had never missed a deadline.

After making hurried arrangements to fill the space left by Temple's absent athletics article with a story about skiing taken from some news agency copy, Nawrat left the busy sports desk to seek the privacy of an office in the paper's business news section. From there, he tried again to contact Temple, and then he phoned Temple's ex-wife, Clare. It was no later than 6.15 p.m. Within half-an-hour, Nawrat's worst fears would be confirmed.

After receiving Nawrat's phone call, Clare Temple drove the short distance from her new home to Sussex Barn, the house where she and Cliff had brought up their family of four children, Kristen, Kenza, William and Joss. On her arrival, she met one of the neighbours who had helped the police gain access to the house earlier in the day. The neighbour automatically assumed that she must already know the terrible news. The assumption was wrong: in tears, Clare Temple drove into Folkestone, to Joan Temple's flat, and from there she phoned *The Sunday Times* to confirm the news which Nawrat had feared.

Of the five letters found at Cliff Temple's home that day, four had been to members of his family. The fifth was to David Moorcroft, the former Commonwealth champion and world record-holder whose biography Temple had helped to write in 1983. Moorcroft was Temple's closest friend in athletics.

In the letters to his children, which Temple wanted saved for them until they were grown up, he merely said his farewells and apologised for what he knew his death would put them through. But in the notes to his mother and to Moorcroft, Temple referred to rumours which he believed were circulating about him. Temple's letters categorically denied the rumours.

'I have no option but to do this,' Temple wrote to his mother, 'because even my friends in athletics no longer trust me.' There was no explanation for this apparent breakdown in trust, nor any details of the rumours. But those in athletics who knew Temple would soon know exactly what he meant, and even without reading the letters, nor even knowing of their existence for more than a week after Temple's death, many soon drew their own conclusions. 'It was obvious what he was referring to,' Moorcroft said. 'Anyone who had been close to Cliff would have known that he was talking about Andy Norman and the fact that he had been telling people that Cliff had sexually harassed Shireen Bailey.'

For a coach in any sport, the trust of their charges, and of their families and friends, is essential. Often unpaid, coaches usually give of their time just for the vicarious pleasure that they get from helping someone else to achieve their potential. Cliff Temple's motivation as a coach was just that. An attempt to smear him could destroy the trust which he enjoyed with the athletes he coached. It could also wreck any professional relationship he might have built up with athletes that he might interview for his job as athletics correspondent with *The Sunday Times*. For Temple, the consequences of such smears were too horrible to contemplate.

In two decades, of all the achievements of all the athletes Temple had coached – from Mike Gratton, the winner of the 1983 London Marathon, through to Sarah Rowell, whom he turned from being a college hockey player into an Olympic runner and British marathon record-holder – the one in which Temple probably took most pride was when Shireen Bailey made the final of the 1,500 metres at the Olympic Games in Seoul, South Korea, in 1988. So when Temple first heard the allegation of sexual harassment, he immediately called Bailey. She made it abundantly clear to him that there was never any suggestion of a sexual approach to her by Temple. But according to Moorcroft, such assurances were not enough for Temple.

'Even though she promised Cliff that she had never complained and that he had done nothing wrong as far as she was concerned, he was worried sick that he was finished in the sport.

'On top of everything else that had happened to him in the previous couple of years, he just couldn't cope with this slur on his character.'

In the three-and-a-half years leading up to his death, there had been two sides to Cliff Temple. One side of Temple was what the athletics world knew as the laughing, wise-cracking, brilliant writer, who each year gave a wonderful stand-up act at the British Athletics Writers' Association awards dinner. The polished professionalism of this performance owed much to the fact that Temple's material – all original, all his own – had been honed and practised from his teens in his secondary career as a comedy writer providing sketches for BBC radio shows such as *Weekending* and *The News Huddlines*.

It was this wit and his perceptiveness which made Temple the finest athletics writer of his and perhaps any other generation. He had a huge following in athletics, thanks to his work in *The Sunday Times*, where he had been instrumental in establishing the National Fun Run as the country's largest annual participation event, and from his regular magazine coaching columns in *Running* and *Athletics Today*, as well as his numerous books.

But since his separation from his wife in 1991, there had also been a darker side to Temple. The break-up of his marriage had depressed him. Temple was badly affected when Clare had moved out of the family home, together with the children, in order to live with a Dutchman she had met when she was on holiday while Cliff was away on work.

Temple felt that his domestic worries were affecting his work. He wrote to Chris Nawrat at *The Sunday Times*. 'He said that he had tried to keep his marriage together, but after a year, he argued quite logically, that his work must be suffering. But there was no basis for that in fact. His work was just as good as it had always been.'

It was just the first of a series of resignation offers and threats which Nawrat would receive and reject over the course of the next two years. Temple's efforts having failed to stop his marriage from breaking up, he then tried desperately to cling close to what he held dear: his children. In order to stay close to his offspring, he remortgaged his house and bought another home in the same area where Clare and the children could live, together with the out-of-work Dutchman.

The desperation of that move was soon apparent financially, however. The combined burden of two mortgages, plus maintenance, placed Temple under tremendous strain. Seeking to work more regularly, he had left *Running* magazine to write instead for *Athletics Today*. But in June 1993, *Athletics Today* closed, and with it went another source of Temple's income. A salary increase at *The Sunday Times*, to £27,000 per year, could not stave off the inevitable day in December 1993 when Temple's accountant advised him that the only sensible course of action for him was to put the family home up for sale and move into somewhere smaller. It was the last thing Temple wanted to do: emotionally, he had invested a great deal in the house. He felt his children would think badly of him if they were unable to visit him in the house where they had grown up.

An incident a week before his death illustrates just how dire Temple believed his finances to be. He was at King's Cross Station, waiting for a train to Newcastle, where he was to cover the televised cross-country event at Beamish, County Durham. A young girl beggar approached him, asking if he could spare some change because she could not afford to pay her rent. Temple turned to a colleague, 'If I carry on for much longer, I'll be like that,' he said solemnly. When asked what he meant, Temple changed the subject.

The race at Beamish on New Year's Day 1994 was an important one for Temple. The previous August, after returning from the World Championships in Stuttgart, Germany, Temple had a nervous breakdown. The collapse of his marriage, the resulting financial troubles, his insecurity at work, all had been compounded by a further pressure which he had never expected. This additional pressure arose while Temple was preparing an article for *The Sunday Times* on the often controversial role in British athletics of Andy Norman, the British Athletic Federation's promotions director, and his fiancée, the former javelin thrower, Fatima Whitbread.

While researching the feature, which was to be the back-page lead story of *The Sunday Times* on 1 August, Temple was phoned at home by Norman. During the phone call, which came in response to a series of questions Temple had put to Whitbread in another telephone conversation earlier that same day, Norman threatened that allegations that Temple had sexually harassed Shireen Bailey would get out. Temple was shocked and astonished, at first struggling to absorb Norman's exact meaning. 'I'm not sure what you mean, Andy, I'm not sure what you mean,' he said, over again.

What Norman had not counted on was that Temple taped their conversation. It was not something Temple was practised at, but he did it on the advice of *The Sunday Times* sports desk. In part, it was as additional proof for his researches, and in part as protection, in anticipation of receiving some form of threat.

Later that evening, after he had driven to Crystal Palace for the annual athletics Grand Prix meeting there, Temple played the tape on his car stereo to three colleagues: John Rodda, of *The Guardian*, Duncan Mackay and *The Times*'s athletics correspondent, David Powell. Tony Ward, the official spokesman for the British Athletic Federation, was also invited by Temple to listen to the tape but, busy with the events of the night, was unable to take up the offer.

On one occasion as Temple played the tape, Linford Christie, the Olympic 100 metres champion, happened to walk close to Temple's impromptu meeting in the car park. Christie had been cajoled and helped to the very pinnacle of world athletics by Norman and now was unlikely to have a word said against his adviser. Temple, spotting Christie, quickly turned off the tape machine. Temple also played to his colleagues Bailey's taped repudiation of Norman's foul slurs. 'It's laughable,' Temple told his friends, 'I've really got Andy on the run.'

But a month later, at the World Championships in Stuttgart, after the article had been published, Temple was horrified to discover that Norman had carried out his threat by telling other journalists his fabricated allegations. 'What's this about you touching up your runners, then?' a tabloid reporter asked the shocked Temple in their Stuttgart hotel bar one evening. On the last Friday of the championships, Temple was part of a large group of British journalists, including Peter Hildreth of *The Sunday Telegraph*, Patrick Collins of *The Mail on Sunday* and *The Independent*'s Mike Rowbottom, who were interviewing Norman and Whitbread shortly after Colin Jackson's victory in the 110 metres hurdles final. Inadvertently, Temple's arm brushed against Norman. The burly former London police sergeant turned round sharply and snapped: 'Don't touch me, you fucking pervert.'

Temple spent most of the rest of his time in Stuttgart drinking heavily, staying in the stadium bar until nearly four o'clock in the morning on the final Sunday. As they returned to England the following day, Moorcroft, who had been in Stuttgart as a commentator for the BBC, was so concerned that he insisted Temple travel back home with him to Coventry to stay with his family for a few days.

Soon, Temple returned to his own home in Kent. Moorcroft had persuaded Temple to consult his doctor. Temple also arranged a meeting with his sports editor, Chris Nawrat. Their lunch in a Chinese restaurant in the Commercial Road lasted four hours, as Temple unloaded his problems and they agreed that he should take some time off. 'I think I've just had lunch with someone having a nervous breakdown,' Nawrat confided to a colleague when he returned to the office after five o'clock.

The amateur diagnosis was accurate. Temple's GP referred him to a psychiatrist, who prescribed a course of anti-depressants. They seemed to work, and after three months' sick leave Temple returned to writing in November. The New Year's Day cross-country race in Beamish, however, was to be his first major 'live' assignment, where he would be expected to deliver a long report in a short space of time.

On the eve of the race, Temple was in good form in the company of colleagues, including the photographer, Mark Shearman, a close friend for more than 25 years who had helped to encourage him back to work. As the evening progressed, Temple seemed to be genuinely enjoying mixing with the athletes who were gathered in the hotel bar after their evening meal. He spent long periods in the company of Sarah Rowell and Carl Thackery, another top British athlete Temple had coached. 'I knew he had been ill, but he seemed really perky,' Rowell said. 'Not quite his old self, but certainly not someone who was about to commit suicide.'

During the evening, Temple finally admitted to one colleague how ill he had been. 'You'll never believe this,' Temple said. 'I was even given a caution by the police in September for walking along the railway line. Can you believe I was so stupid? I've promised myself that I'll never let myself get in that kind of state again.' With just a few hours to go until the New Year, Temple, it seemed, was looking forward to a new start. The next day, however, sitting on the coach that would take the press out to the course at Beamish, and again Temple was quiet and introspective. 'I don't know whether I can still do this,' he said. 'I don't know whether I still *want* to do this.'

The cross-country course at Beamish wound its way around an outdoor museum dedicated to the region's industrial heritage. Once there, Temple seemed to cheer up again. Walking around the muddy course, seeing young children petting the shire horses which formed part of the exhibit, and watching as families were enjoying a day out together, Temple was stopped regularly by friends in athletics who knew nothing of his illness but were nevertheless glad to see him. With each of them, Temple exchanged an aside or a wisecrack. In the women's race Paula Radcliffe enjoyed her first major victory as a senior by beating the 1988 Olympic 10,000 metres champion, Olga Bondarenko, of Russia, and Zola Pieterse, once Britain's Zola Budd, now running again for her native South Africa.

Most of the journalists who travelled south on the 5.20 from Newcastle that evening were in good moods because Radcliffe had made their long journey north worth while by giving them plenty to write about. But Temple was not so happy. He spent much of the three-hour trip slumped alone in a corner, staring out of the window into the blackness of the winter night, occasionally sipping from a can of flat beer. Temple was unhappy with what he had written, though *The Sunday Times* had had no complaints. 'I wrote crap today,' he told a neighbour on the journey. 'I just haven't got it any more. My heart's not in it. Andy wants me out and there's nothing I can do about it, is there?' He told another friend of a dark fear that, with large sums of cash 'floating about in the sport, anything can be said, anything can be done. In ten, 15, 20 years, Andy'll still be haunting me, telling lies about me. The only way I can solve the problem is to get out and let Brasher do it. There's some in the sport who would like that.'

This was a reference to Christopher Brasher. Himself a great athlete – 1956 Olympic steeplechase gold medallist, one of Roger Bannister's pacemakers in the historic first sub-four-minute mile – after hanging up his spikes, Brasher went into journalism and television, running BBC's *Man Alive* programme, winning the Sports Journalist of the Year award and editing the sports pages of *The Observer*. Brasher even went on to be the founder of the London Marathon. On the eve of the 1992 Olympics, Brasher suddenly quit *The Observer*, and offered his services to *The Sunday Times*. Brasher's arrival was hailed as a coup by the then *Sunday Times* editor, Andrew Neil. 'It's one in the eye for *The Observer*,' Neil told his staff.

Temple was furious about Brasher's arrival, because he felt undermined and worried that Neil wanted to replace him. Brasher and Temple were complete opposites, Temple concerned that his new colleague would be difficult to work with. Temple fired off a series of memos and wrote to Andrew Neil complaining about Brasher's appointment. In one memo, Temple noted, 'I have spent my entire career going head-to-head with Brasher. . .' In Barcelona for the Olympic Games Temple suffered the final indignity of having to share accommodation with Brasher. They soon clashed over how to handle the biggest story of the Games, about Jason Livingston, the young British sprinter sent home from Spain after having tested positive for anabolic steroids. Brasher was assigned to cover the story for the news desk, while Temple was to write for the sports pages.

According to Chris Nawrat, this was a device to cover all aspects of the fast-developing story while providing his colleagues working on the news pages with the difficult problem of handling the notoriously abrasive Brasher. Temple did not see it that way: 'You can give me all the work you like,' he pleaded with Nawrat, 'I *want* to work, this is my biggest moment in four years.'

It took a lot of persuasion for Temple not to pack his bags and catch the next flight home before the Olympics had even started. Temple worked through the Games, though he behaved in an odd fashion: he was rarely seen at the house *The Sunday Times* had hired for its correspondents, often leaving at midnight and not returning until six o'clock the following morning, apparently out walking the streets of Barcelona all night, alone with his thoughts.

On his return from the Olympics, Temple sought and was given assurances that his job with *The Sunday Times* was safe. So why, more than a year later, on New Year's Day 1994, was Temple still worried about the threat to his job from Brasher?

On the train journey to London, Mark Shearman and David Powell were worried. When they reached King's Cross, they persuaded Temple to join them for a coffee in the burger bar opposite the station. His spirits seemed to lift slightly, but it was still a depressed figure who stumbled off into the Saturday night on his way home.

It was the last time any of his colleagues were to see Cliff Temple alive. British athletics was destined never to be quite the same again.

Five

Over the Edge

THE Euston Plaza Hotel must have seemed like the ideal venue for the sort of meeting no organisation wants to admit to having. Close to the London mainline station which links the capital to Birmingham, the Midlands and the north-west, the Plaza's unprepossessing car-exhaust grey façade gives it an anonymity which allows tens of thousands of bustling commuters to pass it by each day without a second glance. It was here that Andy Norman, the promotions director for the British Athletic Federation, was effectively put in the dock at a disciplinary hearing over his conduct, specifically his part in events which led to the suicide of Cliff Temple.

The only thing that distinguished the £95-a-night four-star hotel that Wednesday morning at the end of March 1994 was the assembly on the hotel steps of television crews and the huddle of reporters and photographers. Unsure of their prey, their lenses zoomed in on any approaching car or taxi that paused for more than a moment. So it was that Norman broke cover for the first time in more than three months. His taxi fare paid, Norman, dressed in a grey suit with a fashionable, floral tie knotted too tightly – the hallmark of a man who had worn a policeman's narrow tie for more than two decades – he turned on his heels and found his path to the hotel door cluttered by the press corps.

Never one to waste too much time on needless public relations, Norman issued a sharp comment to quickly clear his path, and he swept up the steps and through the door with a robustness that seemed to belie the fact that he had just spent the previous month on sick leave, too ill to attend any such hearing. Presumably, the Euston Plaza had also been chosen by BAF's executive chairman, Professor Peter Radford, as the venue for the hearing because of the management's absolute discretion, carried to the point of obstinate surreality. Witnesses who had been summoned, but who had arrived earlier than Norman, milled around in the lobby, wondering if they really were in the right place – after all, the venue had already been switched twice in the previous three days in order to keep the hack pack off the scent.

'Don't tell your colleagues,' Radford told the witnesses when he telephoned them the evening before the hearing. Since three of them were journalists, this was a pretty hopeful request, and one that failed.

With the media pack out in force, it all nearly descended into pantomime when Norman arrived. As he entered the lobby with the entourage of cameramen, it prompted a call of 'It's showtime!' from among a group of waiting teenaged American tourists, who had been taking great pleasure from watching the journalists' watching and waiting.

Norman went to the reception desk to ask where the hearing was being held. But the staff there denied all knowledge that BAF had booked any of their suites for a meeting at all.

For one mad moment, Norman froze, like a startled rabbit caught in the flashlights of the photographers, not knowing whether to turn this way or that. Then a hotel manager appeared in a doorway. 'Mr Norman?' he asked, and with that, he and his charge disappeared into the sanctuary of a darkened corridor. The assembly that was left in the lobby was bemused, the day's action virtually over in the flash of a lightbulb, while the strains of Tammy Wynette's *Stand By Your Man* oozed from the hotel's muzak, as if specially requested.

Just then another taxi drew up to divert the press corps' attention for a few minutes. It carried Mel Batty, the former distance running world record-holder, more recently the coach to the 1993 London Marathon winner Eamonn Martin. An avuncular publican from Essex, Batty apologised for his crumpled suit – he had left Paris at 5 a.m. in order to attend the hearing, he said, having been to see his beloved Arsenal play in the European Cup Winners' Cup semi-final the night before.

Batty is a life-long member of what is now Thurrock Harriers, the club Norman has more recently aligned himself with through his association with their most celebrated member, Fatima Whitbread. Batty had also dealt with Norman frequently in his role as ITV Sport's regular 'catcher', the person on the in-field whose job it was to bring the top athletes over for interview once their event was over. This time, it was Batty who had the microphones thrust towards him. As he stood on the pavement outside the hotel, the only witness willing to give a television interview before giving evidence, Batty was clear about his purpose for attending the hearing. 'I am here to confirm the statement I have already given,' Batty said, 'that Norman accused Cliff Temple of sexually harassing athletes. He made the comment last August on a plane going to a meeting in Cologne. I was totally disgusted. It has proved to be not true. I believe, without a doubt, that Andy Norman should go. This was the final straw in his behaviour.'

Once inside, Batty and three other witnesses, journalists Randall Northam, Neil Wilson and Duncan Mackay, who had all heard similar remarks by Norman during the previous summer, were finally led into the basement, through freshly painted passageways to a windowless room to wait with a cup of coffee and biscuits until they were called. All four were surprised by the late appearance of John Lister, the BAF's honorary treasurer and one of those officials who had most often supported Norman in the past. Was Lister there to offer a financial insight to the cost of dismissing the promotions director, who was said to be on an annual salary of £65,000? 'I'm here for the same reason as you lads,' Lister said on entering the ante-room containing the other witnesses.

The witnesses were kept in the room for at least half an hour before any of them were called to the adjoining room to give their evidence. They were tense. No one knew who would be first to be summoned. As they waited, the witnesses spoke about anything other than athletics: Batty gave a kick-by-kick account of the previous night's match, they talked about mobile phones (Batty's rang incessantly with questions about his newly opened pub), even about the plate of croissants that had been left for them.

Outside, meanwhile, the hotel management had put a manager on duty at the end of the corridor to turn away the over-curious. When Mackay left to go to the toilet, he had to argue his way back into the waiting room. 'You can't go in there, there's a private function going on,' he was told. 'I know,' said Mackay, 'I'm part of that.'

From his very first phone call to the witnesses at the start of his inquiries, within a week of Temple's death, Radford had stressed that all discussions were strictly in confidence. All witnesses were reminded that the confidences related within the four walls of the hearing room should not be repeated outside.

Suitably, in a year which promised repeated athletics showdowns leading to the European Championships in Finland, the hearing was held in a room called the 'Helsinki Suite'. In that stuffy, 15ft x 15ft room, the 'court' was assembled. On one side sat Radford, flanked by legal assessor David Pannick QC and the hearing chairman, Charles Woodhouse, from Farrers, the Queen's firm of solicitors who also represent BAF.

On the other side was the 'accused' – Norman, his solicitor, Patrick Isherwood, and his clerk. In the middle, barely six feet from Norman, on a narrow, uncomfortable chair, would sit the five witnesses called that morning. More than one commented that they felt intimidated as Norman glowered at them from under his hooded eyelids. 'If looks could kill. . .' said one. The cod courtroom had no standing in law – no oaths were taken, nor did anyone have judicial immunity from comments they made in the hearing.

Norman's solicitor did much of the cross-questioning, sometimes aggressively, attempting to throw doubt on the accuracy of the evidence, sometimes trying to lead the witnesses down other lines of questioning, such as Temple's state of mind after the collapse of his marriage. Woodhouse gave him little opportunity: 'I don't think that's what we are here to discuss,' he said more than once.

First into the room was Batty, whose evidence took about half an hour before he returned to the ante-room to describe the 'court' awaiting the other witnesses. By this time, Lister had made it known that he had a pressing business appointment, and so he was called next.

Wilson and Mackay followed one another, the *Daily Mail* correspondent questioned particularly over a conversation which he had had with Norman in Brussels the previous September. Over a convivial coffee in a café, Norman and Wilson had chatted, the official, in expansive mood, filling the reporter's tape recorder with his knowledge of the sport.

'Only when he asked me about Temple,' Wilson later wrote, 'did the tone harden. I offered the opinion that Temple had enough on his plate with his divorce and financial problems without the unwarranted allegations that Norman had been putting around the athletics world about his coaching of female athletes. Time to lay off, I suggested.'

Wilson was one of the journalists who had worked in athletics longest and dealt with Norman most. When he interceded on Temple's behalf, some felt that perhaps Norman would listen. Norman's response, therefore, was all the more shocking. 'If there is anything I can do to push him over the edge, I will,' Norman said to Wilson. 'He did not elaborate,' Wilson later wrote in the *Mail*. 'It was brutal, calculated and callous.'

Wilson's report of this conversation appeared in the *Daily Mail* just a day before the BAF Council was due to discuss the Norman affair. One council member said that the report, plus the broadcasting on television and radio of Temple's tape recording of his conversation with Norman the previous July, weighed heavily in their discussions.

That tape was at issue again during the hearing. Who had Temple played it to? Had any BAF officials heard it? Listened to now, there is an eerie, unsettling feel to the recording, perhaps from the hectoring tones of Norman, but more probably because of the stunned helplessness in Temple's voice. The threat was made during a lengthy telephone conversation, after Norman had phoned Temple about a story he was pursuing regarding what he described as 'the extraordinary conflicts of interest' in the relationship between Norman, as the sport's promotions officer, and his role within the élite Chafford Hundred athletics club, which was run by his fiancée, Fatima Whitbread.

Norman is captured on the tape suggesting that it was not a good idea for Temple to publish material harmful to Whitbread. Somebody, says Norman, 'might have a go about Miss Bailey. You think about it Cliff, and we'll leave it at that.'

'No, I'm not sure what you mean. I don't know what you mean,' Temple replied.

'Of course you don't. You'll deny it emphatically,' said Norman, his tone becoming noticeably impatient.

'Deny what emphatically?'

'Sexual harassment,' Norman was angry, forceful, barking at Temple down the phone. 'You know what the fucking hell I'm talking about, if you want me to spell it out, right? The lady made complaints in certain areas and we'll leave it at that.'

Temple's tone, by contrast to Norman's, sounded genuinely shocked, confused. And worried. 'Who made complaints?'

'An athlete. You know who made the complaints,' Norman said, but then he seemed to restrain himself, halt short of going too far. Perhaps it was his years of training in the police: 'But I'm not threatening you, I'm just pointing out hard facts of life, that some people don't sit back and take it on the chin.'

Although stated not to be a threat, the effect was the same. And the threat was also carried out, which is why Mackay and Northam were interviewed by the BAF inquiry. Norman, close at hand to the witnesses in the small hearing room, was still intimidating.

As Mackay related the story of Stuttgart the year before, when Norman swore and called Temple a 'pervert' in front of several witnesses, Norman leaned over to his solicitor, Patrick Isherwood, and whispered something. Isherwood asked for permission for his client to speak, and Woodhouse nodded his assent.

'He's a fucking liar,' said Norman, 'it's lies.' Woodhouse, a charming, softly spoken man, as befits someone whose firm of solicitors acts for the Queen, intervened, gently pointing out that he did not feel that such outbursts would assist the deliberations. He then got on with the questioning.

Northam was the last to be quizzed, with Norman's representatives trying to discredit his evidence because, now that he was a freelance journalist, it was in Northam's interests, they argued, to make capital out of Norman's plight.

Throughout, Radford's questioning of the witnesses was, in the least, robust. He tested their testimony as often as possible. In order to avoid any later legal ramifications, the impartiality of the tribunal had to be firmly established in front of Norman's solicitor by the BAF chief executive. Since Norman had already been warned once before about his conduct in relation to Temple, following a complaint from *The Sunday Times* the previous August, which had led to a seven-hour meeting of BAF's management board, Norman could not be dismissed for the same misdemeanour. What needed to be established was whether Norman had gone back on his undertaking not to repeat the false allegations about Temple.

In considering Norman's position, Radford possibly also had in mind other instances in which his federation's officer had been said to have made threats: 'The police always get their man,' Norman told one scribe who had crossed him; 'if he thinks he's got anything on me,' Norman had told another official about a third journalist, 'tell him that I've got something on him . . .'

But Norman's tactic of attempting to intimidate or discredit others was not reserved for journalists alone. He also used the tactics against the athletes he was supposed to be responsible for helping. One case in particular is believed to have been put before the tribunal. A senior athlete had been seen to undermine Whitbread's Chafford Hundred club in a business deal. Norman subsequently approached a journalist with the suggestion that he should publish a story about how this same athlete, though married, had had an affair with another competitor. 'I can't print that, Andy, I've got no evidence,' said the reporter. 'I'll give you the evidence,' Norman said, and then wrote out a terse statement on a scrap of paper, naming both athletes supposedly involved in the affair.

Following the last of the evidence, the panel took a brief lunch break before the hearing resumed, in order to hear Norman's case.

How Norman marshalled his defence is not known, though there were some clues. For, despite the evidence amassed against him and a reputation, according to another senior BAF official, for routinely using 'bluntness and bullying' to get his way, Norman was not without his advocates. Adrian Metcalfe, the former Olympic athlete, claimed in a letter to *The Times* that Norman had acted quite properly when he had notified three senior athletics officials of 'the controversial allegations at the heart of his now infamous conversation'. It was only after closer examination that Metcalfe's claims on behalf of Norman were shown to have only marginally more substance to them than the smear of sexual harassment against Temple. Of the three officials mentioned in his letter, Metcalfe could not remember the name of the first. The second was dead, while the third was to deny that he had ever received an official complaint against Temple.

This third official was Ewan Murray, the former chairman of the British Amateur Athletic Board, one of BAF's predecessor organisations. Murray's only recollection of any such instance which might have matched the account in Metcalfe's letter was from around 1985, when Norman had commented that Temple was training one of his athletes very hard. Murray denied that there was ever any suggestion of sexual harassment by Temple.

This seemed to make a nonsense of Metcalfe's letter, and although the writer admitted that he had not been present when Norman said that he filed this complaint, Metcalfe refused to divulge who it was who had given him the information for the hearsay claims made in his letter.

Another probable line of defence for Norman was that he was a victim of an orchestrated press witch hunt. Certainly, that was the thrust of a letter which was widely circulated by Peter Orpin, of Whitbread's 'real' athletics club, Thurrock Harriers. This theme was repeated in a letter from the offices of Frere Cholmeley Bischoff, Norman's solicitors. 'Whatever Mr Norman may or may not have done or said, he has been the victim and continues to be the victim of a malicious press and media campaign,' wrote his lawyers. Despite Norman's solicitors' claims that articles in national newspapers had been defamatory of their client's reputation, no action to repair such damage was ever taken.

This legal bluff was another tactic used by Norman before. Two years earlier, just as the BBC television programme *On The Line* was about to broadcast a report on Norman and the way he ran British athletics, his solicitors circulated all the national papers with a letter stating that they intended to sue the programme for libel. They added that they would sue any newspaper which reported the claims made on television. No legal action was ever taken against the television programme. But then, they did not need to, since the tactic had worked: no newspaper followed up on the Norman story. Until, that is, Cliff Temple's own investigation appeared in *The Sunday Times* more than a year later.

At the end of the six-hour hearing, Charles Woodhouse emerged from the 'court room' to provide an anodyne statement to the press on behalf of BAF, and also act as a decoy while Norman effected his getaway to a waiting taxi. Norman, his lips tightly sealed into a near-smirk, refused to answer any questions about whether he was fully recovered from the illness which had delayed the hearing, nor whether he intended to resign.

There was no immediate announcement of the decision on his fate. Many in the sport felt that the outcome was inevitable. Steve Ovett, the 1980 Olympic champion at 800 metres who had had his talent developed by Norman, was in no doubt. 'People aren't going to forget this one. It's about time the sport started making decisions, shake itself out of its complacency, shake Andy Norman out of the sport, so that we can breathe again in a sport based on sound moral values.'

Even one of Norman's closer and oldest allies, Brendan Foster, seemed to acknowledge that a time had come for change. Writing in *The Observer*, Foster said: 'You go to an athletics meeting today and it is not a pleasant experience. Suspicion and cynicism abound, there is envy everywhere and no one seems to trust anyone else.

'It is an awful, almost evil feeling and athletics must act swiftly to stop it before the sport is destroyed . . . It is now clear that because of circumstances the Norman era has ended, and we have to look to the future without him, for better or worse.'

After a week of uncertainty, the long awaited decision came early in the evening of 8 April, after Radford had presented his report of the hearing to the BAF management board at the sport's headquarters in Birmingham. The chief executive emerged from the meeting to read a carefully prepared statement: 'Having considered all that was said at the hearing, including the submissions made on Mr Norman's behalf and having considered the papers and other materials before me, I have concluded that Mr Norman's conduct in certain matters was not appropriate for someone employed as director of promotions with BAF and that it would be inconsistent with the interests of the BAF for Mr Norman to remain in our employment.'

Radford then went on: 'I would like to emphasise that it was no part of my function to inquire into the causes or circumstances of the death of the late Cliff Temple. However, I should add in fairness to the reputation of Mr Temple and the athlete (Shireen Bailey) concerned in the allegation and Mr Norman himself that Mr Norman stressed to me that the term "sexual harassment" which he had used in a particular telephone conversation with Mr Temple was not intended to imply any sexual impropriety between Mr Temple and the athlete.'

To anyone who has heard the tape recording, it seems impossible to put any construction on Norman's statement other than that he meant sexual impropriety. But Radford's statement went on to explain that a settlement had been reached with Norman which would see him waive his right to appeal and work through to the end of the month 'to assist in an orderly hand-over of his responsibilities'. Norman gave a number of undertakings in a secret deed of covenant, which was believed to include some form of 'gagging clause' to prevent him from selling his story to the tabloids. In return, he was expected to get a pay-off, suggested to be as much as £100,000, though BAF sources were later to refute that figure as being a gross over-estimate.

In his statement, Radford also included another passage about Norman: 'Through enormous personal effort and dedication and no little skill,' Radford read, 'he has played a major part in putting British athletics in its current successful position . . . I also hope that in future a more balanced view of Andy Norman's contribution to British athletics will emerge in the media than has sometimes been the case recently.'

If by a balanced view, Radford meant consulting some of the athletes who had worked closest to Norman for longest, then Steve Ovett seemed to have a clear view of Norman's contribution. After Curtis Robb, the country's leading 800 metres runner (and who is managed by Norman), had expressed his view that Norman, and only Norman, could run British athletics, Ovett said, 'I suppose even Hitler had his good points.

'What Norman did for the sport was good, but I don't think it was exceptional,' Ovett said. 'I think he sold what people wanted, and he had talented athletes available to him that everybody wanted to see. He came in and saw that there was material there to be used – and abused to a certain extent – and he saw that he could get a lot of money back, and it was fairly obvious how to do it.

'I don't even think Andy Norman is a great promoter. When you've been given a vast purse, as Andy was given, it's not difficult to produce good meetings. The difficult thing would be to be to do it with hardly any money and without the reservoir of talent to call on. Andy is a good administrator, that's his strong point, but he's a man of limited vision.'

Ovett had cause to complain of treatment he felt he had received at Norman's hands. In August 1989, Ovett had broken down in tears in front of millions of television viewers at that year's AAA Championships in Birmingham. The championships, being used to select the England team for the following year's Commonwealth Games, had as its highlight a 1,500 metres final including both Ovett and Sebastian Coe. This was the race the whole world had wanted to see, but it came to fruition perhaps five, even ten years too late. By 1989, both great champions were in the twilight of their careers. It was the only time in their senior careers that Coe and Ovett met in a race outside major championships: despite all the power and influence he exercised as a promoter, Andy Norman had never managed to get this race organised. How he finally achieved this coup was to be the subject of some close scrutiny.

The AAA Championships, the world's oldest, organised annual athletics meeting, had always tried to remain robustly amateur, even after payments had been allowed in athletics, and professionals had been allowed in the Olympics. Some top competitors had been paid subventions in the past but generally the administrators would get the athletes to compete for nothing at the AAAs. The reasoning was simple: often, as in 1989, the AAAs were also team selection trials for the next major international event, so if an athlete wanted to be chosen, he or she had to compete at the AAAs.

Ovett alleged that, in the week before the 1989 Championships, he was telephoned and offered a share of £40,000 to compete in the 1,500 metres against Coe. It was only after they had both qualified from heats on the Saturday afternoon that Ovett approached Coe and told him that he was being paid. Coe told him that he was not receiving any payment.

What no one could understand was why anyone would complain about being paid. As the 1,500 metres final was staged, won by Coe with Ovett down the field in ninth place, the reason became apparent. Ovett really was not in the sort of shape to challenge for another AAA title. He might have chosen not to race at all, so the money may have been persuasive. But once he discovered he was the only person being paid at a non-paying trials event, Ovett's alarm bells sounded: he feared that the reason he was offered cash was that he might have been set up.

The night before the final, it took a great deal of persuasion to get Ovett to race at all. After the race, Ovett jogged over to his kit, and then gave an emotional interview to his ITV commentary colleague, Jim Rosenthal. Frustrated and angry, Ovett told millions of television viewers, 'There's people in this sport who are trying to use it for their own ends. They've got to be stopped.'

Only when AAA officials said that they would not investigate his allegations did Ovett name Norman as the person who had made the tele-phoned offer. Norman, of course, denied that any offer had ever been made. Mike Farrell, then secretary of the AAAs, hardly helped to clarify the posi-tion when, the day after the championships, he said, 'Andy did it without permission if he did it, and he's denying it.'

By the time an inquiry was set up, further financial problems had also come to light: $39,000 in cash had been stolen from Norman's room at the Queen's Hotel, Crystal Palace, a month before the AAAs. There was nothing untoward about Norman having the cash, which he said he had been given to pay athletes following another meeting in Nice. It was suggested that the money was in fact to pay Linford Christie, Colin Jackson, John Regis and Yvonne Murray, but Norman said, 'You can't pay people like Africans with cheques, it has to be cash,' adding with a surprising degree of calmness for someone who had just lost £25,000, 'The money is insured, so no one loses.'

Eventually, the AAA set up an inquiry into Ovett's allegations, con-ducted by Robert Reid QC and David Pickup, a senior Sports Council official. It was the second investigation into allegations against Norman in the space of just two years.

In 1987, Peter Coni QC had chaired an investigation into allegations by international hammer thrower Martin Girvan that Norman had colluded in the evasion of a drug test. 'We found this all very unhappy,' Coni was to say later, 'but we were quite unable to say that it was true. Nor did we feel able to go as far as to say that we were absolutely satisfied it was untrue.'

Despite clearing Norman, Coni – who described Norman's behaviour as 'extraordinary' and 'consistent with somebody who doesn't think and who just bulldozes in a singularly inappropriate way' – was unconvinced by the official's testimony. 'He made one or two comments which were entire-ly inappropriate. One of the comments was: "I wouldn't put myself in jeopardy for an athlete of Girvan's standard", which you or I could turn around and say, "Well, what standard of athlete *would* you put yourself in jeopardy for?"'

The Reid-Pickup Report ended up being largely inconclusive. 'A 0-0 draw,' was the way one official described it. Its release was delayed by nearly three weeks, apparently to allow Norman's legal advisers to scrutinise it first. Eventually, the report was published in late January 1990, nearly six months after the AAA Championships, and also just after most of the athletics journalists who had been following the case had left the country to cover the following month's Commonwealth Games in Auckland.

Norman, according to the report, was 'the most probable candidate for the maker of the call'. But they could not *prove* that he had made the cash offer to Ovett. In seeking to offer an explanation, the 60-page report even made the unlikely suggestion that Ovett might have been victim of a hoax caller who was impersonating Norman, the official who had been his business partner and best man at his wedding. The findings did not shake Ovett's opinion: 'I'm pleased the inquiry admits I was telling the truth when I said I had been offered money. I know who phoned me – it was Andy Norman.'

The report did point out, though, that because Norman's methods of operation were condoned by the governing body, the promotions officer believed 'his powers of discretion could be stretched'. Reid and Pickup offered a series of recommendations for future business practices, including the introduction of confirmations of all Norman's deals with athletes, to be written by another association officer. The Reid-Pickup Report also said that Norman should be barred from acting as an agent for athletes.

If Reid and Pickup felt that Norman's actions had been condoned by the sport's governing body before their report, then the governing body's decision, just months after the report's publication, to register Norman as an accredited agent with the International Amateur Athletic Federation, could only be interpreted as yet another pat on the back for the former policeman.

Thus, the meeting in Euston in 1994 was the third inquiry into Norman's conduct. After that hearing, and following the death of Cliff Temple, there seemed little future for the promotions officer within the British federation. After his dismissal was announced, it took Norman ten days before he finally issued his own statement. As had become his custom, the statement was released through his lawyers, thus avoiding any possibility of the need to answer direct questions. In view of what Norman had to say, it was probably just as well.

Despite the tapes and witnesses, and the findings of the BAF inquiry, Norman still protested his innocence. 'The allegations which have appeared are entirely unfounded and . . . there was no campaign of any kind by me against Mr Temple. Various elements in a complicated story have been taken completely out of context and I want now to put on record a number of facts which I hope will enable a more balanced view to be taken of my dealings with Cliff Temple.'

These facts included a restatement of the unsubstantiated story alluded to in Metcalfe's *Times* letter (though Norman's version, unlike Ewan Murray, placed the incident in 1987-88), claiming that other athletes had been concerned about Shireen Bailey and told Norman 'that they believed Cliff Temple was trying to exercise more control over her private life than was appropriate'. Norman admitted to not ever discussing the matter with Bailey, and did not name the other 'concerned' athletes.

Norman said that he had a 'friendly conversation' with Temple at Crystal Palace about the matter at the time and that he told him that 'in America Mr Temple's conduct might be viewed as "sexual harassment".' This did not tally with the intimidating tone of Norman's remarks in his taped telephone conversation with Temple some five years later.

Having been sacked by BAF, Norman's pleading was difficult to reconcile with everything else that was in the public domain. Perhaps he was hoping that, for the third time in seven years, a sporting inquiry into his activities would again be disregarded as 'inconclusive'. The difference this time, though, was that there still had to be an official inquest into the death of Cliff Temple.

The inquest into Cliff Temple's death was deliberately delayed until after the sport had conducted its own inquiry. When Folkestone Coroner's Court eventually convened later in April 1994 Norman was not available to give evidence. There, the jury returned a verdict of suicide, identifying as contributory factors the break-up of Temple's marriage and the allegations which Norman had made against him. The coroner said that he felt that Norman's threats had 'tipped the balance'.

This time, Norman was not going to be able just to shrug off the allegations. As Steve Ovett said, 'People aren't going to forget this one.' The role played by Andy Norman in the suicide of Cliff Temple had become an indisputable matter of official record.

Six

Take the Money and Run

WHEN Sergeant Andrew John Norman took charge of the Metropolitan Police athletics club in the late 1960s, the most popular cop show on British television was *Dixon of Dock Green*. By the time Norman had risen through the ranks of the unpaid volunteer officials of British athletics to become the first professional Promotions Director of the new national federation a quarter of a century later, the top-rated TV police programme was *The Bill*. That shift in society, as shown by television – from the smiling bobbies and bicycle clips of 'Dixon', through to the high-speed car chases, all-guns-blazing cynical realism of *The Bill* – was fully reflected in the changes in British athletics over that same period. Many of those changes were wrought by Andy Norman.

Norman's rise to become the most powerful man in British athletics was rapid. Born during the Second World War into a working class family, he grew up in Ipswich, Suffolk, where he attended the local grammar school. When he left in his late teens, he joined the Metropolitan Police. By this time, Norman had already begun to show some ability as a runner over a quarter- and half-mile, representing his county. Norman had chosen his sport well, for television's coverage of the 1960 and, especially, the 1964 Olympic Games had given athletics a popularity boost with the general public. Norman was doubly well-starred in the police force because a senior officer who shared his enthusiasm for the sport was Gilbert Kelland.

Kelland, who led the famous Operation Countryman inquiry into police corruption, was Deputy Assistant Commissioner (Crime) at Scotland Yard from 1977 to 1984. He was also a senior ranking freemason.

Freemasonry, though never overt, has for a long time played a role in the management of athletics in Britain. The Athlon Lodge – No 4674 – was founded in 1925 as 'a masonic home for all those with a deep interest in sport, particularly athletics, walking and cross-country'. The Athlon wanted to call itself the Amateur Athletic Association Lodge when it was established, but was prevented from doing so. Instead, the badge of the AAA was adopted as the Athlon Lodge emblem.

The Athlon's membership in its early years drew heavily on the athletics establishment. They have included Harold Abrahams, the Olympic 100 metres champion in 1924 whose story was featured in the 1981 Oscar-winning film *Chariots of Fire*; Jack Crump, the formidable post-war athletics administrator was a Lodge member; Sir Harry Barclay, an early secretary of the AAA, was a mason; as were E.J.H. 'Billy' Holt (the director of organisation of the 1948 London Olympics, who also served as secretary and treasurer of the IAAF), record-breaking marathon runner Jim Peters, and former Olympic sprinter Terence Higgins, who is now the Conservative MP for Worthing.

Even in 1996, the Athlon's officers still included some influential figures in British athletics administration, but although it met at the same masonic hall as a police lodge, there was never any evidence that Kelland attended its meetings, nor that Norman was ever a member. But Kelland and Norman met frequently enough in other capacities, both on and off the track as well as inside and outside the police station.

Kelland was president of the Metropolitan Police Athletic Club when Norman was the club secretary. Thus Norman, who at 23 was one of the Met's youngest sergeants, found he had plenty of latitude to organise the affairs of the force's athletics team. 'I was third in the Southern Youths 440 yards at Hurlingham and fourth in the 880 as a first-year junior,' he was to recall later, 'the best I ever did was 1min 54.1sec, but that couldn't get me into the Met Police team.' Instead of running for the police team, Norman began to *run* the police team.

Norman was an extremely successful team manager, despite relying on only serving officers who might always be called out at the last moment on riot duty or to police an official engagement. By 1974, the MPAC even managed to gain National League status, London's fastest 'flat feet' joining the ranks of Britain's top 30 élite athletics clubs. But perhaps because of Norman's overwhelming involvement in athletics, and despite such a promising start to his police career (including a spell on the Chelsea drugs squad), when he eventually resigned from the force in 1984, he was still only a desk sergeant at the quietly suburban Bromley police station.

As secretary of MPAC, Norman had soon found himself involved in the wider affairs of the local area athletics organisation, the Southern Counties AAA. Under their auspices, he began organising regular open meetings, midweek events to which entry was unrestricted, so that club athletes, and some fringe international hopefuls, could try to improve their best performances. Norman's open meetings at Crystal Palace during the summer months were legendarily successful, with vast numbers of athletes turning up on the night to take part. Those who were there are almost misty eyed when they recall how the queue for numbers and pins on race night used to stretch around the main stand, and how the over-subscribed meets used to run well over time.

'We used to have over 2,000 athletes there on a Wednesday night,' Norman recalled. 'We used to have 65 to 70 in the 5,000 metres at ten o'clock at night. I was always getting complaints from the timekeepers that they never got home until midnight.'

Most importantly, though, Norman's meetings gave the athletes what they wanted: good racing. And they also gave SCAAA something which it craved: a regular, dependable source of income. Norman had discovered his niche. 'The way he shouted and talked to people sometimes was disgraceful,' remembers another London-based AAA official of that time, Doug Goodman, 'but he was really helpful to a lot of athletes.'

An Achilles tendon ruptured when playing a friendly game of basketball had permanently ended his own active athletics career, and it seems as if Norman then started to channel his spare energies, perhaps his frustrations, increasingly into the administration of the sport. For like nature, Andy Norman abhors a vacuum, and by the late 1960s the management of British athletics at a national level had fallen into a poor state.

The great Olympic successes of Tokyo in 1964 – with gold medals won by Ann Packer and Mary Rand, Ken Matthews and Lynn Davies – and four years later in Mexico City – David Hemery winning the 400 metres hurdles in world record time – had been achieved more by individual endeavour than through any great assistance from the governing body. What Tom McNab, the chief coach in the 1970s who later became a successful author, called 'the Blazerati' were in charge of the sport in Britain, and frequently they were at loggerheads with the people they were supposed to serve, the athletes.

Even at this early stage of his career, Norman was developing a reputation as one who did not suffer fools gladly. Yet he found himself surrounded by the Blazerati. He held them in utter contempt. 'They're only ever interested in which table they're sitting on at the reception after the meeting,' is one of his famously dismissive one-liners.

The weak administration of athletics at around that time is perhaps best characterised by the decision to abandon the White City and move the major events of the summer track season across London to the new, all-weather track at Crystal Palace in 1971. It was the equivalent of soccer moving the FA Cup Final from Wembley to Millwall's New Den ground just because it was an all-seater stadium.

In the 1950s, White City had regularly been packed by hordes of spectators, eager to watch the exploits of their heroes of the track. The stadium was redolent of great deeds: the White City had been the venue for the 1908 Olympic Games, where Dorando Pietri staggered on to the track at the end of the marathon only to be disqualified for receiving assistance, although his deeds helped to create much of the legend and folklore that now surrounds the long distance event. Half a century after Dorando, the lucky ones who managed to get inside the same White City stadium for one of the all-star athletics meetings saw the greats of British athletics – Chataway, Bannister, Ibbotson, Pirie – take on the rest of the world and beat them. But by the mid-1960s, those stars had retired and the crowds had begun to drift away from athletics. When the 1970 Amateur Athletic Association Championships were staged at the White City, shortly after the Edinburgh Commonwealth Games, there was a record low attendance of only 4,721.

Faced with this diminished appeal, the Amateur Athletic Association took a fateful decision. Rather than ensure that an all-weather track was laid at a modernised White City (which had only recently been upgraded to stage matches in soccer's 1966 World Cup), and instead of taking steps to bring back the crowds to athletics, the AAA decided that the stadium at the new national recreation centre at Crystal Palace, which then had a capacity of less than 12,000 but had Europe's first all-weather track, was to be the future home of athletics in Britain.

It was a decision which the governing body finally admitted in 1995 was a damaging mistake. At this time Britain was once again one of the world's leading athletics nations, but was unable to bid to stage a European or World Championships simply because it did not have a stadium large enough nor a track suitable for the purpose. Sadly, by that time, it was far too late to return to the White City. The old stadium of legends had been bulldozed, to be turned into nothing more than a staff car park for BBC employees.

As an unpaid administrator with the Southern Counties in the early 1970s, Andy Norman began to organise events at the new Crystal Palace. He and his athletics colleagues all gave of their time freely, but Norman always seemed to have more to give. He had the energy, the street-wisdom, to put on some of the biggest meetings in the calendar. The first big, commercial meeting Norman was asked to organise was the 1974 Coca-Cola meeting. Organised by the International Athletes' Club, 'the athletes' union', all the profits from the meeting were ploughed back into a warm weather training fund or to provide medical assistance for injured athletes. The Coke meet was by then already established as a traditional, end-of-season jamboree, with medallists from that year's major championships brought together to perform one last time in front of packed stands.

Norman's early promotions at Crystal Palace – just a short drive up the road from his police stations at Bromley and Penge – had soon shown the shortcomings of the new stadium, as runners such as Dave Bedford, Brendan Foster and then Steve Ovett saw, once again, people wanting to be at big athletics meetings to share the excitement of close races and record-breaking endeavours.

'My thinking was partly influenced by Brendan Foster,' Norman said in an interview with *Athletics Today* magazine in 1991. 'That was in 1974 and Foster was training at Crystal Palace before the Commonwealth Games. I went up to him, told him I had taken over the Coke meeting and asked if I could talk to him.

'Foster's complaint was that the first time he ever came up against any of the world stars was when he reached the Olympics in 1972.' Norman's promotions over the next two decades would ensure that British athletes never had that same complaint again.

Like a successful theatre impresario whose shows always have a trade-mark style to them, Norman's athletics meetings had a pattern that was refined over the years into a successful, crowd-pleasing formula. Get the meeting started with a bang, with an attractive, exciting event once the television cameras had joined for live coverage, then stage a series of other events in rapid succession to keep the momentum going, before another 'star' attraction halfway through to focus attention, followed by a steady build-up to a final event which would feature the biggest available stars, preferably in a highly-publicised showdown against a rival or in an attempt on a world record.

With the Palace's original, single stand brim full, crowds of people who had not been able to buy a ticket would often line the old motor racing circuit road which butted on to the athletics track's back straight. From there, they would strain for a view of the meeting. On one occasion, the crowd outside was so huge that the fencing built to keep them out collapsed under the weight, giving these illicit spectators a uniquely clear, close-hand view of the night's events. In 1977, a second stand was opened at Crystal Palace, raising the stadium's regular capacity to 18,000. Norman was soon staging meetings which filled the new Jubilee Stand, too.

In order to bring in the crowds, Norman had to circumnavigate the obstructions which officials often sought to place in his way. To this end, he never shirked from taking on any job, however minor. As with most volunteer organisations, often there was no other candidate. Norman could do the job because he had the time to spare while at work. Though Norman always denied it, legend had it that telephone calls to Bromley or Penge police stations were often answered with a sharp 'Athletics?'. But by taking on that extra responsibility, Norman also managed to exclude others from positions of influence.

According to Harry Wilson, the coach who guided Steve Ovett to his Olympic 800 metres gold medal in 1980, the key move for Norman was when he took over as the Southern Counties' coaching secretary in the early 1970s. 'It was the first time he had handled any money, with the small budgets which the coaching committee managed for staging coaching weekends, organising invitations to up-and-coming young athletes to train together,' Wilson says. 'Suddenly, he became a man of quite considerable power.'

It was also in the early 1970s that Norman learned an important lesson about the athletics governing bodies attitude to controversy. In 1972, the British Amateur Athletic Board staged its own appeal fund to raise money to send its team to that year's Olympic Games in Munich. Heading the appeal were two of the leading lights in the athletics hierarchy: Arthur Gold (later Sir Arthur) and Marea Hartman (who became Dame Marea in 1994, shortly before her death).

A scurrilous, roughly-hewn magazine called *Athletics Truth* was in circulation at the time. This typed and photocopied magazine sometimes gently poked fun at officialdom, sometimes sniped at the Establishment in a more vicious manner. It was also accused of being anti-semitic. One of the magazine's attacks was particularly scathing about Hartman, and Gold judged that the article might also damage the Olympic appeal.

Gold, suspicious of the source of the magazine, wrote a formal complaint to the Metropolitan Police Commissioner. There were never any further editions of *Athletics Truth*.

Norman has always denied that he was in any way involved in *Athletics Truth*, but without doubt he would have learned a useful lesson by its demise. Despite the damaging slurs against Gold and Hartman, the athletics administrators chose not to take any further action. Norman must have realised that all too often, when faced with controversial circumstances, the fear of adverse publicity would deter the athletics powers-that-be. Besides, Norman's attention was by now keenly fixed on the future, and he seemed to have a clear idea of where it lay: with Steve Ovett.

Norman's business savvy, his ability to recognise the commercial possibilities for athletics, had already forced one leading athlete to conclude: 'There's only one man in British athletics who really understands what's going on, and that's Andy.' The plaudit came from Brendan Foster. By the mid-1970s, Foster's career was close to its peak, culminating with his gold medal at 5,000 metres in the European Championships of 1974. But the teenaged Ovett, the European Junior 800 metres champion of 1973, offered Norman a decade or more of opportunity.

The first meeting between Norman and the young Ovett was less than auspicious. Norman was in Rome for the European Championships of 1974. Having been asked by the International Athletes' Club to organise that year's Coca-Cola meeting, Norman was busy recruiting athletes. Ovett seemed exactly the sort of exciting new talent which the meeting needed.

The Coke meeting was something of a triumphal homecoming for British medal-winners at that summer's big championship event, a chance for the home crowd to offer its congratulations. Yet Ovett turned his back on Norman.

Ovett had won the silver medal in Rome, one of Britain's rare successes at that time. The day after the final, Norman approached Ovett while he was sitting in the Italian sun on the verandah of the team hotel, chatting with some other athletes, doing what sportsmen in any 'village' environment have to master when at a major championship event: avoiding boredom and somehow pass the time until the next meal. Norman asked if he could have a word. The young runner was probably glad of the diversion.

In his biography, Ovett recalled: 'He asked me if I wanted to run in the Coke meeting and I simply replied, "No, it's not possible." This brought a puzzled look and "Yes, of course it is". Whereupon I explained that I was not returning directly to London since I was going on holiday with my Italian girlfriend . . .

'He seemed not to be put off and adopted what I now realise is his policeman's look: by the time the conversation ended, with me not running in the Coke meeting, my girlfriend and I could have had a free holiday in Barbados, or anywhere else in the world for that matter.'

According to Robert Harland, of the Coca-Cola organisation who was with Norman during that conversation with Ovett, as they walked away from the future Olympic champion, Norman turned to the Coke executive and said: 'Right, you wait, if that so and so wants to run next year . . . we'll see about that!' Norman's threat tactic was something that would be heard many more times by other athletes over the next 20 years.

Despite such an unpromising beginning to their relationship, Ovett and Norman were to work very closely together. Norman would find the runner the right races, at the right price, at the right time, and Ovett would deliver the goods, usually in terms of a devastatingly quick final 150 metres off the last bend to leave all his rivals struggling behind him down the finishing straight.

Between 1977 and 1980, Ovett and Norman were almost inseparable. Certainly, there was a time when Ovett appeared invincible at the mile and 1,500 metres. He went 42 races unbeaten, breaking the mile and 1,500 metres world record three times. Outside championship events, Norman had arranged all the races for him. Ovett's winning sequence only came to an end in the Moscow Olympic 1,500 metres final, an event which even Norman had no control over.

As they forged their world-beating partnership, it had not taken very long for Norman to realise that Ovett was such a rare, precious commodity for other promoters in Europe that his presence at a meeting could be valuable in many ways. Ovett could be used to barter places in overseas meetings for other British athletes. 'I started to point out to the promoters that we had a lot of good athletes in Britain and that if the overseas meeting took them, British television would come. We created Oslo like that,' Norman said. One year, the organiser of the Oslo meeting took 40 other British athletes because Norman promised that Ovett would compete there.

'When it all started, it was just a bit of fun, $200 a race, or an air ticket or two,' Ovett has said, showing an attitude that could be characterised as almost Corinthian compared to the avarice that seems common to so much of the sport 20 years later. Yet Ovett's admission is significant, because it unveils the system of shamateurism that operated at that time, with payments being made to athletes with brown envelopes stuffed full of used notes.

Ostensibly, the sport in the 1970s and early 1980s was still run, quite strictly, by the *Amateur* Athletic Association for men in England, while Britain's teams were organised by the British *Amateur* Athletic Board, and the sport internationally was administered under the auspices of the International *Amateur* Athletic Federation.

Yet despite his status as a senior official within the sport, Norman had no qualms about bending, even breaking the sport's amateur rules by paying athletes to compete at his meetings. 'Nobody was breaking the law,' he said, 'just the regulations of the sport.'

There were those, however, who took a different view of how the rules of the sport ought to be applied. Sebastian Coe was Ovett's great rival who ended the unbeaten sequence in that 1980 Olympic 1,500 metres final. Looking back on his track career, Coe viewed the under-the-counter payments of the pre-1985 era somewhat more piously than Andy Norman did. 'It's a situation which makes honest men dishonest,' Coe said.

Just how dishonest the sport was to become though, only time would tell.

Seven

A King's Ransom

WHAT only a very few people had realised before the Moscow Olympics of 1980 was that athletics, especially in Britain, was about to enter a golden age, with spectators, sponsors and television all eager to see more events, more stars, more records. What's more, the spectators, sponsors and television were all quite prepared to pay, and handsomely so. Andy Norman was one of those who was wise to such changes, and he made sure that it was not just the sport that benefited by this new flow of cash into athletics: the Bromley police sergeant made certain that he got his share.

'Marketing' had become the buzz word in all sports, and track and field was not slow in catching on. Athletics had to market itself properly: in 1978, the International Amateur Athletic Federation launched its 'Golden Series' – the Golden Mile, the Golden 5,000 metres, the Golden this, the Golden that. Individual athletics events were staged at various venues around the world, paid for with cash from the oil-rich Emirates, and drawing together the best athletes of the world in special one-offs. All were televised around the globe. These competitions ultimately meant very little (can you name more than one 'Golden Series' winner? But how many Olympic champions do you remember?), yet at that time they served an important purpose in the development of athletics as a modern, international sport, generating a great deal of publicity.

There was no athletics world championships: the IAAF did not have title to any major events which it could use to 'sell' the sport to the public, through television. More importantly, this meant that the IAAF did not possess any event around which it could raise funds for its own organisation through the sale of TV rights and sponsorship deals. Instead, the IAAF merely concerned itself with administering minor rule changes, looking after the programme of athletics events at the Olympic Games, and overseeing its new policy of drug testing. What seemed to be lost on Adriaan Paulen, the Dutchman who was president of the IAAF in the 1970s, was that by not having an athletics world championships, his sport was investing the Olympics with added importance. It was not a mistake his successor as IAAF president, the aggressively ambitious Italian, Primo Nebiolo, would repeat.

Under Paulen, the IAAF did at least make some efforts to modernise itself and catch up with the sort of changes which had been altering sports such as golf and tennis, launching them into a new era of professionalism. Under Paulen, the IAAF staged the World Cup, although this international, inter-continental team event failed to capture the imagination of the world's top athletes and the public, even up to its staging in London in September 1994. But the World Cup was notable, at its first staging in Dusseldorf in 1977, for a phenomenal 1,500 metres victory by Steve Ovett, which marked him out quite clearly as one of the world's greatest milers, not least because of the way that the devastating Ovett finishing kick prompted John Walker, the then Olympic champion, to walk off the track 120 metres from the finish in bemused resignation.

By the early 1980s, Norman's reach as an athletics promoter spanned the world. Through his dealings with Ovett and other top British athletes, Norman had been expanding his powerbase. Despite his continuing duties in the police as a desk sergeant, he seemed to be a fixture at athletics venues around Europe during the summer, moving from London to Oslo – his wife of that time, Gerd, is Norwegian – to Stockholm, Koblenz, Brussels and Rieti, all regular stops on the new athletics circus's merry-go-round.

He also became involved with the careers of athletes from other countries. Don Quarrie, the Jamaican who won Olympic gold at 200 metres in Montreal in 1976, was a mainstay of the sprint events at meetings in Britain. John Walker, the tough New Zealander who had won the 1976 Olympic 1,500 metres, was almost a fixture and fitting of Norman's promotions. Walker, the first to run a mile in less than 3 min 50 sec, was one of the first athletes to adopt the 'have spikes will travel' approach to competition. But then Walker had to: coming from New Zealand, his chances of top quality racing at home were limited, so he often spent eight months of the year on the road – or, more accurately, in often uncomfortable motels and airport lounges. Norman once said of the ever-travelling Kiwi that, if he parachuted into the Sahara, he would find a race, win it, and then make sure that the meeting promoter paid his air fare home.

In those early days, the barter over airline tickets often became as important to the athletes as the discussions of their personal best performances. Flight tickets offered a range of possibilities to athletes – if the ticket was of the right type and could be exchanged, perhaps, for a cheaper flight on another airline, the athlete would often cash-in their better ticket and pocket the difference. It was all part of the 'game' of making a few dollars without getting caught, because if that happened, it would jeopardise the athlete's status as an amateur, and could prevent them from competing at the Olympic Games.

Norman utilised the negotiating power of air tickets as well as any European meeting promoter. He also used his pre-eminence in Britain to a major advantage. Unlike most meeting promoters in Europe, who staged perhaps two meetings at most each summer, often independently of their national federations, Norman – with financial backing from his governing body – had a near monopoly of the organisation of all the main meetings in Britain.

All but one of the major track events staged in Britain each summer in the early 1980s were organised by the governing body, then either the Amateur Athletic Association or the British Amateur Athletic Board. Because he was always available, Norman usually had a pivotal role in the staging of each of those events. And even for the one meeting *not* staged by the governing bodies, Norman was meeting director of that for ten years, too. That made Norman the most powerful meeting promoter in the world, with the biggest available budgets. Like a shopper in the athletics supermarket, Norman made sure that he bought athletes 'in bulk' to keep their prices down.

As he staged more meetings, so a pattern began to develop to the way Norman would structure the British season. Often, Norman would arrange for a match to be staged in Britain at the start of the European circuit and featuring a number of the top American athletes. Using sponsors' money, he would pay for the Americans' transatlantic air fares to Britain to ensure he had a great event to kickstart the season. By doing this, Norman also won the gratitude of the American athletes and other European promoters: the key to this equation was that, once in London, the Americans could get to other European meetings far more easily and cheaply than if they flew in directly from the United States. That obviously endeared Norman to those European meeting promoters who 'picked up' top American track stars more cheaply because of the cut in costs. And Norman was popular with the American athletes because he looked after them so well.

At a time when many meeting promoters gave their international competitors accommodation that was often little better than a youth hostel, with a meagre *per diem* allowance for food, Norman, by contrast, cosseted visiting athletes, putting them up in their own rooms at a local hotel, making sure that in-bound and onward air tickets were arranged to the athletes' requirements, even making sure that there was always transport at the airport to collect arriving athletes.

'If you had to get some place, needed a ticket, Andy could take care of it,' remembers one stalwart of those early years. 'He seemed to have an inside track on everything.' According to Steve Williams, the top American sprinter who was a regular in Norman's meetings, 'Andy was a godsend for many of the athletes who needed someone to connect the dots for them. It was a sort of one-stop shopping affair, you could call Andy to do these things.'

Not that all dealings with Norman went smoothly. According to Williams: 'Put it this way: when you have a business relationship that is not based on the usual precedence of business – offer, acceptance, contract – there is always room for disagreements, misunderstandings. Andy was particularly heavy handed in his negotiations and on many occasions would not honour some of the things he said, about a set price or a set amount of races, things like that.'

Kriss Akabusi, the former European 400 metres hurdles champion, confirms that this style of business was still being used by Norman well into the 1990s. 'My first run-in with Andy was in Oslo 1985,' Akabusi recalled. 'I'd run well in the 4x400 in the Olympics the previous year and it was one of my first trips. I'd heard the going rate for people like me was $300 and I knew that some of the big names, the established athletes, were getting $700. I ran a personal best and then paced the 800. I think Peter Elliott did the fastest time of the year. Anyhow, all I got was $20.

'The following year, I knew $300 was the minimum. He offered me $20 again and I said: "I'm going home if I don't get $300." He said: "OK, you get $300, but you'll never run in Europe again." It was the beginning of my problems with Andy.' Even after Akabusi had won European gold and Olympic bronze, those problems with Norman seemed to continue. A promised $50,000 for a 'farewell tour' of British meetings by Akabusi before he retired in 1993 never materialised.

Like footballers and cricketers, old athletes, too, need 'benefit' seasons at the end of their careers. But Akabusi even pulled out of one meeting at Crystal Palace in his final season because he felt Norman had unreasonably loaded the field against him by including the Olympic champion and the world champion in the line-up. 'I didn't want to say goodbye from the back of the field,' Akabusi explained. 'Ultimately, I got $42,000 for five meetings. If my face had fitted, I'd have got $100,000, but I've always refused to be his puppet.'

By buying and selling athletics talent 'in bulk', and by careful and clever use of his sponsors' money, Norman won himself the respect and loyalty of many other people, from athletes, to promoters, even some national federations. As Norman knew to his advantage, such loyalty cost him nothing.

All Norman asked in return was a 'favour': if Norman had arranged for an American star to come over to Europe at the start of the summer, he would expect that the athlete would come back to London at the end of the season for his Coca-Cola meeting. Norman's 'favours', though, were not boy scoutish good turns, done for athletes out of some deep sense of altruism. Norman's 'favours' always had to be honoured and returned, and these, too, helped to ensure that his promotions always had the best athletes.

Often, his promotions were not even in Britain. One example of Norman's ever-lengthening influence came when Jeff Gutteridge, the pole vaulter who was later to become the first British athlete to be banned for failing a drugs test, phoned the organiser of a meeting in Texas. After a brief exchange of pleasantries, Gutteridge was told to contact the person putting the meeting's fields together, a Mr Andy Norman in London, England . . .

As well as using favours and airline tickets as bargaining chips with athletes, Norman was prepared to do more than just 'bend' the amateur rules that forbade cash payments in the sport. Norman was also prepared to break the most fundamental principle of the sport – that of fair competition, of athlete against athlete, both doing their utmost to win their event fairly.

Alan Pascoe, 13 times a winner of AAA titles, indoors and out, at 60, 110 and 400 metres hurdles, had been a mainstay of Norman's early meetings in the 1970s, a popular figure with the crowds. But after a lengthy track career which included Commonwealth and European titles at 400 metres hurdles and an Olympic relay silver medal, Pascoe decided to bring the curtain down in front of his home crowd at Crystal Palace at the end of 1979. Unlike Kriss Akabusi 15 years later, Norman ensured that his friend, Pascoe, would go out on a high note. To do that, Norman arranged that Pascoe's last 'race' was in fact a carefully orchestrated event, a sham, played out in front of the packed Palace stands, with one of the competitors paid to ensure he *did not* win the race.

By careful selection of which athletes would compete in any given event, any half-competent promoter can ensure, to a certain degree, the outcome of the events at his meeting. In 1985, when Mary Slaney and Zola Budd received £150,000 between them to race in one of Norman's meetings at Crystal Palace, the Olympic champion, Maricica Puica, was offered an unacceptable £1,200. Had the Romanian been in the race, the re-match between Budd and Slaney might have been overshadowed. But that was by no means the first time that such a ploy had been used for a Crystal Palace meeting.

For Pascoe's farewell race at Norman's 1979 Crystal Palace meeting, the world's top two 400-metre hurdlers of that time, Ed Moses and Harald Schmid, were conspicuous absentees. Otherwise all appearances suggested that Pascoe was going to have a tough contest. Yet according to James King, the American who finished runner-up that night, Norman had approached him before the race and offered $500 to ensure that he did not win.

King, these days a decent veteran – over-40s – performer on the United States masters' circuit who works in Los Angeles as a short-order cook, recounts the approach: 'Andy wanted to make sure that I would give Alan a great race. You know, make it close. He wanted Alan to go out on a really good note, and make it look good for the public. Andy was a real good friend of mine, and he gave me the decision, did I want to do it? Since it was Alan, and he's a close friend, I decided to go ahead and do that favour for him.'

A review of the video tape of the BBC television coverage of that race – which includes the unfortunate, unknowing commentator David Coleman describing Pascoe's farewell appearance with the words '. . . and they've given him no easy ride . . .' – shows that King came to the last barrier just in the lead, but then looked across to Pascoe. As the Briton made a big effort on the run-in to the finish, he managed to pass King.

'Alan was a great runner,' King goes on, 'but at that time he was getting slower and all Andy wanted me to do was just to keep it close, not to run away from him, and so that's what I did. I sort of backed up a little just before the finish to make sure he got in.'

Steve Williams, who was there that night, remembers a conversation with King at the time: 'He in essence told me that he was not supposed to win today. It was important for Alan Pascoe to win and that Andy had arranged for him not to compete to his best abilities.'

There is nothing to suggest that Alan Pascoe knew of this arrangement between Norman and King. But the story of James King and Pascoe's last race soon became an open secret in British athletics, though it was not reported for 13 years. Norman, a man who knew how to use threats or favours to get his own way, had already cultivated a strange love-hate relationship with the small corps of athletics journalists, dispensing stories to one or two whenever it suited him. Thus the story of Pascoe's last race was never pursued for more than a decade.

Despite his best efforts to keep a low profile during the 1980s, Norman increasingly become the subject of press attention, which is hardly surprising considering the importance of his role. He, however, takes a different view: 'He regards his influence within British athletics as exaggerated by the media,' his solicitor, Patrick Isherwood, has said.

But when he had something to say, Norman commanded a captive audience. In 1984, Norman was part of British athletics' negotiating team for a new, four-year, multi-million pound television contract. The BBC, broadcasters of all meetings in Britain for the previous 25 years, suddenly found that they had competition from ITV. The BBC bid offered the *status quo*, years of experience and excellence, and just under £10 million in cash, nearly five times the sum which had secured the previous four-year deal. ITV, keen to buy-up the rights of this burgeoning, successful sport, bid £10.5 million. But ITV's trump card was the knowledge that a change in the broadcasting laws being prepared at Westminster would soon allow the sponsors of sports events to buy advertising time in the commercial breaks between their sponsored fixture. This would transform sponsorship opportunities for events shown on commercial channels such as ITV. It also, at a stroke, made sponsoring an event to be televised by the BBC much less attractive to potential backers.

Thus, there was also several sports marketing companies keenly pitching for the potentially lucrative contract to sell sponsorship for British athletics. Leading the way was the powerful International Management Group, the company set up by the American lawyer Mark McCormack initially to look after the interests of golfer Arnold Palmer, and which grew to encompass many sports, including the Wimbledon tennis championships. IMG at one point even represented the interests of Pope John Paul II, earning McCormack's company the sobriquet of 'God's agents'.

While IMG may have suited God, they were less favoured by Denis Howell, the veteran Labour MP and former minister for sport, who had investigated and reported unfavourably on IMG's style of operation. Howell was opposed to IMG's methods, which often saw them represent all the key players, own the marketing rights to a tournament in which those players competed, and running the television production as well. The timing of Howell's report was not auspicious for IMG's ambitions in British athletics. Thus British firms, such as West Nally, the company headed by BBC television presenter Peter West and which had been in the forefront of marketing athletics for both the IAAF and European Athletics Association, seemed to have a better chance of winning the British athletics marketing contract. And then there was a new, small company, called MSW, run by former athlete and sometime ITV athletics commentator, Alan Pascoe.

Obviously, if the BBC was to win the contract, the commercial value of any marketing deal with the sport could be much reduced. Sponsors, denied the chance to advertise around their meetings, would want to pay much less to be part of British athletics. Before the final meeting of the sport's top officials to decide on which television offer to accept, the BBC was still the favourite to win. Yet behind the closed doors of that final meeting, Norman addressed the room in a decisive manner.

According to one of the officials present at the all-important committee, 'Andy's arguments changed the course of the meeting, without a shadow of a doubt. Going in there, I was convinced that we would stay the way we were. But there was a very forceful argument. They were financial more than anything else, plus opportunities for the future, the development of the sport, bringing it out of the 19th century, we heard all those sort of things. Andy spoke about the possibilities that the deal would present to us, and at that stage we were being pressed to be more commercially professional. It hit a mood. Plus Andy was the man who was driving everything at that time, and he was saying that he really couldn't continue to help take us forward unless we took up the opportunities that were going to become available through commercial television. At the end of the meeting, we didn't vote, there was just a look around the table.'

Thus, without even a vote, British athletics was sold to ITV. Even John Bromley, head of ITV's flagship sports programme of the time, *World of Sport*, admitted he was 'flabbergasted' at the turn-round.

Not long after ITV's coup, and just before the Los Angeles Olympic Games, Norman was attending a press briefing held at the British team's pre-Games training camp at Point Loma College, San Diego. After the formal interviews with the team had been concluded, Norman got chatting to a handful of journalists. To the surprise of the newspapermen, during this impromptu press conference of his own, Norman held forth with an astonishing outburst against the BBC. 'Their commentators had begun to think they were bigger than the sport,' Norman told the amazed reporters, including Ken Jones of *The Sunday Mirror*, and Neil Wilson of *The Daily Mail*. 'They thought they were above the athletes. They were acting too high and mighty with us.'

Norman's comments brought a threat of legal action from BBC television commentator Ron Pickering, and an angry response from Bill Cotton, then head of BBC television. 'It comes a bit ill from a full-time policeman and part-time athletics official to start telling us how to run television coverage of a major sport,' said Cotton.

Yet Norman was to continue as a full-time policeman and part-time athletics official for only a short time after the Olympics. Although at the time ITV denied that Norman's appointment as the sport's first full-time, professional promotions officer was a condition of their contract, Bromley had marked the athletics administrators' cards when he described Norman as 'someone we can do business with'. Within a year of the new ITV deal being agreed, Norman had resigned from the police force to work full time in athletics. This, however, may not have been solely because of the influence of ITV. At the end of the Olympic summer of 1984, Norman had been working with the International Athletes' Club, who organised their own international spectacular meeting. Norman had, for the previous decade, been the IAC's Coca-Cola meeting's director.

In the IAC office a week before the meeting, a telephone call for Norman was taken by another IAC official, Dave Bedford, the former 10,000 metres world record-holder. According to Bedford, the call came from a Jane Quigg, from a Portsmouth accountancy firm called Edward Leaske. Bedford took a message: Quigg told him that Norman's payment of $10,000 into a company called Fay Promotions was now due and should be made immediately. Acting like an innocent message taker, Bedford took the bank account details and made notes of the conversation. Bedford was already suspicious over Norman's conduct (Norman was to quit as meeting director after an acrimonious row with Bedford and the IAC over the running of that year's Coke meeting). With the details he had been unwittingly provided with, Bedford resolved to investigate Norman's business affairs.

Fay Promotions, Bedford discovered, had as directors Eric Nash, another senior Southern Counties AAA official, and Margaret Whitbread, mother and coach of Fatima. There were links with other companies, such as Elite Management Ltd (directors Svein Arne Hansen, the meeting director from Oslo, and Mrs Gerd Norman), Ovett Ltd (in which a minor Southern official, Graham Martin, held shares bought for him, ostensibly as a gift for his son, by Andy Norman), and Zed (Portsmouth) Ltd, in which Norman was named as a director along with Steve Ovett. Most of the companies named as their accountants Edward Leaske – a firm set up by a former Olympic yachtsman who was a business associate of Alan Pascoe.

Some of the companies Bedford traced seemed to be dormant, having not traded for some time, while others were active. Armed with his dossier on Norman's businesses, Bedford arranged a secret meeting. One dark night in early November 1984, Bedford, along with two club colleagues, confronted Norman at a motel by the South Mimms junction of the A1. The atmosphere was tense. The three men pointed out to Norman the conflicts of interest between his position within the sport and his businesses. They gave Norman an ultimatum: either he ceased to be involved with these private companies while holding positions of influence in athletics, or they would inform his employers, the police authorities.

It was not long before Norman quit the police but he would never go short of money. Norman was already on a £30,000 annual retainer with the sportswear firm, Nike, whose European operation was run from Newcastle by his old friend, Brendan Foster. In 1985, Norman joined John Hockey Associates in the role of a paid 'consultant'. Meanwhile, Norman had also been receiving regular retainers from others, including West Nally. It was not long afterwards that the British Amateur Athletic Board and AAA appointed Nike as the official kit suppliers to British athletics, and they also entered a contract with John Hockey Associates for them to supply Norman's services as the sport's promotions officer.

Many of the press reports about Norman's demeanour and attitude tended to be unflattering, reflecting the description of him made by the AAA general secretary, Mike Farrell, of 'an honest rogue'. But when *The Times* ran a series of stories about Norman in 1987, alleging that he had 'fixed' drug tests by ensuring that 'clean' urine samples were provided for athletes who feared that they might test positive for a banned substance, the allegations went well beyond mere 'roguishness'. According to Norman's own lawyers, this was 'the most damaging allegation which could be made against him'.

The governing bodies set up an inquiry to look into *The Times*'s allegations. Peter Coni QC, a rowing enthusiast who had introduced strict drug tests in that sport, chaired the three-man committee, which included retired RAF officer and senior Midlands official, Dan Davies, and – extraordinarily for an 'independent' inquiry – Gilbert Kelland, Norman's former commanding officer and his fellow enthusiast for police athletics.

It was no surprise when the resulting Coni Report was inconclusive. Without 'judicial' powers, no one could be summoned to give evidence, and none of the testimony given was privileged. The report cleared other officials of some of the allegations made by the newspaper. But not all. Graham Martin (the minor official who was also connected with some of Norman's business interests) was subsequently dropped from the Sports Council's rota of approved doping control officers because of other complaints about his conduct. Even Norman was later relieved of responsibilities for drug testing at AAA meetings.

None of this seemed to matter to Norman, though. He did not crave nor need public approval for what he did: he just got on and did it. His disdain for the Blazerati was now also felt for the small group of journalists who followed Norman's athletics caravan around Europe – 'those arseholes', as Norman called them.

If Norman did believe that he was irreplaceable, he might have had a point. As the sport became more successful, and Norman's influence became ever wider and stronger, so the officials who were supposed to be in control of Norman instead became all the more dependent on him. One of Norman's talents as an organiser is an incredible memory for all sorts of details, from the most obscure athlete's personal best performances, to the times of flights from Heathrow to New York. Norman's memory meant that very little of what he did was ever committed to writing. There were rarely any files or records of any of his deals or arrangements that he made. When, in 1994, he was dismissed by the British Athletic Federation, it took two BAF staff members three days at Norman's home to go through his official affairs with him and emerge with some sort of order for the coming season.

Norman's other great attribute, despite his own modest career as a runner, is that he is a terrific judge of a race, and of the personalities of the runners in that race. In Moscow in 1980, it was his tactical advice to Ovett which helped him win the 800 metres Olympic gold as much as Seb Coe's desperately bad-run race.

'There's no natural leader there,' Norman told Ovett, 'Guimaraes, who doesn't know the European scene, will probably find himself in the lead in something around 53 seconds. If Coe goes before the bell and you're boxed, you're dead. Warren will probably put in a burst out of bravado, and Kirov will go from 280 out, as he always does. Take Kirov and *go*, don't slow down and wait for someone else's kick, keep at it.' Now, as an account of what happened in the Olympic 800 metres final, it is so accurate that it is hard to believe that Norman told this to Ovett *before* the race.

The British team's golden exploits at those Moscow Olympics, through Allan Wells in the 100 metres, Ovett, Coe at 1,500 metres and Daley Thompson in the decathlon, turned athletics into front page news. The drama of those Coe v Ovett races, Ovett's 'ILY' signal to his fiancée, Rachel (meaning 'I love you'), all made good tabloid stories.

Moses Kiptanui won a third steeplechase world title in Gothenburg, easing up to save the world record for Zurich's lucrative meeting the following week.

Peter Radford (right), the beleagured executive chairman of BAF, explains a point to ITV's Jim Rosenthal.

Primo Nebiolo, all-powerful president of the IAAF, and described as 'probably the most detested man in world sport'.

Australian official Maurie Plant, although banned in his own country after he tried to fix a drug test, by 1995 was employed by the BBC and appointed to the IAAF's Grand Prix Commission.

Christopher Winner could not continue working as IAAF press chief after he uncovered that the ballot for the 1994 Athlete of the Year had been rigged.

Fatima Whitbread threatened legal action against the Sports Council when doping control officers accompanied her to hospital after this 1990 Cardiff meeting.

Sunday Times *journalist Cliff Temple (in red) interviewing Peter Elliott. Temple's suicide in 1994 would have repercussions throughout world athletics.*

Andy Norman's partnership, on and off the track, with javelin thrower Fatima Whitbread would cause continuing controversy for British athletics.

Despite being sacked by BAF early in 1994, Andy Norman (centre) remained an influential figure with top British athletes such as Linford Christie.

Linford Christie with his manager, Sue Barrett, and IAAF official Ernest Obeng at the 1995 World Indoors in Barcelona.

Former European 200m champion John Regis was a victim of British athletics' new economics in 1995.

Diane Modahl (No 323) spent 20 months battling to clear her name after a doping ban following a meeting in Lisbon in June 1994.

Jonathan Edwards transformed triple jumping with his record-breaking performances in 1995. But could he also change the fortunes of British athletics?

But Norman's friendship with Ovett, on and off the track, was about to take a decided turn for the worst, and the women in the two men's lives would play a pivotal part in a bitter break-up of a successful team.

Norman and Ovett were extremely close friends. As well as athlete and agent, runner and race organiser, they were business partners. Norman was even best man at Ovett's wedding in 1981, when it was Norman who somehow managed to persuade Ovett's parents – who had fallen out with their son over his relationship with Rachel – to attend the wedding reception. Yet after Rachel first met Norman, she turned to her husband-to-be and told him: 'I do not like the man and I will never like the man.'

Things started to go awry between Norman and Ovett around 1983. Ovett's plans for the 1982 track season had been ruined one dark night the previous November when he ran into some church railings near his Brighton home, badly damaging his knee. The following track season was a wretched one for a man who in the summer of 1981 had lowered the world record for the mile to 3min 48.80sec. Instead of racing, he had to work as a television commentator as Steve Cram succeeded him as European champion at 1,500 metres.

By 1983, though, with a full winter's training behind him, Ovett was getting back to his old form. The only question was whether he would get back soon enough to win the 1,500 metres title at athletics' first World Championships, staged in Helsinki, Finland. Norman thought he would not, and perhaps by this stage had thoughts of hitching himself to Cram's rapidly rising star. Both Norman and the young Geordie, after all, were soon to be represented by the same agency, John Hockey Associates.

Norman's judgement at that time was that Ovett needed more races to be at his sharpest going into the final in Helsinki. Ultimately, from the way Ovett, the arch-racer in his prime, ran in the 1,500 metres final, Norman's view was vindicated. For while Cram was primed ready to follow the break of the little Moroccan, Said Aouita, with 500 metres of the race to run, Ovett was trapped at the back of the pack, a position he would never normally languish in. In a desperate effort around the final lap, Ovett chased after the leaders, running a faster last 400 metres than any of his rivals. But he never got back on terms with the leaders, who had got a vital head-start as the bell sounded for the last lap, and so Ovett finished out of the medals in fourth place, as Cram became the first world champion at 1,500 metres. As if to reinforce Norman's judgement of Ovett's preparations, five races later, the Olympic 800 metres champion again broke the 1,500 metres world record in Rieti, Italy, with 3min 30.77sec.

But any differences Ovett and Norman may have had on the track were as nothing to the estrangement that was to come because of Norman's involvement with another Helsinki medal-winner and rising young star of the British team, javelin thrower Fatima Whitbread.

The Ovetts, through their friendship with Andy, had also become friendly, and loyal, to Gerd Norman, Andy's wife. So when they invited the Normans to stay with them in Brighton, they were shocked when Andy arrived not with his wife, but with Fatima Whitbread. The Ovetts' relationship with Norman became distinctly chilly thereafter.

Ironically, the Norman-Whitbread liaison which ruined his friendship with Steve Ovett would also become something which would ultimately contribute to Norman being toppled from his position as the most powerful man in British athletics. But even after his dismissal by BAF in 1994, Norman still retained important positions of influence with the IAAF and European AA.

Indeed, just four months after he was dismissed, in August 1994, Norman, as a member of the EAA Council, was given the honour of presenting the medals to the first three in an event at the European Championships at Helsinki. At first, Norman was designated to make the presentations for the women's 400 metres hurdles, until it was pointed out that it might be insensitive, if not completely inappropriate, for him to attend Sally Gunnell's victory parade. Instead, Norman was asked to make the presentations for the women's long jump: somehow, there was something very apt about the former Met policeman hanging the gold medal around the neck of Heike Dreschler, the former member of East Germany's Stasi secret police.

When the EAA next held elections for its council, in October 1995, BAF nominated its treasurer, John Lister, rather than Norman. But at the same Paris conference, Norman nonetheless maintained his great clout in international athletics when – in spite of representing no one but himself – he remained a member of the EAA's marketing committee, while the IAAF reaffirmed his position on its influential Grand Prix Commission. The foundations for this important position in world athletics had been laid at a conference in Athens in 1982, when Norman gave a speech which effectively cleared the way for athletics to turn professional.

Eight

The Beginning of the End

AS THE Olympic flame flickered and died above the vast bowl of the Lenin Stadium at the end of a long August day in 1980, it was symbolic not only of the end of the Moscow Games, but also the end of a cankerous hypocrisy in athletics. For at the same time, amateurism was being extinguished by the custodians of the principal sport at the Olympics.

The Moscow Olympic Games were just the latest to be blighted by a political controversy. From the student riots in the Place of the Three Cultures in Mexico City in 1968, to the Black September assassinations at Munich in 1972, through to the African nations' boycott of the 1976 Montreal Games, all had demonstrated that when the focus of the world was on a major sporting event, then other interests could use that global attention to highlight their cause.

Such wider politicisation of sport was very damaging to the Olympic movement, and the International Amateur Athletic Federation realised this and grasped its opportunity. Until 1980, the Olympic Games had been *de facto* the athletics world championships. In many ways, athletics was extraordinary among major sports in not having its own world championships. But from 1983, the IAAF was to stage its own sporting festival. The first World Championships in athletics were staged in Helsinki, Finland. Within ten years, as well as the obligatory gold medals to all winners, athletics – for so long a bastion of amateurism – was offering luxury Mercedes-Benz cars to its individual world champions. In 1997, 101 years after Baron Pierre de Coubertin staged the first modern Olympic Games in Athens, that city is to stage the sixth World Championships in athletics and, for the first time, prize money is expected to be paid to finalists.

Athens was also the venue, in 1982, for the greatest revolution in a century of modern athletics. There were no races run, no jumps leaped nor implements thrown: the revolution took place in a conference hall, where the IAAF took the first tentative steps towards allowing athletics to go professional.

The process had begun at the IAAF's conference in Moscow prior to the 1980 Olympics. There, the federation established a nine-man working group on 'eligibility' – in other words, to examine the amateur status of athletes.

During the 1960s and 1970s, amateurism, although increasingly regarded as an anachronism in the modern sporting world – cricket had abandoned its 'Gentlemen and Players' distinction, and the Wimbledon tennis championships had gone open – it had still been strictly applied by the International Olympic Committee, first under the autocratic leadership of the American, Avery Brundage, and then under the Irish peer, Lord Killanin. The Games were still the most important event in any amateur sportsman's career, so no athlete could risk being banned for receiving money. But with Michael Killanin set to retire as IOC president in July 1980, the ground was laid for a moderniser to succeed him. The Spaniard, Juan Antonio Samaranch, duly became the IOC's first full-time president. Fittingly, he was to preside over a period which made it increasingly possible for Olympic competitors to become full-time, professional athletes.

The mood at the IAAF's congress in Moscow had reflected this turning point in world sport. When the IAAF working party on eligibility delivered its report to the governing council when it met in Cairo the following March, its findings were hardly a surprise. The tone of the report was categorical: the very future of the IAAF was in the balance. The shamateur game was up, according to the working party. 'The year 1980 has brought to a head the fact that the future of the IAAF and its members is at stake,' the report began. 'It is felt that at international level, athletics is a semi-professional (in the widest sense) sport already, with many leading athletes in top countries training for at least 30 hours per week. The Group aims, however, to make a clear distinction between a professional sport and athletics, which, by its very nature, can never become this.

'It is recognised that there is dissatisfaction among the élite athletes and meeting organisers with the present rules on eligibility, and in different countries, violations of the rules occur, which causes accusations of hypocrisy to be levelled against the whole sport of athletics.'

Conscious of the need to prevent an amateur-professional schism in the sport, but also subjected to political pressures from the eastern bloc nations – who wanted the *status quo* maintained, so that their state-funded athletes would maintain their apparent advantage over part-time western athletes – the working party proposed a set of rule changes which would openly allow payments to athletes, through a system of prize-money and trust funds. The recommendations, though, were only a majority view of the working party.

The proposed new eligibility rules were debated heatedly when put before the IAAF Conference, held just before the European Championships in Athens in September 1982. The reactionaries on the working party, who wanted to avoid change, seemed to have swung opinion among the IAAF Congress – the sport's 'parliamentary' body, made up of representatives of every national member federation, with the authority to make or change the sport's rules.

Compromise was offered. Although the working party had favoured prize-money over appearance fees ('An athlete receiving money merely because he is a champion is felt to be an unfair and unworthy system for the sport. Appearance money inevitably takes the stimulus away from competition, just as it may be argued that prize money gives added stimulus'), it was the latter, appearance money scheme which had attracted more support. Yet even moves towards this new system of appearance payments seemed to have stalled until a rousing address by a member of the British delegation. The man who turned the day in favour of appearance fees was Andy Norman.

Before breakfast, sensing that the mood of the Congress might reject all proposals for athletes' payments at that afternoon's debate, Norman had banged on the door of the hotel bedroom of *The Guardian* reporter, John Rodda. After a typically journalistic late night, Rodda was feeling a little fragile when he was awoken by the knock on the door from the policeman, but he was persuaded nonetheless to help Norman by writing what Rodda later described as 'a blatantly provocative speech' in favour of change.

Standing in front of all the IAAF's power-brokers at the Athens conference, and with Rodda's speech to guide him, Norman warned that if the national governing bodies continued to pretend that under-the-counter payments were not happening, then what they all feared most – a breakaway, professional circuit – might happen. Norman 'knew what the athletes wanted,' Rodda recalled, 'and how it was obtainable'.

'Rule 17 – Athlete's Funds', the new payment rules, went through by 367 votes to 16, though not without hitch. The IAAF very quickly rushed out a two-page, ten-point 'Explanatory Statement', it said 'to make the Athens decisions completely clear'.

The first point of the explanatory statement read: 'The IAAF is against the introduction of commercialism and professionalism in our sport, and the IAAF Council will always actively struggle against any such introduction.' Not only did that seem to contradict the entire argument in Athens, but the evidence of the next 14 years showed the IAAF to be the prime movers in the commercialisation of international athletics. The explanatory statement was just shouting at the gale. While the IAAF tried to give the appearance of shoring up the position of its members by ruling that all deals and payments for athletes must be routed through the national federations, any qualifications to the new rules proved to be unenforceable. The tide had turned professionalism's way.

No one knew that better than the man who had argued so persuasively in Athens for reform. After all, Andy Norman had been breaking the sport's rules on amateurism for years.

In the late 1970s, Patrick Nally was a young entrepreneur who had helped to develop the whole concept of marketing promotions through sport. His company, West Nally, which he founded with the BBC television presenter Peter West, dealt with such blue chip sponsors as Ford, Kraft Foods, Esso, NEC, Canon, Seiko and Adidas. Nally introduced these companies to sports organisations, sometimes developing a wholly new event just as a vehicle for the sponsor (the Benson and Hedges Cup limited overs cricket competition, for example), and he made sure that they wrung every penny's-worth of value out of their sponsorship pound. It was Nally who in 1976 brought together FIFA, football's world governing body, and Coca-Cola in the world's largest single sponsorship agreement, a liaison which was still going strong 20 years later. And it was Nally who devised the concepts of the Golden Series and the World Cup for athletics. Suited, booted and very professional, dealing with so many highly financed companies meant that Nally had a certain, correct way of doing things, particularly when it came to handling money. But with athletics, Nally was a little perplexed by the somewhat unorthodox approach some of the sport's officials had to payments to the competitors, especially since the athletes were supposed to be amateur at the time.

Giving evidence in 1995 in a libel case won by the London Marathon organisation, Nally was in no doubt about the need to secure the appearances of big name athletics stars, even if that meant breaking the rules. 'Even prior to the rule changes by the IAAF permitting payments to athletes,' Nally testified, 'it was always extremely important to the events and to sponsors that star runners took part. With the full knowledge of the IAAF, payments were made to athletes to ensure they competed at principal events. The IAAF were aware that payments had to be made and positively encouraged these arrangements at their own events.

'West Nally also worked closely with a number of marathon organisers at the time . . . and all major Grand Prix event organisers, all of whom were fully aware of the importance of securing top names. This was an integral part of their responsibility to sponsors, television and the general public.'

Andy Norman was one of the officials organising meetings during this period, and he received cash from Nally, on behalf of sponsors, in order to make the rule-breaking payments to athletes. 'We would agree a budget, either in cash or payment to a company, and Andy would make sure the athletes turned up,' Nally said.

As the unpaid, honorary coaching secretary for what was called the Southern Counties AAA in the early 1970s, Andy Norman had successfully

argued for more money to be made available for the area association's train-
ing camps, which he organised. The reason Norman's plea was successful
was because he had already devised a plan to raise more money for the
SCAAA: he would stage an all-star, televised meeting at Crystal Palace.
The TV rights, sponsorship monies and gate receipts from such a meeting,
Norman believed, would combine to turn a nice profit, which could be
ploughed back into coaching. Twenty years later, and that same meeting at
Crystal Palace, now Britain's only annual Grand Prix event, is still going
strong.

In the early days, it was Nally who brought in the meeting's sponsorship funding. 'There was a need for somebody to work with the athletes,
make sure that they appeared, deal with the problems of their air tickets,
accommodation . . . all necessary if the sport was to expand,' Nally recalled.
'The administrators shunned it, they shied away from it, and Andy Norman
filled that void. He had an important role in the development of athletics. It
was a dirty job, but someone had to do it.'

Nally remembers on several occasions handing over to Norman a briefcase full of cash from the sponsors, effectively the agreed 'budget' for the
meeting, and leaving the full-time policeman/part-time sports administrator
to go off and deal with the athletes. The deals had to be paid in cash:
shamateurism had created a sort of athletics black economy, with no paper
trail of cheques or bank transfers to show that any athletes were receiving
money for competing. Nor did Nally ever receive any breakdown of how
the money was spent. Once Norman had provided Nally with a simple
written receipt for the cash, as far as West Nally and the sponsors were concerned, the part-time athletics official was in complete control of how the
money was spent.

As Steve Williams, an American sprinter who was a regular in
Norman's early meetings and who admits to receiving cash payments
before they were allowed under the sport's rules, says: 'I think it was universal. We all knew there was a huge double standard existing in the world
of track and field. I felt no particular need to penalise myself by not taking
the money.'

Nor did Norman apparently feel any need 'to penalise' himself for all
the spare-time effort he put into organising the meetings. Although Norman
was still a serving officer in the Metropolitan Police, and gave the appearance of being an unpaid official doing all this work for his love of the sport,
Nally says that he made regular payments to Norman to ensure that the
sponsors were properly looked after. 'We paid him a quarterly retainer,'
Nally says, 'and I'm certain we weren't the only ones. He was doing a big
job, doing a full-time job before it was a full-time job.'

Norman was nothing if not a quick learner. The ploys which he saw
used by Patrick Nally, the personality management skills of his own agent,
John Hockey, or the general sports marketing which he may have learned

during his lengthy visits to the offices of Alan Pascoe's business empire, would all stand him in good stead in years to come. Norman, the master of doing several jobs at one time, developed plenty of business sidelines to keep himself busy, and to help him become exceptionally wealthy through athletics.

As a marketing coup, Chafford Hundred Athletics Club was a masterstroke. As an athletics club, it was just the latest manifestation of the greed and money motive that threatens to corrupt athletics forever. From its creation in 1991, Chafford Hundred AC overnight almost certainly became the richest athletics club in Britain. Yet it enters in and competes in no team competitions. Chafford Hundred AC was established purely as a marketing ploy, a one-stop shop for sponsors wanting to become involved in one of Britain's most successful sports.

There was no longer any need for potential sponsors to trek around the country's athletics clubs in order to get their logo plastered across the vest of a high-profile athlete, when, with Chafford Hundred AC, in one go they could secure the endorsement for their products of Linford Christie, Colin Jackson, Sally Gunnell, Steve Backley, John Regis and Yvonne Murray. All those athletes were also represented by British athletics' promotions officer Norman. The Chafford Hundred club, meanwhile, was managed by what one press release described as 'the mastermind behind its formation', Fatima Whitbread, the former javelin world champion who, by then, had become Norman's fiancée.

All businesses want to be seen as the best, and to be associated with the best. There is usually very little value to a commercial company in sponsoring, say, the world's 40th ranked shot putter. Thus, when Chafford Hundred was launched, by signing up most of the leading names from British athletics, it was immediately able to offer exactly what prospective sponsors might want, while having none of the national federation's responsibilities for funding development programmes and club athletics.

All of the crowd-pulling members of Chafford Hundred AC had emerged through the traditional British club system. By allowing Chafford Hundred to operate, however, the sport was effectively choking hard-up clubs of vital income. The Chafford Hundred concept broke no rules, but just exploited a loophole. Its members were all 'second claim', allowing them to continue to compete for their original clubs in team events. Those events rarely attract television interest, however; but at Grand Prix meetings, with the TV cameras covering their every move, Chafford Hundred athletes would wear Chafford Hundred kit, adorned with their sponsors' logos.

Even a conventional club as relatively high profile and successful as Belgrave Harriers, the Battersea-based winners of the British League, were to feel the cold economic effects of the emergence of Chafford Hundred. Boasting several internationals among their members, undoubtedly the star performer in their clubhouse was John Regis, who at the European

Championships in 1990 won a record four medals, including golds in the 200 metres and 4x400 metres relay. The prospect of Regis wearing a corporate logo on his club vest during televised meetings during the European summer track season had enticed Lucozade to offer Belgrave a deal worth £18,000 over two years. The club secretary had even received a letter of intent. Such an amount would have proved invaluable to Belgrave, but with the offer less than three weeks old, Lucozade pulled out. 'As you know a vital part of the package was for John Regis to wear the Lucozade Sport logo on his running kit at a range of meetings throughout the season,' said a second letter from a senior executive at Alan Pascoe Associates, who were brokering the deal for Lucozade.

'Recently, John has been signed up by the Chafford Hundred AC as his secondary claim club. This effectively would prohibit him wearing the Lucozade logo at any meetings apart from those he is committed to wear his club vest. For this reason, our client has decided that it is no longer practicable to pursue a sponsorship arrangement with Belgrave.' Instead, Lucozade 'pursued a sponsorship arrangement' with Chafford Hundred AC, worth £220,000 over three years to the club that never competes. Similarly lucrative deals were also arranged with Interflora and Vaseline, effectively diverting money away from British athletics as a whole, and instead benefiting a handful of the country's élite athletes.

Norman has always vigorously denied any involvement in Chafford Hundred. 'It is totally Fatima's project,' he said. 'Andy has nothing to do with the Chafford Hundred club,' said Whitbread. Sponsors and their agents were also always at pains to stress how 'hands-on' Whitbread's involvement with negotiations had been, while noting how totally absent Norman had been from discussions. Although Norman has not been involved in the management of the Chafford Hundred, some in the sport questioned his role as promotions director of a governing body whilst acting as agent to the majority of Chafford Hundred's members while also being engaged to marry the club's manager.

Despite Whitbread's claims to be the 'mastermind' behind Chafford Hundred, it was soon apparent that one of her partners had also laid claims to the idea. 'I thought of it,' Colin Jackson, one of the sharpest men in British athletics, has said. 'I suggested it to Linford. The idea was to put together all the best athletes the UK could offer, then pull in the businesses that would want to be involved.'

There were other events around the time that Chafford Hundred was established which suggested that perhaps no single person could claim all the credit for its foundation. When this new club was set up, it took its name from its original backer, an otherwise unassuming Essex housing development many miles away from Jackson or Christie's homes, but close to Orsett, an expensive surburban neighbourhood in the countryside to the east of the M25, London's orbital motorway. It was in Orsett that, following his divorce from Gerd, Norman set up house with Whitbread in 'Javel Inn', a large, new double-fronted house, bought for around £250,000. A 'his 'n hers' pair of Mercedes saloons were routinely parked in the driveway.

For all that Norman, Whitbread and the club's sponsors' denied that Norman had any involvement in the club, one person had given an account to suggest that the British athletics promotions officer was very much involved in its establishment: Norman himself.

In June 1990, Whitbread's career as a javelin thrower had reached an end. After the disappointment of winning only the silver medal at the Seoul Olympics of 1988, injury and illness had curtailed her international appearances. At the UK Championships staged at Cardiff's Leckwith Stadium on a damp afternoon early in the summer of 1990, she made her tentative return to competition, hopeful that it might lead to a successful defence of her European title in Split, Yugoslavia, later that year. Yet after five rounds of her event, Whitbread found herself in the unusual position for a domestic meeting of being only third, behind Sharon Gibson and the teenager Mandy Liverton. Whitbread's best effort of 51.50 metres was a long way short of her best form, the 77.44 metres she had thrown in the qualifying round of the 1986 European Championships in Stuttgart, Germany, which had broken the then world record.

So with her pride and her status at stake, Whitbread sprinted in for her sixth and final throw of the event, determined to retrieve the competition. As the eight-time UK champion let go of her spear, there was a sudden, loud 'crack' noise, audible to all of the 5,000 spectators in the new stadium, quickly followed by a yell of pain from the thrower. Whitbread clutched her shoulder in agony. Ever the competitor, she was careful not to cross the foul line so that the throw would still count. It did, but at just 48 metres, it had no effect on the outcome of the event.

She was rushed to a local hospital, where surgeons operated overnight on her shoulder, which, under the tremendous strain of her final throw, had been dislocated and fractured. The sheer power which she had generated had proved too much for her skeleton to contain. It was Whitbread's third operation in three years.

Ten days after the competition, Norman made an angry telephone call to *Athletics Weekly*. That morning's latest edition had included in its 'trailer' of articles to appear in the following week's issue a teasing headline: 'Whitbread: My future'. Norman was convinced that the article would be taking a negative slant, and he vented his anger at the editor. Yet it had been Norman himself who had arranged the interview when, in the aftermath of the Cardiff injury, the magazine's staff had been trying to contact Margaret Whitbread, Fatima's adoptive mother, hoping to interview her, as Fatima's coach, about the consequences of the injury for one of Britain's biggest athletics stars.

Without having seen the article – which, at the time of his call, was still being written – Norman first complained to the young reporter who had been assigned to the interview, David Ogle. It was wrong, Ogle was told by Norman, to take liberties like this. After all, had Fatima not given him a lengthy interview at her home, and even shown him the latest scar across her broad shoulder?

Eventually, Ogle transferred the call to his editor. After about 20 minutes of airing his concerns again, Norman seemed to be placated. 'It's not easy for her, you know, when the sport's been your life for 15, 16 years, just to stop and move on,' Norman said. 'I'm trying to set something up to keep her involved,' Norman added. Seeming satisfied with the explanations offered by the magazine editor about the article's intentions, Norman ended the conversation with: 'You will make sure you use a nice picture of her, won't you?'

The seed of the idea which was to become Chafford Hundred Athletics Club, Norman's 'something to keep her involved' was already germinating, with Whitbread poised to reap the benefits. 'We don't make a profit,' Whitbread has said in defence of Chafford Hundred. 'What we aim to do,' she explained, 'is create a financial opportunity for the athletes to be able to prepare for their competitions and financially secure them for the years when they have finished athletics.'

In other words, Chafford Hundred AC was a management agency for athletes. But by the time it was set-up, there was a very good reason for Norman's involvement to be played down as much as possible. In 1989, Norman had once again found himself at the centre of a storm when Steve Ovett alleged that his former business partner had offered him £20,000 to race the 1,500 metres against Seb Coe at the AAA Championships, a meeting at which appearance money was supposed never to be paid at all. Ovett's allegations were investigated by Robert Reid QC and the Sports Council's David Pickup, and among the resulting report's recommendations was that Norman, while promotions officer for British athletics, should be banned from operating as an agent for athletes, organising their competitive programmes. Undeterred, the governing body went ahead and registered Norman as an international athletes' representative, reasoning that it was an essential part of his duties as promotions officer, and that as long as he was not paid for such work, there could not possibly be any conflict of interests.

Clearly, what the Reid-Pickup Report would not allow was for Norman, while working for the BAF, to have any involvement with an organisation which took commission payments from athletes, as Chafford Hundred does.

Fatima Whitbread, it seemed, had simply applied some important lessons about making business deals in athletics. BAF never took action because they could not show that Norman was working for Chafford Hundred. 'We cannot take action against our promotions director because of the business activities of his fiancée,' explained a federation spokesman.

But Norman already had a history of entering into his own, private business arrangements and keeping his employers in the dark.

There were some important parallels between the way Chafford Hundred was set up as a business, and the way some of Andy Norman's earlier ventures had been established. Records at Companies House show that FLC Marketing (where FLC is believed to stand for Fatima, Linford and Colin), was a joint venture between Whitbread, Christie and Jackson which was created at the same time as Chafford Hundred AC. The accounts of FLC Marketing list Chafford Hundred as principal creditor.

The chartered accountancy firm which handled FLC's accounts is Edward Leaske, the Portsmouth-based business which seems to have cornered the accountancy business in the athletics market rather well – over time, they have audited the accounts of several companies associated with the sport, many of them run by or listing as a director Andrew John Norman. One of the first companies with athletics links which hired Leaske to look after its accounts was a consultancy firm known as Zed (Portsmouth) Ltd. Norman set up this company with his then friend, Steve Ovett. On the official registration forms for Zed (Portsmouth) Ltd, held by Companies House, Norman's occupation was given as 'Consultant'. There was never any mention of his then job, as a serving officer with the Metropolitan Police.

Norman remained a director of Zed (Portsmouth) Ltd until 1983. In fact, Norman was listed as a director of several companies. Usually, his occupation was listed as 'Consultant'. His employment as a police sergeant was not mentioned. This declaration of his occupation is a minor breach of Company Law, hardly becoming of someone who at the time was supposed to be a guardian of the law.

Norman's reluctance to come forward to the police with details about his outside business interests did not stop him from conducting business transactions in police time. One associate from that period remembers the police sergeant holding a business meeting in the cells of the police station where Norman worked at the time. The company being discussed at the meeting was Ovett Ltd. Even though someone else other than Norman was nominated as a director of the company, it was the policeman who at the meeting paid for a tranche of company shares with a stack of used notes. This, apparently, was as a gift from Norman for the son of the nominee director.

More than a decade later, the man who received this payment from Norman in a brown paper bag can still vividly recall the transaction because of the highly irregular circumstances. 'It's the only time I've ever been in a police cell,' he said. He was also in no doubt that Graham Martin, the man who was formally recorded as a director of the company, had only a nominal role in the conduct of the business. 'It was clear that Martin was only a nominee director for Andy. We'd regularly get calls from Andy, telling us where to deliver stock.'

Another reason for this businessman's good memory of events is because of the unsavoury manner in which Ovett Ltd was eventually wound-up, costing him and his business partner many thousands of pounds. Ovett Ltd, despite the cachet of an Olympic champion's name as its trademark, and Ovett's own involvement in promoting its sportswear products, struggled to establish itself in a very competitive market. Eventually, Norman and the company accountant, Edward Leaske, persuaded the businessmen to put £10,000 into the company and to buy up all the surplus stock for sale through his chain of sports shops, in order to avoid Steve Ovett's name and reputation being damaged by association with a bankruptcy.

Yet after Ovett Ltd was formally wound up, the businessmen discovered to their horror that, without their knowledge or authority, they had been nominated as directors, and therefore were liable for all the rest of the failed company's debts, over and above the £10,000 payment and stock purchase.

Insults were to be added to the businessmen's financial injury, however. A new company bearing a similar name – Ovett Sports Ltd – had been formed shortly after Ovett Ltd was wound up. Despite the new company's apparent lack of a business history, it quickly announced that it had won the potentially lucrative contract to be official clothing suppliers to the 1985 London Marathon. Norman, meanwhile, went public in the press about two London businessmen who had taken Steve Ovett for a ride.

Seven years later, and Chafford Hundred AC was also being accused of sharp business practices. In the spring of Olympic year, 1992, Fatima Whitbread approached Roger Black and Kriss Akabusi with an offer of £7,000 each to appear with John Regis and Derek Redmond, the rest of Britain's 1991 World Championship-winning 4x400 metres relay squad, in a television commercial for Mars chocolate bars.

The relay team had become national heroes the previous September, when they declared that they had 'whupped ass' by beating the crack American squad in the World Championship final in Tokyo. Mars's promotion plan in 1992 was to jet the four British runners out to Barcelona to film an advertisement for use before that summer's Olympic Games. As half of the relay squad, Black and Akabusi were essential to the plan. However, they were not members of Chafford Hundred AC, which had received the original approach to make the advertisement. When they were approached, Black and Akabusi referred Whitbread to their own coach and manager, Mike Whittingham, a former international hurdler who had just been appointed as national event coach for 400 metres.

'I remember that there were a number of inconsistencies and the deal was very vague,' Whittingham recalled. His suspicions had been raised by the fact that Mars had approached Chafford Hundred with the deal in the first place, when it was well known within the sport that he managed the affairs of half of the relay squad. Whittingham wondered whether there was someone within the British Athletic Federation who was favouring Chafford Hundred by steering business deals their way, regardless of who or what was required.

The four relay runners nonetheless went ahead and filmed the advertisement – by anyone's standards, £7,000 is still a substantial pay-day. But as they were nearly finished in their work, they discovered from the ad agency working for Mars that the chocolate confectionery company had in fact paid Chafford Hundred a total of £40,000. The four runners checked notes: it did not take a rocket scientist to realise that, somewhere along the line, there was £12,000 unaccounted for.

The athletes were outraged. Whittingham, on behalf of the athletes, took legal advice and publicly confronted Whitbread at the final meeting to the season at Sheffield. She broke down in tears, saying that she had been 'naïve'. Norman stepped in shortly afterwards, asking Whittingham to back off because Whitbread was 'new to this game'. The missing £12,000 was paid over to the runners.

A year later, and Norman was typically vitriolic about critics of Chafford Hundred, 'They're just jealous little nobodies,' he said. But within the next 12 months, even Chafford Hundred's founder members were beginning to have second thoughts about the so-called 'élite super-club'. It was Cliff Temple's investigations into the affairs of the club for *The Sunday Times* which led to the threats from Norman which contributed to the journalist's suicide in January 1994. By February 1994, Chafford Hundred's three biggest star names, Linford Christie, Sally Gunnell and Colin Jackson, had all drastically changed their position within its structure.

Christie and Jackson resigned their directorships – according to their spokeswoman, 'they wanted to concentrate full time on athletics', without considering what that says about Chafford Hundred's position as an *athletics* club – and they established their Nuff Respect agency, where they soon had John Regis as a client, although all three continued to appear in track meetings in Chafford Hundred club vests. Gunnell quit Chafford Hundred altogether 'to pursue her own business interests', while also dropping Norman as her race manager.

Undeterred by these defections, however, Whitbread had established another promotional deal, this time involving her own, 'real' athletics club, Thurrock Harriers. A three-year contract was signed with the Flour Advisory Bureau under which a group of Chafford Hundred athletes now also joined Thurrock Harriers, again as 'second claim' members, in order to wear a prominent 'Bread For Life' logo at televised meetings.

According to Whitbread in a taped telephone interview, the deal was worth £250,000. Thurrock Harriers was set to receive £30,000 over the three years. For appearing in four televised meetings and two personal appearances for the sponsors, each athlete in the scheme would receive

£1,000 per year – making the total spend on athletes of around £40,000 per year. That ought to have left Chafford Hundred with something like £180,000 of sponsors' cash, which she said in the interview was to be spent on promotional activities and development seminars for young athletes, while 'a lot would be spent on the awards scheme'. In 1993, '94 and '95, the Bread For Life award scheme gave cash awards to four young athletes, totalling just £4,000 each year, plus a year's supply of bread.

When these figures were reported in *The Sunday Times*, Whitbread wrote a letter to correct the 'impression that I am deriving a disproportionate personal benefit'. In her letter, Whitbread said that the deal was in fact worth a total of £207,500, and that £2,000 was used in administration, while she would herself be taking a ten per cent commission on the deal, that is, something slightly over £20,000. By no means was she getting too much of the Bread For Life scheme's dough.

Even taking Whitbread's second, lower total figure for the deal, the sums in her letter did not add up. Just as with the Mars deal, there were tens of thousands pounds apparently unaccounted for – about £25,000 in this instance.With so many athletes involved in the Bread For Life deal, it was impossible for them to ever get together and compare their average £1,000 annual grant with the total value of the deal. But there are always those athletes, not quite at the superstar level, for whom such hand-outs are vital, while the whereabouts of other cash is an irrelevance. 'We're not going to complain about the man who hands out the money,' as one young athlete remarked.

Indeed, there was a view that perhaps the sport needed more initiatives like Chafford Hundred AC. As British athletics, like the British economy, became stuck in recession in the early 1990s, Peter Radford, head of the BAF, was heard to muse: 'There are times when I wonder whether the DSS could end up as the biggest sponsor of athletics.'

Increasingly, to succeed in international athletics requires a full-time commitment, even from the most talented of athletes. Rarely, though, are emerging talents in a financial position to be able to afford such a commitment. Sebastian Coe and Steve Ovett's track successes were supported throughout the early years by their parents. Until he began to earn big money from his track performances, Linford Christie worked in an accounts office at the Co-op, and had his girlfriend pay for his physiotherapy treatment. As Roger Black has warned, in the modern world of professional athletics, an injured athlete is an unemployed athlete: 'If you don't run, you don't get a penny.'

Perhaps because of moves made by groups such as Chafford Hundred, Black's fear may finally be alleviated. Ten years on from payments finally being (openly) accepted, the sport in Britain is getting itself ready to take the final step towards professionalisation by putting the top 100-or-so international athletes under contract.

In the past, most of Britain's international athletes had been subject to a haphazard system of payments and benefits: a £200 training grant here, a medical insurance scheme there. An entire generation of Britain's brightest juniors through the 1980s were lucky enough to benefit from the personal benevolence of Sir Eddie Kulukundis, a multi-millionaire who indulged his passion for the sport by personally funding training for promising youngsters.

Once they reached the senior ranks, though, only the fortunate few seem able to survive and thrive at international level, and fewer still progress to championship honours. Too often, athletic talent has slipped through the net for the want of a little cash. The new contract system, warmly embraced by Radford as 'the shape of the future', would seek to organise all the services offered to athletes by BAF in a structured manner.

The scheme was the product of six months' work by Mike Whittingham. He used as his blueprint the successful, state-funded schemes in Spain, Portugal and Italy, when annual grants, a sort of athletes' salary, are paid to those assessed to have medal-winning potential. Like these continental counterparts, the British scheme includes merit awards for athletes attaining world rankings, bonus payments for winning medals, and a separate scheme to assist those suffering from long-term injuries. But the principal problem which faced BAF as it attempted to introduce the scheme in 1996 was fundamental: it did not have the finance to pay for it.

The sponsors and backers of British athletics in the halcyon days of the Golden Decade of the 1980s had deserted the sport. Alan Pascoe Associates, hired to bring in sponsorship packages for athletics, found its task increasingly difficult. British athletics' reserve fund was worryingly low. The public rows and disputes in 1995 saw the federation make a pretax loss of £256,000, leaving even less cash in the kitty to fund development schemes. Even the meagre £600 training grants which had been paid to top athletes in 1995 were cut to just £500 for the Olympic year of 1996.

Within a decade of going professional, what some IAAF officials had feared when Andy Norman made his decisive speech at Athens in 1982 to usher in paid athletics had come to pass. National federations were losing their influence, as the sport's financial might had now come to rest with the promoters of the big-budget invitation meetings and with athletes' agents. People, in fact, such as Andy Norman.

Nine

The Never-Ending
Money-go-Round

AFTER THE first ten years of professional athletics, the first decade of cash prizes in the International Amateur Athletic Federation's Grand Prix circuit, strange things have begun to happen in the sport. An athlete with the chance of breaking a world record deliberately slowed down before the finishing line of a World Championship final, while another, much fancied to double his own collection of gold medals, just did not bother to turn up for the heats of his second event, preferring to save his energies.

Very often in a major championship final, especially in the sprint events where the margin of victory can be so small, an athlete just *has* to break the world record to secure gold: Sally Gunnell in Stuttgart in 1993, Carl Lewis in Tokyo in 1991, Ann Packer in Tokyo in 1964. There are other examples. But where, by the final stages, the outcome of an event is clear cut, surely no athlete would stint of that final, extra effort to achieve the ultimate performance – an Olympic gold, or world title, sealed with the world record? No one in 1968, for example, could have imagined David Hemery jogging across the line of the Olympic 400 metres hurdles final, safe in the knowledge that he could not be beaten for gold, and certain that he would break the world record the following week.

Yet, with a lap to go in the final of the 3,000 metres steeplechase at the Gothenburg World Championships in August 1995, Moses Kiptanui was the length of the home straight clear of his nearest rivals. Clearly, he was about to win the title for the third time. The only question was: could he break his own world record? Renowned for his strength at the finish of races and his ability to run close to 60 seconds on the final circuit of his race, barriers and all, somewhere down the back straight of the Ullevi stadium, Kiptanui seemed to lose power, his pace slacken. The sigh from the packed crowd as Kiptanui stopped the clock at 8:04.16 amply expressed the anti-climax. Unchallenged, the Kenyan had run only (*only!*) the third fastest time ever seen.

An hour later, with the gold medal around his neck in the post-race press conference, Kiptanui mentioned the unmentionable: the Kenyan admitted in an unguarded comment that he had eased back on the final lap, so as not to unwittingly break his own world record and thus jeopardise any bonuses that might be on offer to him later in the week at the Weltklasse meeting in Zurich.

The purists criticised Kiptanui for losing his sense of priorities, for being motivated more by greed than speed. They said Kiptanui valued gold more than gold medals. The truth, as ever, is slightly more complicated.

After all, there's only so much you can do, living in the bush outside Nairobi, with a second Mercedes-Benz C-180 saloon. The IAAF had grudgingly put up the luxury cars as first prize bonuses for the first time at the 1993 World Championships in Stuttgart, home city of Mercedes, after some of the élite athletes threatened a boycott over the lack of prize-money. But the cars did not address the rumbling discontent among the athletes. 'Can an athlete pay his mortgage with a Mercedes?' was the way Kiptanui's British manager, Kim McDonald, put it. 'Being crowned world champion might be important to someone who has never won a title before, but Moses had already won twice, so, just by being in Gothenburg, he actually had more to lose than to gain.'

Running that last lap in Gothenburg, Kiptanui was also being mindful of his responsibilities at home, to his ten brothers and sisters. 'I want them to have a proper house to live in and a proper education, not like I did,' he said. He also remembered his former training partner, Paul Kipkoech, world champion over 10,000 metres in 1987, who died early in 1995, aged just 33, from cerebral malaria.

Kipkoech died a long, painful death, with little by way of what the western world would recognise as proper medical care, because he was penniless, despite his massive winnings during his competitive career. It was Kiptanui who led a group of Kenyan athletes in setting up a trust fund for Kipkoech's widow and three children.

Thus Kiptanui, the world's greatest ever steeplechaser, was only showing that he had realised that if he did not capitalise on his fleeting fame as a fleet-footed celebrity, no one would. Therefore, on a steamy August night in Zurich the week after the World Championships, running without a pacemaker – steeplechasers prefer a clear run at the solid 3ft barriers, and besides, there is no one on Earth who can run at the Kenyan's pace for much more than a mile – Kiptanui became the first man to run 3,000 metres steeplechase inside eight minutes, a feat on a par in terms of athletics significance with Bannister's first sub-four-minute mile.

Yet the really important statistics that night were the rich rewards such endeavour yielded. Kiptanui was probably receiving around $50,000 as an appearance fee from the Zurich promoter, Res Brügger, who would have also paid a win bonus of $5,000. Then Brügger would have had to shell out another $50,000 as a world record bonus, and a further $20,000 bonus for breaking eight minutes. The meeting sponsors also put up a 2lb 8oz gold bar for the world record – worth another $15,000. And finally, Kiptanui's contract with shoe manufacturers Reebok also included world record bonus clauses which would have amounted to another $60,000.

In total, Kiptanui's night's work in Zurich probably yielded him about $200,000, or £130,000. It proved an expensive night at the Letzigrund stadium for Brügger, because later in the evening, the Ethiopian, Haile Gebresilassie, who had retained his 10,000 metres world title in Gothenburg, broke the world record at 5,000 metres, which Kiptanui had set earlier in the summer. But since Brügger is a retired banker, and since the Zurich meeting is staged in the centre of Swiss banking, it is very likely that all the record bonus payments would have been covered by a very careful insurance policy.

The way Gebresilassie was running, they needed to be. Many felt that had the tiny Ethiopian raced in the 5,000, as well as the 10,000 metres, at Gothenburg, a championship distance double was there for the taking. Such a double gold feat had not been accomplished in fifteen years, not seen since another Ethiopian, Miruts Yifter, won both races at the Moscow Olympics.

Gebresilassie, though, opted out of the 5,000 metres at Gothenburg to save himself for Zurich. There, he produced *the* running performance of the year by knocking 10.91 seconds off the world best, the biggest single improvement in the event for 63 years. It is said that pole vaulter Sergei Bubka earns $80,000 in bonuses every time he breaks the world record, an achievement he has turned into an art form, improving the world record 35 times, usually by the minimum margin of one centimetre. Thus Gebresilassie's 12 min 44.39 sec 5,000 metres world record in Zurich was hardly the calculating performance of an athlete conscious of collecting as many world record bonuses as possible. He might have been accused of wasteful extravagance.

'He could have made more money if he had run more slowly, and set another record at the next meeting,' Jos Hermens, Gebresilassie's manager, said, 'but you have to take these chances while you can.'

Sandro Giovanelli, the promoter of the Rieti meeting in Italy, who also works in the IAAF's promotions office, accepts that 'where athletes know there is money around, they are looking for as much as possible'. It was a situation which had been of the IAAF's own making. In 1982, the IAAF's own working party condemned appearance fee: 'Appearance money inevitably takes the stimulus away from competition, just as it may be argued that prize money gives added stimulus.' Gothenburg saw those words made flesh. For the IAAF has over the past dozen years greedily expanded its championship programme, in pursuit of millions of television dollars, while passing on little of its profits to the athletes. With athletes now professionals, it is little wonder that they should seek to maximise their earnings from their brief careers in the sport.

According to Kim McDonald, 'The bottom line is that the IAAF are trying to slow down a process which it is too late to slow down. We are already involved in a professional business, yet they still want to call it an amateur sport.' That it is unarguable is shown by a quote from Leroy Burrell, the world's fastest man, holder of the 100 metres world record, who was interviewed by the *Wall Street Journal*: 'We aren't in this sport because we like it, or we want to earn our way through school. We're in it to make money.'

To all athletes, an Olympic gold medal is priceless. But with world championships now being staged every two years, the IAAF is debasing its own currency. McDonald's professional body, the International Association of Athlete Representatives, has been lobbying since 1991 for at least $11 million in prize money at each world championships, with $100,000 for every champion, down to $5,000 for eighth place. They recommend a $100,000 world record bonus, too. Instead, the IAAF has opted to increase prize money on its Grand Prix circuit. It is not difficult, therefore, to see where the IAAF's priorities lay.

In launching the Grand Prix series in 1985, the IAAF had sought to bring some shape and purpose to the annual merry-go-round of international invitation meetings. Unspoken, but no less real, was the international federation's desire to have more control over this burgeoning, high-profile and lucrative area of the sport.

Thus, instead of just having a set of independent events that invited the top athletes to perform in one-off competitions, the IAAF tried to co-ordinate the dates of the meetings, their programme of events, even determining the number of different nationalities of athletes that were supposed to compete at each meeting. In this new Grand Prix, the top performers through the season would accumulate points according to their finishing positions, and then be invited to compete at an annual showpiece final. In 1985, that final was held in Rome, naturally enough since the IAAF was now presided over by the Italian, Primo Nebiolo.

The template for the modern, televised athletics spectacular meeting had been the International Athletes' Club's annual Coca-Cola Meeting, the end-of-season, floodlit event which, from its first staging in 1968 always played to a guaranteed packed house and always delivered some form of athletics fireworks. So it is the ultimate irony that, once the IAAF launched its Grand Prix series to catch up with this idea of big-time athletics, it was the venerable Coke meet which was the first and biggest casualty.

The fact that Britain went into the first Grand Prix season in 1985 with two Grand Prix meets – what was then called the Peugeot Talbot Games (events' identities change with changing sponsors), organised by the Southern Counties AAA and staged at Crystal Palace, and the IAC/Coca-Cola International at the same south London venue – was a fair reflection of the country's status in international athletics, and of the two meetings' standings on the European summer circuit of invitation meetings.

Eventually, though, the IAC's innovative Coke meeting was killed off. Other countries with less claim to stage more than one Grand Prix somehow managed to continue to have two or more events in the élite top 16 invitation meetings. In 1995, Switzerland and Germany both staged two of the top events; America saw two Grands Prix played out in front of half-empty stands in New York and San Jose; and France, if you include the tiny Principality of Monaco, hosted four out of 16 of the year's Grands Prix. Yet Britain had just one meeting included among those showcases for star athletes. This was a direct result of the internecine rivalry and feuding which existed in the sport in Britain in the 1980s.

Although it was part of that inaugural IAAF circuit in 1985, the IAC/Coca-Cola meeting soon found itself being undermined. Over time, the IAC meet was denied its traditional end-of-season date (needed for the Grand Prix final, the IAAF's Grand Prix Commission had decreed), it was denied its traditional venue (you can't stage two events in the same city, the Commission said), and finally, it lost its Grand Prix status altogether. That lost, so the meeting was abandoned by sponsors and television.

As Andy Norman, a member of the IAAF's Grand Prix Commission throughout this period, was to observe so accurately: 'No television, no sponsors; no sponsors, no money; no money, nobody gets paid.' And if nobody gets paid, in this day and age there can be no meeting.

The seeds of the destructive inter-meeting rivalry had been sown at Crystal Palace one evening early in the autumn which followed the Los Angeles Olympics. Well into the programme of the Coca-Cola Meeting on that clear late summer's evening in September 1984, with not a spare seat to be had in the Crystal Palace arena, David Bedford found himself perched on a bench between the long jump run-up and the track itself, as close as you can get to the action without donning a vest yourself.

'And now let's have a warm welcome for one of the great favourites here at Crystal Palace . . .' came over the public address system as the announcer worked his 18,000 audience, '*Mike Boit.*' There was an irony in the smooth, warmth of the welcoming introduction for the Kenyan, for it masked just one of the incidents which had made the previous four days anything but smooth.

When Boit had turned up at the Queen's Hotel in Sydenham two nights earlier, his arrival was greeted with more surprise than warmth. Boit, the 1972 Olympic 800 metres bronze medallist and a regular at the Coke meeting since 1975, this year had not been invited to compete. The ageing Kenyan's out-of-the-blue appearance represented just another problem for Bedford, who was officially working as 'Meeting Co-ordinator', which basically meant that in a backroom, bloodless coup, he had supplanted Norman as the Coke's meeting director.

Organising the event for the first time, and despite his title, it was Bedford's job to act as dogsbody to everyone else involved in the meeting, ensuring that every detail was just right, from organising inter-continental air tickets for Olympic medallists, to sticking stamps on envelopes containing car park passes for the meeting's timekeepers. When asked whether he had a job description, Bedford had a pat reply. 'Yeah, a one-word job description,' he said, 'Gofer. You know: gofer this, gofer that . . .'

And so it fell to Bedford to find space for Boit both at the hotel – the IAC had taken over all 180 rooms in the slightly down-at-heel Queen's Hotel just up the hill from the stadium – and to fit the Kenyan into the meeting's most controversial event, the men's mile.

Bedford had been involved in the first ever Coca-Cola meeting 16 years earlier, as a competitor. That year, in Ron Clarke's world record-breaking two miles, the young Bedford had come nearer last than first, but his days of gloriously winning national titles and breaking records were still to come.

A long-time member of the IAC, the 'athletes' union', Bedford's own rebellious outlook during his running career seemed perfectly matched with the organisation's own rumbustious attitude to authority. With problems anticipated, Bedford had been brought in to help with the organisation of the meeting earlier in the summer. At that time, Bedford was running his own nightclub in Luton. His workload on the Coca-Cola meeting grew considerably, however, when a dispute over TV contracts between the IAC and the British governing bodies, as the IAC sought to negotiate its own television deal, festered into a full-scale row with Norman. Relations with Norman had been strained because although he was the IAC's meeting director, at the same time he was also one of British athletics' official negotiators for the new television contract. Some within the IAC suspected that he could not serve both masters fairly.

The weekend before the 1984 Coca-Cola meeting, the world's athletics fixers had met in Rome to hammer out details of the new Grand Prix circuit which was to be launched the following summer, when for the first time fast runners would pursue fast bucks. With athletics now open about making cash payments to its participants, the world governing body put its weight behind a scheme to pay $500,000 in prize-money. Norman was in Rome to discuss the scheme as a member of the IAAF's Marketing Committee and as meeting director of the Coke.

Amid growing rumours that the Coca-Cola meeting might not be given vital status as part of the Grand Prix, Bedford and Derek Johnson, the IAC's secretary, had flown to Rome at short notice to confront Norman over the negotiating table. An argument ensued about the quality of the athletes that Norman had attracted to compete at that year's meeting, which developed into a full-scale row over the event's longer-term future. Soon afterwards, Norman, whose appointment as meeting director in 1974 had seen the start of his rise to pre-eminence among European event organisers, announced that the 1984 Coke would be his last.

On his return from Rome, Bedford's first task was to prepare for the midweek press conference which traditionally launched the event into the public's consciousness, though its primary objective – to sell tickets – had been rendered redundant weeks earlier when the last ticket had been sold. It was still necessary to get some good pre-publicity for the sponsors, however, the Bottlers of Coca-Cola who had loyally backed the meeting from the outset in 1968.

So, 60 hours before the event would get underway, Bedford had an assembled party of athletics writers in the elegant tea-rooms of London's Waldorf Hotel. Bedford and Norman sat uneasily beside one another, together with representatives of Coca-Cola and two Olympic champions from Los Angeles, Al Joyner and Valerie Brisco-Hooks. But Fleet Street was interested in only one event – the mile – and in two men – Steve Cram and Said Aouita. Behind-the-scenes negotiations had been going on for weeks to try to achieve what every big athletics meeting craves for, a 'head-to-head' competition between two major track stars.

At first, Aouita, newly crowned as the Olympic 5,000 metres gold medallist in Los Angeles, had been booked for the two miles, while Cram had been signed up for a 1,000 metres race. Step one, to get them both at the meeting, had been achieved, at least. Then the 1,000 was scratched from the programme and Cram shifted into an 800 metres instead. The next phase of negotiations – to get the two rivals both into the same event – would test the negotiating skills of Henry Kissinger.

At the press conference, Norman, playing the diplomat, was at pains to stress that neither athlete would have anything foisted on him. Yes, he had been on the telephone to Steve Cram's Jarrow home immediately before the conference. And yes, he would be going to the airport straight afterwards to meet Aouita's flight from Paris. Yes, perhaps he would know more later that day, and then again, perhaps nothing would change.

The arrival of other athletes from across Europe during the course of the day shifted Bedford's centre of operations from central to south London, and the Queen's Hotel. All afternoon, cars, taxis and mini-buses shuttled between Heathrow, Gatwick and the hotel, with Bedford there to meet each arriving athlete, see that they were checked into their room, and checked off his list of items to worry about.

During Thursday, there were other arrivals at the Queen's, the various volunteer helpers who would meld into the team which would run the

Friday evening meeting. Len Smith, then the secretary of the Southern Counties AAA, was in charge of ensuring that the event had the requisite number of officials; Eric Nash was in charge of accommodation; international athletes such as Graham Savory, Mike Winch and Kath Binns were there to assist with the transport and other administration; and the IAC's full-time office staff, Joan Allison and Marlow Hadler, were, like Bedford, on call for each eventuality.

Just down the corridor from the hotel reception was Room 65. Bedford's bedroom doubled as the IAC office and a storage shed for the week. It was here that athletes' numbers were sorted and hundreds of T-shirts and Coca-Cola clipboards ('freebies' for competitors and the Press) were stored, while the IAC's computer, brought from their central London office, was set up to bring some order to the list of 200 competing athletes from 21 nations. And it was from Room 65 that Bedford was to make the most important telephone call of the week.

On Thursday afternoon, just over 24 hours before the meeting started, amid many more mundane problems – such as Poles (competing) arriving without visas, and poles (for vaulting) not arriving at all – the more important matter of the men's mile required resolution. In order to get Cram to agree to race against Aouita in the mile (the Moroccan had agreed to the race almost immediately), Bedford spent 30 minutes on the phone to Cram's hotel, discussing the problems facing the IAC, the importance of 'head-to-head' events and the future of British athletics. At some point, they might even have touched on the meaning of life.

That Bedford had become involved in the negotiations at all was unusual. This, after all, was supposed to be Norman's territory. But the basic breakdown in trust between Norman and Bedford had already become irreversible. After all, Bedford reasoned, Norman and Cram's interests were perhaps too close for his meeting director to achieve the best possible deal for the meeting. Norman, although then still a serving policeman, had his 'interests' in athletics represented by John Hockey, the same London businessman who managed the affairs of Steve Cram.

It was during Bedford's telephone conversation that Cram was given the option of running in the mile and being paid – the 1,500 metres world champion could command up to £12,000 per race at this high point in his career – or running in the 800 metres for no appearance fee. Cram resented the ultimatum, and Hockey issued a strongly worded press statement during the evening complaining of undue pressure being applied to his client – 'the sort of thing', Cram was to say later, 'that a body like the IAC should help to relieve, not create'. Cram resigned from the IAC, saying that he would run in the mile the following evening, but that he would never grace an IAC event again.

Bedford's phone never stopped ringing the night before the meeting as the press sought further quotes and comments for their Friday morning stories. Other arrangements for the meeting, such as guest tickets, prize pre-senters and return airline tickets, were left undone until the early hours of Friday morning as a result. It was not until some time after 2 a.m. that Bedford cleared his bed of surplus XL-sized T-shirts (which had gone unclaimed by the majority of the skinny athletes at the event) and tried to get some sleep.

Five hours later, Bedford was up again and off to the shops to buy the morning newspapers, a fresh shirt, underwear and bathroom kit: he had not expected to have to stay away from home overnight. But just as he *had* expected, perhaps almost hoped for, the row over Cram featured promi-nently in the sports pages of that day's newspapers. If there was a villain of the piece, then Bedford fitted the bill quite nicely. He seemed unconcerned. 'Let's see what sort of reaction I get when I do my presentation tonight,' he said over breakfast.

The morning was filled with more of the same, basic administration and attention to details. Bored athletes, whiling away time, clogged the hotel foyer, playing cards or reading magazines. They were also waiting to col-lect their 'expenses' (overt payments to athletes would not be legal under the sport's rules until the following year). And the paymaster was late. Norman had been keeping a low profile all morning, avoiding the publici-ty that the previous day's events had attracted. Once at the Queen's, he took his attaché case full of currency into Room 65, laid it on the bed, clicked the locks and was open for business. The queue of athletic talent which lined up down the hall ready to collect payment was impressive indeed.

In the afternoon, as the pace picked up towards the start of the meeting, Bedford made his way down the hill from the hotel to the stadium. He took with him one of the poles which had finally found its way through Customs, and one of the Poles who had emerged from immigration in desperate need of a pre-competition massage.

Then it was into the on-site requirements. Despite having a radio walkie-talkie and use of at least two telephones at any one time, Bedford also had to make a continuous shuttle from main stand to the Jubilee Stand on the back straight and back again, keeping tabs on everything and every-body. With less than two hours before the first event of the evening, the rush and panic had begun to get to Bedford. No more the courteous smile and pause to sign an autograph. With everything supposed to have been done five minutes earlier, it was a case of no more Mr Nice Guy.

There were late withdrawals by athletes, runners with the wrong race numbers, unexplained blank spaces in the 12,000 programmes which had just arrived straight from the printers, the ink still wet. A crackling message came over the walkie-talkie. 'Can you arrange an extra heat of the 100 metres hurdles?' he was asked less than a minute after he had agreed with the BBC's producer, John Shrewsbury, that there should be no late changes of the timetable. And then the key question: could the giant scoreboard generate a hyphen, so that it could be inserted between 'Coca' and 'Cola' to give the sponsors their correct title when flashed above the stadium across the black of the night to the spectators and millions watching the meeting on their televisions at home?

Barely an hour before the start, at 6.10 p.m., you could have heard a pin drop in the Portakabin that served as Bedford's operational headquarters. You could have heard a pin drop, if there was a pin to be had. 'No safety pins? Where's the fucking safety pins?' With all the numbers neatly arranged on trestle tables near the athletes' warm-up area ready for collection, someone had discovered that there were no pins to fix the numbers to the athletes' vests. 'It's all right, Dave,' came a reply as near to being calm as was possible under the circumstances, 'they're in a box under your bed at the hotel.'

With a car despatched back to the hotel to collect the pins and salvage the situation, Bedford now had time to check that everyone was where they were supposed to be. Well, nearly everyone. 'Excuse me,' asked a man with gold braid on his uniform as he poked his head around the door. 'I'm a trumpeter with the Life Guards. Do you know where I'm supposed to report?'

An hour later, though the time passed in what seemed like five minutes, and the Coca-Cola theme was faded out on the PA system and the announcer introduced the long jumpers, high jumpers and hurdlers in the evening's first events. Meanwhile, on some nearby astroturf football pitches, Aouita and Cram paced around, pointedly at opposite ends of the warm-up area.

It was not long before Cram, Aouita and 14 other middle distance runners were called forward for the main event, the men's mile. Bedford, who until that high point of the night had only caught occasional glimpses of the action, was also required trackside at this point, too, for after the mile he was to present the prize for the women's 800 metres, staged earlier in the evening.

So Bedford took a place on a bench beside the long jump run-up, alongside the IAC chairman, hammer thrower Paul Dickenson. There, in the centre of the arena, with some 36,000 eyes trained on a small group of people as they shed the various layers of their tracksuits, strangely everything seemed silent: how could so many people be so quiet? No one in the stadium said a word, so drawn were they to the events unfolding before them as the starter called the runners to their marks.

The explosion of the starter's gun eased at least some of the tension, the crowd's cheers echoing into the pit of the arena, perhaps helping to loosen the knot in Bedford's stomach. 'All we need now,' he said, 'is for Crammie to go down and get injured . . .'

After the race was run, and once the track had been cleared of the victorious Aouita's fervent Moroccan supporters, it was on with the show. But before the next event could be started, there was to be an awards ceremony. Perhaps it was Steve Cram's tumble early in the race which had shocked the crowd, but when Dave Bedford was introduced as the prize-giver for the women's 800 metres, the renewed hush of the crowd was more eerie than that which had preceded the men's mile. Ten years earlier, it was said that Bedford had brought cheering crowds back to British athletics. But on this evening, the crowd was no longer on his side.

While the presentation went ahead, the two principal performers from the men's mile were ushered to the room at the back of the main stand which served for press interviews. There, Cram gave vent to his feelings. 'I was pretty annoyed at what happened. Dave Bedford never once rang me to say, "What event would you like to run at the Coke?" He assumed people were acting on my behalf and he never once said, "Will you consider this?"'

Cram explained that he had not been able to pull out of the meeting. 'I'd made a promise to the BBC to run tonight because they're televising my meeting at Jarrow on Sunday.' As his mentor, BBC commentator Brendan Foster, had done at Gateshead a decade earlier, Cram wanted the opening of his own local track to be marked with a world record. Cram's record attempt at his home track two days later was as ill-fated as his run in the Coca-Cola mile, the strong northerly winds making any target times impossible to achieve.

Bedford was unrepentant about getting Cram to run in the mile. And the world carried on turning, and the meeting carried on, strictly according to schedule. While the press, who had taken their notes and filed their stories, headed for the bar for a drink while waiting for the notorious Crystal Palace car park to clear, Cram jogged into the semi-darkness around the astroturf to warm down

As the last competitor of the night, Willie Banks, packed away his triple jumping spikes ready to leave for his hotel, a late meal and an early flight the next day, so the stands were cleared of the last lingering spectators. Bedford's night's work was not yet finished, however. Long after the flood-lights were switched off, there was another round of handshakes to thank officials and athletes, even the schoolchildren who had been involved by carrying athletes' clothing from start to finish during each race. Then it was back to the Queen's, where a reception for 250 guests, sponsors and athletes was being staged.

The reception was well underway by the time Bedford arrived there just before midnight, and tried, in vain, to get a waitress to rustle together a plate of lukewarm food. 'I've just realised, I've not had time to eat anything since dinner last night.' A bread roll, a slice of cold ham and some luke-warm pasta was all he had for dinner that night, but Bedford stayed until the bitter end, leaving for his cluttered bed in Room 65 long after Valerie Brisco-Hooks had finished her dance routine.

The IAC's international meeting that last, pre-Grand Prix year, was staged for a remarkably modest budget of £150,000. Of that, half came from the sponsors, nearly one-third from ticket sales, and the final £27,000 in television rights fees. That money was used to pay for everything involved in the staging of the meeting, from the £7,800 hire fee for the international stadium, all the way down to those troublesome safety pins, with any profit being used by the IAC to pay for warm weather training or medical treatment for its members.

A decade later, and the cost of staging athletics meetings had soared, fuelled by ready cash from television and sponsors. In 1993, Gateshead in north-east England staged the 'Dash for Cash' between America's Carl Lewis and his successor as Olympic champion, Linford Christie. There, in a single, staged-for-TV 100 metres race, Lewis and Christie shared £200,000 between them. Christie won the race, with Lewis a lacklustre third, and another American, Jon Drummond, second. 'The only thing that mattered,' said Greg Dyke, the television mogul who had approved the deal, and the cash, which made the race possible, 'was 13 million viewers on a Friday night.'

Just as the price of everyday purchases is subject to inflation, so the asking price for top athletes' appearances had been spiralling. In the 1970s, when Dave Bedford was a world record-holder, while he knew of some athletes who could make up to £7,000 in 'expenses' in a year, he says that the most he ever got paid for taking part in a race was £500. By 1980, the guesstimated average fee for top athletes appearing at European track meetings had not changed much and was put at between $1,000 and $3,000, though the likes of Coe and Ovett in record-breaking form might expect more.

By the mid-1980s, though, with appearance money in athletics now legitimised and the Grand Prix series established, Steve Cram could command £12,000 every time he raced in Britain, perhaps £8,000 for races abroad. According to Cram's own agent, at the height of his career, between 1984 and 1988, Cram was earning £100,000 per year from racing alone.

Until Lewis and Christie split their £200,000 between them in 1993, the record appearance fee had been set in that first Grand Prix season of 1985, when Zola Budd was paid £90,000 to race against Mary Slaney at Crystal Palace.

Some thought that this earning power detracted from the main aim of any athlete, an Olympic gold medal, the ultimate prize, something which was to elude both Cram and Bedford. Derek Ibbotson, like Cram, once a holder of the world record for the mile, observed the racer's weakness. Ibbotson told *The Times*'s David Miller: 'Cram raced too much for money, and didn't need to. It was the same with Dave Bedford. Dave was at a training camp before the Munich Games in 1972, but suddenly went off to Finland because he'd had a good offer. When he came to Munich, he got stuffed. I said to him: "If you'd won the Olympics, you'd have been made".'

Sebastian Coe, uniquely the winner of two Olympic 1,500 metres gold medals, steadfastly maintained throughout his career that he would only race as and when the event fitted in with his racing plan which he hoped would lead to a championship gold medal at the end of the summer. Such single-mindedness meant that the British public never saw the best of Coe on British tracks – his individual world records were set elsewhere, on balmy summer nights on the continent. *The* race which everyone wanted to see, Coe v Steve Ovett, only took place at the Olympic Games, European Championships, or too late in their careers to really mean anything.

In his book, *Born To Run*, Coe acknowledged with distaste that rapid professionalisation of his sport could yield rewards in many ways other than simple fees for competing. 'Life at the top in athletics now is a totally false one: cheap this, free that, discount flats, fill-your-tank-free and sign an autograph,' Coe said. 'When it all stops, you have to pay. That's why, if I've wanted something, I'd pay for it.'

The explosion in athletes' on-track earning power was often fuelled by a cut-throat rivalry between meetings, each eager to stage the most expensive, the most glitzy, the most record rich promotion. And, in so doing, the meeting director hopes he – there are no female meet directors – will guarantee a television contract and sponsors for at least one more year. Once the worldwide economic recession hit athletics in the early 1990s, however, a clear division began to emerge between those meetings which had secure TV and sponsorship deals, and the other, struggling, poorer meetings which did not. With contracts dependent on Grand Prix status, promoters would sometimes break the bank to ensure they had the best possible meeting.

This was made all the more competitive by the IAAF's own ratings of events on its Grand Prix circuit. This system attributed points to each meeting, mainly according to the athletes' performances. If a meet failed to come up to scratch, it would be dropped from the Grand Prix schedule. Grand Prix meetings in the former eastern bloc, in Moscow and Budapest, did not survive the economic realities once there was no longer any central government finance behind the events.

The IAC's meeting also lost its Grand Prix status: despite finding new sponsors after Coca-Cola pulled out, it had a new date forced upon it and a new venue, Edinburgh. Placed in the middle of the season, the competition for athletes with other meets became much harder. And the damp and cool climate in the Scottish capital too often mitigated against world-class performances. Despite the organisers' best efforts – at one desperate stage, with no sponsor in sight, Bedford even offered to mortgage his own home to fund the event – eventually, the Coke meet slipped off the bottom of the Grand Prix ladder, never to reappear.

Those meetings with plenty of backing behind them, though, prospered. By the summer of 1995, the 16 Grand Prix meetings on the IAAF's circuit put up an estimated £10 million in appearance fees for athletes. Yet of that £10 million, around half of it was paid by just four meetings – Oslo's Bislett Games, the Ivo Van Damme Memorial meeting in Brussels, the Weltklasse in Zurich and the ISTAF meeting in Berlin. They called themselves the 'Golden Four'.

The concept of a Grand Slam of athletics was put together by a German television marketing firm, called UFA. UFA already handled the sale of the European television rights to the All-England tennis championships at Wimbledon and in August 1995, they put in a $1 billion bid for the rights to football's 2002 World Cup.

When UFA looked at athletics, they saw a golden opportunity, literally, and they bought the exclusive rights to sell television pictures from four of the top European athletics meetings with a £15 million, five-year deal which runs until 1997. Even by the end of the 1995 season, UFA executives, having just enjoyed the first summer when the deal had broken even for them, were purring contentedly about having an option to extend the contract. It was also clear who had control. The Oslo meeting director, Sven-Arne Hansen, had no doubts about who determined which meetings are chosen for the exclusive club, the Golden Four, where membership is by invitation only. 'As long as they pay the money,' the Norwegian said of UFA, 'they can say who is in or out.'

Without really trying, UFA had managed to create a Premier League of athletics meetings. Unlike events in Britain, which tended to have one title sponsor backing the meeting, on the continent each meeting had a string of sponsors, all contributing towards the overall budget for the event, each sponsor given title to a particular event during the meeting – something more akin to the way horse race meetings are sponsored in Britain.

In 1995, in addition to the £5 million which Zurich, Brussels, Oslo and Berlin had available between them to spend on athletes, the Golden Four meetings also offered a $1 million prize fund, plus £160,000 in gold bars to be shared by the athletes who went undefeated through the four meetings. Hence the *Golden* Four.

With such riches available, and with athletes being contracted to all four meetings, the Golden Four had developed a built-in advantage over other meetings on the Grand Prix circuit. Simply, they could afford to buy more athletics talent than the other meetings. In London, for example, with its revolutionary performance-related-pay scheme, a world record performance by an athlete would have paid about £20,000, only half the amount of promoter's bonuses available in Zurich. Suffice to say, there were no world records in London.

A league table of the 1995 Grand Prix shows that, while dollars do not guarantee points under the IAAF's assessment system, it rarely did any harm.

The Grand Prix league table

Meeting	Budget for athletes	IAAF points (and ranking)
Zurich (G4)	$3,000,000	87,035 (1st)
Cologne	$1,500,000	85,604 (3rd)
Lausanne	$1,250,000	85,442 (4th)
Oslo (G4)	$1,250,000	84,866 (10th)
Brussels (G4)	$1,200,000	86,156 (2nd)
Berlin (G4)	$1,200,000	85,211 (6th)
Paris	$1,000,000	84,885 (11th)
Monte Carlo	$ 800,000	85,007 (8th)
Stockholm	$ 750,000	83,962 (12th)
Nice	$ 700,000	85,365 (5th)
Rome	$ 650,000	85,000 (9th)
London	$ 600,000	85,087 (7th)
Sao Paulo	$ 400,000	83,230 (13th)
New York	$ 250,000	81,940 (14th)
San Jose	$ 200,000*	80,639 (15th)

G4 = Golden Four meeting; * = estimated figure

Such divisions in available funding forced the Grand Prix itself to be reappraised. For while UFA managed to sell the gilt-edged Golden Four to 126 television stations around the world, Primo Nebiolo, the president of the IAAF, was struggling to win a new TV deal for the rest of his events. Attendances at Grands Prix were down, television audiences were disappearing. Athletics was beginning to suffer from over-exposure. 'After a while, no one cares who wins,' was the Grand Prix heresy which dared to be voiced by Peter Radford, head of the British Athletic Federation. 'It's the same races with the same cast.'

Nebiolo's bargaining tactics on behalf of the IAAF may not have helped. He demanded £110 million for a new TV deal, while the European Broadcasting Union offered just £30 million. Nebiolo's response to the Golden Four's increasing dominance of his circuit came on the day before his 1995 Grand Prix final was staged in Monte Carlo. It was a typically audacious gesture by the Italian, since Mobil, sponsors for 11 seasons, were about to end their association with the IAAF. 'We didn't quit,' said Jim Mann, a vice-president of Mobil, pointing out that negotiating with the IAAF came to an end when the athletics body demanded two and a half times the $2 million per year sum which the oil firm had been pumping into the sport.

Yet without a replacement sponsor to name, Nebiolo announced an increase in prize-money at the 1996 Grand Prix final to £2 million, doubling the amounts available to the winners of the men's and women's overall Grands Prix to $200,000 each, and for the first prizes for the top performers in each event. (In an exceptionally lucrative year for the steeplechaser, Moses Kiptanui had walked away from Monte Carlo with £87,000 as steeplechase and overall winner of the 1995 Grand Prix.)

Where Nebiolo was particularly wily, though, was in his low-key announcement that in future, to qualify for the Grand Prix final (and therefore the lucre), athletes must compete in eight of the summer's meetings, instead of the previous five. The interests of the athletes could not be served by such a move – they were already complaining of weariness. The new Grand Prix rule would force athletes to extend their seasons, with perhaps more competitors making themselves available for the early summer events in the Americas.

This change in the rule was aimed squarely at reducing the burgeoning command which the Golden Four meetings were exercising over the top athletes. Those competitors most in demand – the Christies, Gebresilassies, Torrences, Bubkas and Kiptanuis – had begun to contract-in to the Golden Four, perhaps competing in just one other Grand Prix meeting during the summer to get their full quota of points. The rule change requiring performances at eight meetings from 1996, however, meant that just scoring qualifying points in the Golden Four plus one other meeting would no longer be good enough to guarantee a place at the Grand Prix final. The Golden Four's monopolisation of the star athletes looked to be broken at a stroke.

Despite the shaky start of the Grand Prix, this relatively arbitrary collection of Europe's top athletics meetings, plus one or two events in north and Latin America, had established itself quite firmly after ten years, with the Grand Prix final replacing the old Coca-Cola meeting as the 'traditional' culmination of the track season. All Nebiolo's attempts at investing the Grand Prix final with some form of prestige, though, had failed.

The Stade Louis II in Monte Carlo, just like the Stadio Olympico in Rome for the first Grand Prix final in 1985, was nearly empty of spectators that sunny afternoon in September 1995. The athletes all displayed the heavy-leggedness familiar at the season's end. The arcane points scoring system, with a complex set of tables to compare one woman's triple jump with another's 3,000 metres time, was beyond comprehension for most of those watching, whether in the stadium or on television. 'If Biryukova jumps 15 metres, will that beat O'Sullivan's 8min 39sec?' one harassed hack on deadline shouted across the press box, making more noise than the meagre scattering of spectators. If truth be known, no one in the stands cared less which of the two performances was rated the better, except probably O'Sullivan, who received $20,000 for her fourth place in the Grand Prix's overall standings, $30,000 less than the Russian triple jumper.

The old IAC/Coca-Cola meeting, with nothing much at stake except perhaps a few bob in appearance money, had always rounded off the season with a bit of end-of-term fun, and usually with one or two beltingly good competitions thrown in. After just ten years of professionalism in athletics, the one thing abundantly clear from the IAAF's anti-climatic 'culmination' of the season was that now only money that mattered.

Ten

Primo's Plaything

EVEN AS recently as the late 1970s, the International Amateur Athletic Federation's unpretentious headquarters offices, just across the Common from London's Wandsworth Prison, housed just three staff and two secretaries. There was so little money in the IAAF's coffers that they only needed a single, part-time clerk to keep account of it.

At that time, there was neither an annual Grand Prix to organise, nor a biennial World Championships. There was neither race walking and marathon World Cups, nor was there a World Half-marathon or World Junior Championships. Looking back now, the wonder of it all is quite what the world's athletes did in the years between the Olympic Games.

Until the 1980s, athletics was still run by the *Chariots of Fire* generation. The Marquess of Exeter, the IAAF president for 30 years from 1946, had even had a character in the Oscar-winning film based on his own Olympic hurdling exploits in the 1920s. When Exeter's successor as IAAF president stood down in 1981, the mainly amateur organisation still did not have even £100,000 in its bank account.

Yet by the mid-1990s, international athletics was as far removed from *Chariots of Fire* as the latest Mercedes-Benz saloons are from a Model T Ford. In 1995, the IAAF organised six world championship or World Cup competitions of one kind or another, while its Grand Prix circuit included 25 meetings in 17 different countries on three continents. At the IAAF's opulent new headquarters on the shores of the Mediterranean in fashionable Monte Carlo – where the organisation moved from London in 1993 – the events department alone has between eight and ten people working in its office: twice as many as the entire IAAF had employed 20 years before.

Since 1985, the IAAF has struck sponsorship and television deals worth an estimated £7 billion. In April 1996, it pulled off an audacious negotiating coup when the European Broadcasting Union agreed a £110 million deal to televise IAAF events into the 21st century. The IAAF now has more national athletics federations as members than football's world governing body, FIFA; the IAAF can fly more national flags at its events than does the International Olympic Committee; the IAAF even has more member states than the United Nations. The man responsible for the exponential growth is Primo Nebiolo, the president of the IAAF since 1981. Everything that has happened in international athletics since Nebiolo's election has the Italian's imprint clearly on it.

Athletics had never had such a high profile, never been more popular, never as rich as it has become under Nebiolo. Nor has the sport's integrity and reputation been lower, with drugs seemingly everywhere within the sport, the star athletes gone money mad, while allegations of corruption permeate the sport.

In contrast to Exeter and Adriaan Paulen, his predecessors as IAAF president who had both been world class athletes before they donned the administrator's blazer, Primo Nebiolo, who was born in Turin, Italy, on 14 July 1923, was only ever a long jumper of modest ability. But he developed an ability as an excellent organiser. He was just 24 when he turned his attention from the track to the committee room. It was the beginning of an inexorable rise up the greasy pole of sports administration. Financially cushioned by a fortune made in construction, Nebiolo was prepared to do whatever it took to get to the top. 'If you don't want to have critics,' he once said, 'you must not try to do great things.'

Having slowly built up a powerbase in student sport, where he became head of FISU, the university sports world governing body, by cultivating contacts in the old, communist bloc, Nebiolo moved into the mainstream of athletics administration in the 1970s. In 1981, Nebiolo used his persuasiveness and guile to get Adriaan Paulen to stand down as IAAF president by convincing the ageing Dutchman that he had himself collected sufficient promises of votes that if it came to a contested election between the two men at the IAAF Congress in Rome, the incumbent would suffer a humiliating defeat. Paulen, Nebiolo suggested, should retire gracefully and maintain his dignity. It was a masterful sleight of hand by Nebiolo, a classic bluff. But Paulen only discovered that he had been duped some months later, with Nebiolo already installed in office. If Paulen had allowed the election to go ahead, his upstart Italian challenger would probably have been trounced.

Once in office, Nebiolo was determined to pursue his ambition of making athletics the world's top sport, as popular and high profile as football. Such ambition for athletics would also, of course, ensure Nebiolo became one of the most powerful men in world sport.

Nebiolo is a man who gets things done. Almost from nothing, the IAAF went into a frenzy of organising events. As the sport's most aggressive salesman and publicist, Nebiolo realised that his 'product' must be kept constantly in the public's attention, thus creating a high value in international marketability. Nebiolo became like a conjurer: you never knew which new event he would pull from up his sleeve next.

Paulen had given Nebiolo a head start, having set in train the moves to stage the IAAF's first World Championships in Helsinki in 1983. The IAAF Grand Prix soon followed in 1985, the World Indoor Championships in 1987, the World Junior Championships in 1988, the Marathon World Cup was followed by the World Half-marathon and World Road Relays in 1992, even a global cross-country circuit was established. Between 1992 and 1995, what Nebiolo's marketing machine ungrammatically dubbed the 'World Athletic Series' saw 26 competitions staged around the world, from Peking to Toronto, Gothenburg to Monterey. There were no gaps left in the IAAF's calendar.

When he came to office, Nebiolo had inherited the IAAF World Cup, a track and field event first staged in Dusseldorf, Germany, in 1977. From its beginnings, it had always been of questionable merit, contested between contrived and unequal national and continental teams. It was hardly an original idea: the World Cup merely extended the successful United States v Soviet Union dual meets to include the power-house of East Germany, plus a team made up from the rest of Europe's best athletes, and assortments from Africa, the Americas (Canadians, Caribbeans and a few Latins), Australasia and Asia.

It was in athletics' relatively under-developed areas that the World Cup was most warmly received, and on taking office Nebiolo realised that the up-coming World Championships could make vast sums of money for the IAAF's cash-strapped members. Just how Nebiolo would go about spending the revenue from his successful new promotions would come to trouble a wide variety of people involved in athletics.

The World Championships soon became Nebiolo's plaything. When first staged in 1983, they seemed a welcome return to sporting innocence, sandwiched as they were between the boycotted Olympic Games of Moscow in 1980 and Los Angeles in 1984. For the first time in more than ten years, all the world's athletes were able to gather together and compete without outside political interference. Much was made of the venue, the Olympic Stadium in Helsinki, as the World Championships harked back to a previous, golden era, of those 1952 Games when Zatopek won his three gold medals. And when Carl Lewis won three golds in Helsinki in 1983, it caused further comparisons with another athletics great of the past, Jesse Owens. Nebiolo was not slow in accepting the credit for Paulen's brainchild. Helsinki was a great success. It was a breath of fresh air.

Four years later, when the second World Championships were staged in

Rome, something stank. Most people have a taste for national triumph, for whatever their country, they like to see their compatriots succeed. But few people realised quite what lengths Nebiolo would go to in order to see his fellow Italians succeed. For example, in 1981, when Italy had failed to reach the World Cup final at Rome's Stadio Olympico as one of the two top teams in the European Cup, Nebiolo spared no expense. He had a ninth lane built to allow an extra team, 'the host nation', to compete in the World Cup. Worse was to come, though, when the Roman emperor of athletics presided over another move to ensure Italian success at the World Championships in 1987.

Giovanni Evangelisti was the Italian Number One in Nebiolo's old event, the long jump, and among their best chances of a medal in Rome. But the competition would be tough. Carl Lewis, at the height of his powers, was unbeatable. Robert Emmiyan, of the Soviet Union, was also well ahead of the rest of the world. Then in the pecking order came Evangelisti and another American, Larry Myricks. On the eve of the Rome Championships, a group of Italian officials who would be judging the long jump met to hatch an incredible plan – to guarantee their man a medal.

The late afternoon sun was still beating down on Rome's magnificent stadium when Evangelisti opened the competition. As he sprinted down the runway there was a whirl of camera motor-drives. He leapt into the air, but the huge crowd's cheers were stifled when a judge raised a red flag to indicate a foul jump, as Evangelisti's foot had gone over the take-off board. Myricks did the same thing on the next jump. Lewis followed, and sailed high in the air before landing at 8.67 metres. He had secured the gold medal with his first jump. Emmiyan then jumped 8.53 metres, a distance which he knew practically assured him of the silver. As everyone had predicted, the real contest now would be between Evangelisti and Myricks for the bronze.

The pair had been closely matched throughout their careers, and this event was no different. The Italian led Myricks in the second round when, to the relief of the crowd, he got a good jump in, measured at 8.09 metres to the American's 8.04. Despite Evangelisti improving to 8.19 metres in the third round, he slipped out of the medal positions when, with the next jump, Myricks cleared 8.23. When Myricks then jumped 8.33 in the fourth round after Evangelisti had faulted again, Italian hopes in the crowd were beginning to fade. But Evangelisti had not given up hope. He psyched himself up for one, last big effort in the final round. At the far end of the runway, he was finishing his preparations for the jump when, over the loudspeakers, the *William Tell Overture* blasted out, signalling the medal ceremony for the women's shot putt. Evangelisti was furious at the way his concentration had been shattered. He threw his arms in the air and stormed back to his seat by the side of the long jump pit.

As the medal ceremony took place, most of the long jump officials stood to attention facing the winners' podium. Yet unnoticed amid the pomp of the ceremony, one official continued to busy himself around the long jump pit. Meanwhile, Evangelisti composed himself once again and took his final jump. Even before he left the sand, experienced observers, journalists and statisticians could see that Evangelisti's last jump would not be enough to dislodge Myricks from third place. It looked no better than 7.90 metres, maybe 7.95, but still short of Evangelisti's own earlier efforts, never mind Myricks's 8.33, and therefore not far enough for a medal. The Italians in the crowd groaned.

Then, the distance of Evangelisti's last jump was flashed on to the electronic scoreboard – 8.38. The mood of the crowd changed dramatically: flags were waved, whistles pierced the evening air, for Evangelisti was now in the bronze medal position. When Myricks lined up for his last jump, he was loudly jeered by the partisan crowd, and despite his best efforts, he could not improve on his earlier jumps. The American was only fourth.

Yet some people refused to ignore what they had seen with their own eyes. Evangelisti's last-round jump distance was treated with derision, the Association of Track & Field Statisticians refusing to recognise the jump, consigning it to a footnote in the end-of-year rankings, so convinced were they that a mistake had been made. It was an unprecedented decision for them to take on a performance achieved at the World Championships, the premier athletics event.

With elections for the position of president of the Italian Olympic committee (CONI) coming up, Nebiolo, to his dismay, soon found himself entangled in the controversy of the Evangelisti affair. Nebiolo coveted the CONI presidency and considered himself a clear favourite for the post, but now everything seemed to be in jeopardy. Nebiolo's ambitions suffered a further blow two months after the championships when RAI, the Italian state television network, used state-of-the-art equipment to establish that Evangelisti's last jump was no more than 7.90 metres. Interviewed for the television programme, Luciano Barra, Nebiolo's assistant, conceded that perhaps there had been a mistake with the measurement. But Barra laughed off any suggestions of conspiracy: 'Nobody would dare to cheat that much.'

Further scientific analysis of film and video tape of Evangelisti's long jump proved that, despite Barra's claims, someone had indeed dared to cheat so blatantly. The Sports Institute of Cologne calculated that Evangelisti's last jump was only 7.91 metres. Nebiolo was routed in the CONI elections, but even now, he refused to accept that some action was required on the basis of the overwhelming evidence to show that there had been some sort of fix going on. At an IAAF Council meeting in Monte Carlo, Nebiolo insisted that the result would stand: 'When we saw the video tape of Maradona in the World Cup helping the ball into the net with his hand against England we realised he had cheated – but with us it's also too late, I'm sorry.'

Nebiolo might have thought that that was the end of the controversy, but he was wrong. Very wrong. As the complaints mounted, there was an official police investigation, and CONI decided to launch their own inquiry. The 83-page CONI report, delivered in March 1988, finally got to the bottom of the matter. It did not make happy reading for Nebiolo.

The report revealed that one of the long jump judges, Tommaso Aiello, had used the time while the medal ceremony was going on before Evangelisti's sixth jump to set up the measuring device at 8.38 metres, locking this distance into the event's computer, ready to be produced after Evangelisti jumped. Evangelisti's last jump need never have been measured.

Nebiolo was strongly implicated in the cover-up of the scandal , and the report concluded that there had been 'pronounced intervention by the IAAF intended to interfere with the work of the Committee and prevent the ascertaining of the facts'. The IAAF Council for once took a hard line and forced Nebiolo to correct the result of the competition.

Nebiolo was forced to step down as the head of the Italian national athletics federation, and his assistant, Barra, was sacked, earning him the nickname of 'Unlucky Luciano'. But the IAAF, at whose championships this entire fiasco had been allowed to happen, never conducted any investigation, nor offered any apologies to Myricks or Evangelisti, the innocent athletes caught up in the whole, sordid affair.

Instead, the IAAF released a simple, short statement. 'After a review of the Men's Long Jump Competition in the IAAF World Championships in Athletics, Rome 1987, Council decided unanimously that, notwithstanding the present IAAF rules, the 6th jump of Giovanni Evangelisti should not be counted and the result adjusted accordingly. Therefore Larry Myricks became the Bronze Medal Winner (8.34 metres) and Evangelisti (8.19 metres) dropped one place in the listing.'

Nebiolo even tried to turn the reverse of policy into a PR coup for himself and the IAAF when he brazenly contradicted what he had said just weeks earlier: 'We did what no other international governing body has done. We changed the result after watching TV. Did Fifa do this when Maradona handled a goal against England in the World Cup?' In the otherwise comprehensive official handbook issued to the media at the 1995 World Championships in Gothenburg, there was no mention of the Evangelisti affair, not even as a footnote. It was as if it had never happened.

It would later emerge that Nebiolo had used the power and influence of his position as IAAF president in an earlier cover-up for an Italian athlete. At the 1984 Los Angeles Olympics, hammer thrower Gianpaolo Urlando tested positive for testosteronc, an offence which at the time carried an automatic two-year ban. The IAAF did not formally recognise that any offence had been committed until spring 1986, 18 months after the event.

When the ruling communist regime in East Germany collapsed and the country was unified, the previously confidential files of the secret police, the Stasi, were discovered to contain records of many sports-related meetings, including one in 1984 involving Nebiolo and Professor Manfred Donike, the man in charge of doping control for the International Olympic Committee. The report says the two men 'quarrelled heavily'. Nebiolo asked Donike 'whether anything could be done for Urlando', and why it was necessary to have quite so many positive drug tests. Donike later complained to colleagues that Nebiolo had tried to intimidate him.

A decade later, and the conspiracy to keep the Urlando positive a secret still leaves a sour taste in the mouth of at least one senior IAAF official. 'We thought Nebiolo was trying to protect an Italian athlete because he himself was Italian,' he said. 'Also, we thought he was trying to make himself look important to members of the IOC – as IAAF president, he wanted to make sure that athletics was seen to be a clean sport, free from drugs. The whole affair was very embarrassing. It was felt that he had sacrificed the honesty of international athletics.'

There was even less honesty left in the sport after Ben Johnson tested positive for drugs at the 1988 Seoul Olympics and was stripped of his gold medal. In Seoul, Johnson had set a world record of 9.79sec for the 100 metres, but the record was never ratified because he failed the drug test. A year earlier, in the final of the World Championship 100 metres in Rome, Johnson had set a world record of 9.83sec. That record *was* ratified because Johnson passed the drugs test. In fact, until Seoul, Johnson had managed to pass at least a dozen IAAF drug tests every year during six years of steroid misuse. This was not lost on those already questioning the integrity of the people in charge of the sport.

To cope with its embarrassment over the sport's failure to identify Johnson as a drugs cheat earlier in his track career, once the athlete confessed to prolonged steroid use the IAAF decided to consider the unprecedented step of stripping Johnson of all of his records and titles retrospectively. Nebiolo's unconventional approach to discussion and committee decisions was fully illustrated when, after five hours of fruitless debate at the 1989 Congress on the issue of Johnson's past misdeeds, the matter was still unresolved. Nebiolo called for a lunch break, and when this got a round of applause, he unilaterally interpreted this as a unanimous vote to strip the Canadian of his records and titles.

It might be expected, given the way Nebiolo seems to court controversy, with Evangelisti, Urlando, Johnson, that the sport might do something about its president. Yet when the position was next up for election, in Tokyo in 1991, Nebiolo was elected *nem con*. Unopposed. Nebiolo's survival remains as much a disgrace to the whole sport as the Italian's arrogant and self-important conduct.

Since the IAAF was founded in 1912, the IAAF has had only four presidents and one contested election, when Exeter stepped down in 1976. During his reign, Nebiolo has inevitably made enemies, and during the last few years, at athletics events around the world, but always well out of the hearing of Nebiolo's hand-picked team of assistants, dissatisfaction has been steadily mounting. But no one wanted to be seen to be making the first move against the emperor of athletics.

Then, unexpectedly in May 1995, the IAAF dissenters – a modern-day grouping of the silent majority – thought they had found a man brave enough to stand against Nebiolo. Eisa Al-Dashti was not an obvious choice as candidate for the presidency of the IAAF, but he had much to commend him. The Kuwaiti was a hero of the Gulf War, at 46 was relatively young, and he had seemingly limitless personal wealth.

Nebiolo's inner cabinet, based in Rome, was taken by surprise, but within hours of Al-Dashti's candidature being announced, Nebiolo undertook a hurried clandestine mission in a private jet to ensure that all opposition would be crushed. The IAAF president himself flew to the newly rebuilt Kuwait City and talked with Sheikh Ahmad al-Sabah, a member of the country's ruling family and, like Nebiolo, a member of the IOC. According to Ali Sultan Al-Mazuki, general secretary of the Kuwaiti athletics federation, Nebiolo and Sheikh Ahmad went into a room together and 'emerged in accord'. Al-Dashti's name was withdrawn from the election.

Even if the Kuwaiti had forced a vote, Nebiolo would have been in a strong position. Within a year of becoming president, Nebiolo pulled off a change in the IAAF's rules which he would exploit throughout his term in office. Against the wishes of the United States, the Soviet Union and Great Britain, all of whom had eight votes in the IAAF Congress, Nebiolo introduced a one-country, one-vote system.

This immediately brought him the gratitude of more than a 100 developing nations. Having already developed close personal links with the communist bloc through his position in student sport, Nebiolo now used the IAAF's own development funds for athletics projects in Africa, Asia and South America, which helped to cultivate those countries' future support. Nebiolo makes sure that his friends in what he likes to call 'the athletics family' are always looked after properly when at IAAF events. Nor are they ever allowed to forget to whom they owe a debt of gratitude.

Nebiolo collects sports presidencies like other men collect stamps. While the IAAF post constitutes his most influential position, he is also head of FISU and of the Association of Summer Olympic International Federations, both of which are vital threads in the tangled web he weaves.

The jewel in Nebiolo's crown is his membership of the IOC, sport's most powerful and most exclusive private club. For years, his sporting ambitions were stifled because the IOC already had two Italian representatives. Nebiolo argued that, as head of the principal sport at the Games, he was entitled to a place himself.

Nebiolo was so keen to become part of the IOC that Giorgio de Stefani alleged that in 1985 Nebiolo offered him a 50 million lire bribe to stand down from the IOC to open up a vacancy for another Italian. When he could not join the club, Nebiolo determined to make as big a nuisance of himself as he could. In 1991, he hinted that the IAAF might not readmit South Africa, a move which would have effectively blocked the country's return to the Olympic stage in Barcelona the following year. Nebiolo also began to let it be known that there was a plan under consideration to make the athletics events at the Olympics open only to under-23s. At a stroke, such a move would undermine the importance of the Olympics, while making the IAAF's own World Championships, open to all the world's top athletes, whatever their age, the single most important athletics event.

Nebiolo was also unhappy about his sport's cut of the cash from money-spinning Olympics. The IAAF's $1.5 million share of the Olympic revenue did not compare favourably with the $40 million return from the 1991 World Championships in Tokyo. And anyway, Nebiolo argued, why did the IOC have to turn away offers of more money from advertisers keen to have boards at the trackside in the Olympic stadium? 'The Italian peasant', as one IOC member described him, was a threat to the last bastion of Olympic idealism.

Then, early in 1992, the IOC president, Juan Antonio Samaranch, was granted two 'wild card' IOC selections, in his gift, free of the national two-person quota. No one was surprised when Samaranch offered Nebiolo one of the two places, obviously reasoning the Italian was less dangerous inside the movement than sniping at it from outside. One minute after Nebiolo had been handed his invitation to join the IOC by Samaranch in Lausanne, someone in the IAAF's headquarters in London pressed a button on a fax machine to send the news of the IAAF president's elevation around the world. The IOC secretariat was furious: the IOC and no one else announces who has joined the club.

On the same spring weekend as Samaranch announced Nebiolo's IOC membership, Nebiolo confirmed that South Africa would be 're-admitted to the athletics family'. The Olympic athletics age limit proposal has never been heard of again. 'It is a gesture of friendship and collaboration,' said Nebiolo.

With so many titles to his name, the sun never sets on Nebiolo's empire. In August and September 1995, Nebiolo sat beside the King and Queen of Sweden as the curtain came down on the fifth World Championships in Gothenburg; two weeks later, he watched the Crown Prince of Japan open the 18th World Student Games in Fukuoka; then he flew back to Monte Carlo to watch the climax of the athletics Grand Prix circuit alongside Prince Albert of Monaco.

Nebiolo expects royal treatment wherever he goes. When the IAAF was based in London, Nebiolo complained to one member of staff: 'Why doesn't your Queen ever invite me round to Buckingham Palace? Doesn't she realise how important I am?' In fact, the Queen has probably been fully briefed about Nebiolo by her daughter, the Princess Royal, another IOC member. Even Britain's politicians shied away from the increasingly notorious Italian when, in September 1994, London staged the IAAF World Cup at Crystal Palace. With Nebiolo facing a court case over allegations of fraud surrounding the rebuilding of the Rome Olympic stadium for soccer's 1990 World Cup tournament, no senior government figure – not the sports-mad Prime Minister, John Major, nor the Minister for Sport, Iain Sproat – could attend. Nebiolo was subsequently cleared of the fraud charges, but the snub by the British undoubtedly rankled with him. For usually, when Nebiolo's athletics circus pitches its tent, most countries are only too happy to roll out the red carpet and treat him like royalty. Aides ensure that the IAAF president is chauffeured from the airport by limousine, often with police outriders to avoid the inconveniences of traffic. 'He probably has an ego metabolism that takes more feeding than others,' said LeRoy Walker, the president of the United States Olympic Committee.

Nebiolo's official biography details a list of honours, awards and honorary degrees bestowed upon him from world leaders ranging from Romania's Nicolai Ceaucescu – also known as the Butcher of Bucharest, who was executed by his own people when his reign of terror came to an end – to Cuba's Fidel Castro.

Nebiolo expects to have his expensive tastes indulged. In 1993, when the World Indoor Championships were being staged in Toronto, a television reporter who interviewed Nebiolo in his suite at the exclusive $1,500-a-night L'Hotel, described it as the most palatial digs he had ever seen, with its wraparound view of Lake Ontario, the SkyDome and the CN Tower, plus a separate bar, library and dining-room.

Nebiolo grew angry at a press conference when he was asked how he could justify such extravagant expense for himself, when elsewhere, items such as random drugs testing and development programmes remained underfunded. 'We are considering the idea of putting our members to sleep in the garden to save money for doping control,' Nebiolo said, sarcastically, in his gravelly voice. 'But some people are of a certain age and the climate is not so nice, so sometimes it's not good for these people to sleep in the garden.'

Age does not seem to weary Nebiolo ordinarily. Even though he celebrated his 72nd birthday in July 1995, his appetite for power remains voracious. His vanity, too, will not allow him to make concessions to his age. His closest staff tell of how their master is proud of parading around in his underpants in front of them in his hotel suite. 'Can you believe that someone with such a good body could be so old?' he asks.

'It does not matter how old you are,' Nebiolo said while in Japan in 1995 after being asked if he has any thoughts of retiring from his IAAF position. 'What is important is how you think of yourself. If you think yourself old, you are old. But if not, you are not old.'

Besides, Nebiolo has other interests to pursue, such as the International

Athletic Foundation. Founded in 1986, and based in Monte Carlo before Nebiolo had moved the IAAF's headquarters to the Principality, the IAF is constituted under Monegasque law and has its own, separate bank account, with 'donations' paid directly into it, the money used to fund various 'development projects'.

Twelfth December 1986 marked the first in a series of sumptuous IAF Galas. In front of 200 invited guests at the Hotel de Paris in Monte Carlo, the IAF launched its first projects, which were to celebrate the 75th anniversary of the IAAF in 1987. Some suggested that such projects had more in common with self-publicity and aggrandisement for Primo Nebiolo than any genuine 'development'. But nonetheless, everyone seemed content, since earlier in the day, Nebiolo had been presented with the Medaille de Vermeil de l'Education Physique et des Sports, and he was able to present 75th Anniversary Awards to Prince Rainier and his son Prince Albert.

According to the IAAF, 'a unique creation in the world sports movement, the Foundation's objective is to contribute to the development and appreciation of athletics' by considering applications for grant aid 'covering promotional, media, technical, educational and social aspects'. There were many more projects funded through the IAF during the years following 1987, with a $20 million payment from American television network NBC in return for some requested timetable changes at the Seoul Olympics providing a vast reserve fund, accountable to no one, under Nebiolo's control.

Yet even this organisation, kept well away from any public scrutiny, led Nebiolo into more controversy in December 1995. As the IAAF president arrived in Monte Carlo for the now annual Gala Night banquet, at which Gwen Torrence and Jonathan Edwards were to be announced as the '1995 World Athletes of the Year', allegations of vote rigging had rocked the international federation's headquarters.

The party pooper was Christopher Winner, until earlier in the year the IAAF spokesman, who revealed that 12 months earlier, Sally Gunnell, winner of the 1994 Commonwealth, European and World Cup titles at 400 metres hurdles, had topped the ballot for the second year running. Winner claimed that after the poll had closed, when he informed Nebiolo of the outcome, the president 'expressed his disappointment'. According to Winner, 'I told him about the situation, and he said, "Oh no, not the Englishwoman again".'

Winner said that ten days after the polls had closed, he found 30 new ballots on his desk in an unmarked envelope. Some of the voting papers were incomplete, but all nominated the American heptathlete, Jackie Joyner-Kersee, as the woman athlete of the year. Winner said he was ordered to accept the new votes. 'I did it because at the time I did not have the courage to say "no" to Primo Nebiolo,' he admitted.

With the new votes, 'JJK' had amassed 3,067 points, enough to win the poll, while Gunnell – who had already made it known that she would be unable to attend the Gala – was relegated to fourth place. Instead Joyner-Kersee collected the award from Prince Albert at the Gala, which was paid for by around $200,000 in sponsorship from Coca-Cola and which boasted some television coverage in more than 70 countries.

The vote rigging scandal brought down the curtain on an uncomfortable 1995 for Nebiolo, when he had seemed to be under constant attack. Often, it seemed, he put himself into awkward situations. Such as the time in Sweden, just before the World Championships, when he objected to a television interviewer's line of questioning and responded by asking his inquisitor how many men she had slept with. 'I worked for 23 years as a foreign correspondent and I've interviewed dictators and other nuts, but I've never met anyone who behaved like Nebiolo,' Britt-Marie Mattson, the interviewer, told the Stockholm *Expressen*.

The front-page headline of the *Goteborgs-Posten*, one of the major sponsors of the championships, proclaimed, 'Primo Nebiolo go home'. Norwegian columnist John Hanson described Nebiolo's behaviour as 'disgusting and unworthy of a democratic country'. John Hanson wrote: 'In Europe, dictators have fallen, the free order has won, but athletic despots are still here, more secure than ever with the help of quiet and loyal underlings.'

In October, leading officials of the European Athletic Association turned on Nebiolo, alleging that he had manipulated voters in the EAA's elections so that his supporters would gain important positions. This was no unimportant ballot for athlete of the year: this time, Nebiolo was accused of meddling with the running of one of the most influential independent bodies in world athletics. Anny Schmitz, the Dutch federation president, lost her seat on the EAA and said: 'Primo now thinks he is an emperor who can do what he wants.'

Schmitz, supported by Jose Odriozola, the president of the Spanish federation who also lost his seat on the EAA council, and by the German federation, claimed that Nebiolo made promises of financial help to national federations provided that they supported candidates in the election favoured by Nebiolo. The IAAF president, together with Istvan Gyulai, the IAAF's secretary, put the deal to a meeting of 22 European federation presidents, mainly from the old eastern bloc – Nebiolo's oldest power base – in Budapest just one month before the EAA elections. 'Money is the root of all this evil,' Schmitz said.

Those who agreed to Nebiolo's scheme were given a list of fourteen 'approved' candidates for the 13 EAA council seats. Odriozola claimed he was blacklisted by Nebiolo when he refused to stand against EAA president, Carl-Olaf Homen. The Spaniard alleged that Nebiolo had 'managed to control the European association as a result of money and buying people'. When Heiner Henze, the German who was the honorary secretary of the

EAA but who lost his position on the council, met Nebiolo in a lift shortly after the vote, the Italian said to him: 'It is the way I wanted it. Now you are where you belong. You are nothing.'

The German federation issued an official statement after the elections. 'Anyone who has criticised Nebiolo in the past is put on his hit list. That such politics can be successful should be a warning to all democrats in sporting organisations.

'The way the elections took place in Paris contradicts important democratic principles and almost completely discredits athletics, the most important sport at the Olympic Games.'

Nebiolo and the IAAF rejected the allegations, describing the German statement as irresponsible: 'The IAAF reserves the right to take any necessary action in order to safeguard its own image, that of its leaders and of the sport itself.'

Nebiolo allows no one to interfere with the way he sees fit to run the sport. With less than six months to go before the opening ceremony of the Atlanta Olympics, he had still refused to submit a finalised events timetable, delaying because of indecision over the start time of the men's marathon and whether to alter the schedule to suit Michael Johnson's ambition of the 200 and 400 metres double. It was typical of the man that, having refused to budge on either issue for more than a year, he should suddenly change tack, throwing the organisers, who had already distributed ticket application forms for the Games, and the television companies, who had allocated air time, into confusion and chaos.

Much depends on appearances for Nebiolo: he wishes to be seen as the most important leader in world sport. He has always compared the IAAF with Fifa, the football world body. To ensure IAAF events are seen around the world, he ensures that special television packages are prepared, at no cost to the receiving country. Personal vanity is also very important to Nebiolo. 'He is very vain,' recalled a former aide. 'He once refused to have his picture taken behind a desk because he knew it would only draw attention to how small he is.'

Mattson, the Swedish TV journalist, was just unlucky. You can usually ask Nebiolo a straight question and just not get a straight answer. Nebiolo is a practised master at the ability to ramble on, around the subject, never quite getting to the point, sometimes drifting off into incoherence. He is as eager to discuss a controversial issue as he is to meet British journalists. He once said of the British press: 'They call me a little Mussolini without hair. Why do they always refer to my hair?' That Nebiolo should object more to being referred to as follicly challenged than he would resent being compared to a fascist dictator is something which is not lost on many observers.

He has never quite understood the British press. In 1994, he summoned one IAAF employee to his Lisbon hotel suite, where he was staying during the staging of the World Junior Championships. What, Nebiolo wanted to know, did he have to do to earn the respect of the British media? Would a few free trips to exotic locations help? When informed that the British press could not be bought, Nebiolo, shaking with rage, had the aide thrown out of the room. 'Every man has his price,' was Nebiolo's passing shot as the poor employee was shown out of the door. Nebiolo is convinced that the antipathy towards him by the British press (something which is now by no means a uniquely British trait), is because they resent the loss of a sporting empire. Nebiolo's dislike of the British may also have a deeper, darker side to it. 'The British,' he once confided among some Italians, 'they all hate me. They're all Jews.'

Perhaps it is just that he distrusts any who do not fall in line behind him. Jack Buckner, the Briton who won the 1986 European 5,000 metres title, remembers the occasion when he was a member of the IAAF's athletes' commission and had cause to complain to Nebiolo. A few days later, Buckner received a return letter. 'Dear Mr Buckner . . .' the letter began, 'thank you for your time on the athletes' commission'.

It is all doubtless part of Nebiolo's unique sense of humour. At a press conference on the eve of the 1993 World Indoor Championships in Toronto, Nebiolo was talking about the IOC and referred to its 95 members. 'Mr Nebiolo,' a voice from the back of the room meekly started, 'there's only 91 IOC members.'

There was a pause as Nebiolo, the godfather of world athletics, toyed with his metal framed spectacles in his hand. 'Then,' Nebiolo said gruffly, 'I'm more important that I thought.' As if anybody ever doubted that Nebiolo has always considered himself Primo.

Eleven

From Hero to Zero

'THEY CAN test me every day of the week and they will get the same result. Even if I get a cold, I won't take anything. I think drug users should be banned for life. I know I will never touch the stuff.' Sound familiar? It was shot putter Neal Brunning talking in 1991. Twelve months later, Brunning was tested positive for steroids.

You might expect an athlete using banned drugs to make all the right noises if they have not been caught. After all, 'Deny, deny, deny', according to one drug-using former world-class sprinter, is the mantra of the drug cheat. Thus the disclosure in 1992 that Brunning was using steroids elicited this response from another British international shot putter: 'I am confident he is the only one of the leading British throwers to have resorted to drugs.' Two years later, the man who made those comments, Paul Edwards, was himself banned for four years for using steroids following a positive test taken after he had competed at the 1994 European Championships in Helsinki.

The most surprising thing about Brunning's capture was that, after 15 years of testing at meetings in Britain, he was the *first* British athlete to be caught using drugs. Did the absence of positive tests mean that British athletics during the 1980s and 1990s has been scrupulously clean? Hardly likely. If anything, the lack of positive drug test results on British athletes actually indicated an even greater degree of corruption within the sport, because to go all that time without catching any drug misusers required widescale complicity from some officials to make sure that there were no positive drug tests at meetings in Britain.

'The world was laughing at those results,' Charlie Francis has observed of British drug testing in the 1980s. 'You have to ask yourself how it's possible to have a random testing programme in Britain for years and never catch anybody.' And Francis should know, for he was the coach to Ben Johnson, the man at the centre of the biggest scandal in Olympic history, the most notorious exposed drugs cheat in athletics. So dependent on the use of chemical assistance were some of Francis's athletes, and so expert had the coach become in the use of steroids, that his nickname became an open joke in Canadian athletics: 'Charlie the Chemist'. Yet, until Johnson was caught after the 100 metres at the 1988 Seoul Olympics, Francis had ensured that his athletes always avoided detection. Even when they came to Britain, Francis was able to guarantee that any of his athletes who might 'have a problem' with drug tests were not exposed as cheats.

'What every meet promoter in the world wants is a world record, and what every meet promoter cannot afford to have at his event is a positive drug test. And there's no way you can have the former without some use of drugs,' is the view of Britain's David Jenkins, the 1971 European 400 metres champion who was eventually convicted in the United States for illegal supply of steroid-type drugs, and who subsequently admitted to steroid use during the later part of his own athletics career.

Cynical, perhaps, but Jenkins is not isolated in his opinions. Daley Thompson, the double Olympic decathlon gold medallist, once estimated that 80 per cent of his British team-mates were using drugs. How had they all managed to avoid detection? With the help of officials is Thompson's view. 'They've turned a blind eye. Their feeling is, if we haven't caught any, we haven't got any. Why? Because it means more TV, and more money.'

With such a cash incentive for athletes, officials and promoters, the two reasons most often cited for strict drug testing – to protect the health of competitors against the long-term side effects of steroid misuse, or to ensure a 'level playing field' for competition – were easily overlooked and ignored.

Charlie Francis discovered one way for his athletes to avoid detection by drug testers when at a meeting in Britain in 1979. Francis was the Canadian assistant team manager for a triangular match against England and Kenya at Gateshead that June, organised by the Amateur Athletic Association. In charge of the event was Andy Norman. It was the first time Francis had encountered Norman, 'with his dishevelled hair, a pot belly that peeked through an unbuttoned shirt, and low-slung pants barely clinging to his hips, he looked like a cross between Andy Capp and Long John Silver, with an attitude to match,' Francis recalled in his book, *Speed Trap*. 'For years afterwards, I considered Norman a man to be avoided.'

Before most international events, there is a technical meeting, at which team managers and coaches are given information about the organisation of the events – what make of throwing implements are to be supplied for use, late timetable changes, and lane draws, for example. Last minute questions are also dealt with, including queries relating to doping control. At Gateshead, Francis was astonished to discover at the technical meeting that the team managers were invited to observe the draw by which athletes were randomly selected for drug testing during the following afternoon's events. When the 400 metres was selected for doping control, the number three was drawn, and 'we knew they would test the third placed finisher – and him alone – in that race'.

Whether the organisers' openness was just a case of misplaced trust, or a deliberate attempt to by-pass the rules, it was a crass departure from doping control regulations. Such draws are supposed to be made in secret immediately before the meeting – not the day before – and the information is supposed to remain confidential to just a couple of officials in charge of doping control. Francis, for one, admitted exploiting his access to such information.

One of the athletes Francis had been coaching, Brian Saunders, had been using steroids, but had forgotten when he had taken his last shot. Saunders was one of Canada's 400-metre runners in the match. After the technical meeting, Francis warned Saunders: 'You better make sure you don't finish third tomorrow.' Come his race, and Saunders duly eased up before the line to avoid third place. He was not tested.

Not only can you avoid positive drug tests if you avoid testing those who have been using drugs, but you can also avoid positive tests by simply not carrying out the analyses of the samples taken. For there were other international matches where Britain played the perfect host in order to avoid 'embarrassing' our guests. In June 1982, the mighty East Germans had been invited to Crystal Palace to compete in a prestigious, two-day dual international. But, on the eve of the event, when the visitors' team management discovered that drug tests were to be conducted the following day, they threatened to walk out.

Nigel Cooper, then the secretary of the British Amateur Athletic Board (the forerunner of the British Athletic Federation), decided that rather than cancel the match, he would scrap the drug tests: no East Germans were tested that weekend. A year later, when a Soviet Union team came to compete at Birmingham, Cooper compromised the testing system in a different manner. This time, he insisted that drug testing should take place – it was even written into the agreement which had helped to bring the Soviets to Britain – but on the day after the meeting, he handed over to the Soviet officials a box full of sealed plastic bottles. It was all the Soviet athletes' doping control samples, ready to be taken back to Moscow for examination by their own internationally recognised drug testing laboratory. There were no positive tests from that particular meeting. Cooper might as well have flushed the samples down his hotel bedroom's lavatory: at least that way, he might have saved the Soviets some excess baggage charges.

There were other ruses used by British officials to ensure that known steroid users were not tested. After all, the principle is flawless: with a limited number of tests to conduct, if you test someone who you know is *not* using drugs, you should get a negative test result.

This sort of protection was also extended to top British athletes. When the draw for events and finishing positions is made correctly, the numbers should be drawn from a bag barely an hour before the meeting begins. But one senior official has admitted that on one occasion, he meddled with a drugs test random selection by deliberately omitting from the draw the number which related to a particular event. The official had been approached by one of Britain's most popular athletes, 'He said he might have a problem with a drugs test. I realise now what I did was wrong, but at the time it didn't seem all that important. I knew who was going to be conducting the draw, and he is such an honourable gentleman that he would never dream of looking in the bag to check that all the numbers were there. So I just left a number out of the draw, to make sure that his event was not selected for testing. No one noticed anything was awry.'

A fourth method of evading detection for drug cheats is to substitute their urine with a 'clean' sample taken from somebody else. This can require assistance from an official, but it is not always failsafe: in 1992, when Katrin Krabbe, Germany's sprint world champion, was tested along with two training partners, the scientists' analysis showed that the samples submitted by the three women had all come from the same person. For interfering with their samples, the three athletes were initially banned.

In 1987, in a series of articles in *The Times*, hammer thrower Martin Girvan alleged that Andy Norman had helped him to evade a test at a meeting at Crystal Palace by arranging for a bottle of 'clean' urine to be provided by an off-duty policeman and left in a cubicle in the testing centre. To investigate the claims, the sport set up an inquiry, under Peter Coni QC, with Norman's old friend from the Metropolitan Police Athletic Club, Gilbert Kelland, on the three-man panel. The resulting Coni Report was inconclusive: 'We were quite unable to say that it was true,' Coni was to recall. 'Nor did we feel able to go as far as to say that we were absolutely satisfied it was untrue.'

Coni was unconvinced by Norman's testimony, but had insufficient proof to act on Girvan's allegations. What Coni was able to discover was that, between 1975 and 1982, at least three British doctors had been prescribing anabolic steroids to help their patients – international athletes – improve their sporting performances. As many as 60 British internationals might have received this special service on the NHS, Coni estimated. David Jenkins, for one, has admitted that he got his steroids with prescriptions from a GP in Bromley, Kent. The Coni report did not name the doctors, but observed, 'it would be naïve in the extreme to think that there were neither other doctors monitoring British athletes similarly, nor other British athletes using drugs without the precaution of regular medical monitoring'.

It has since been discovered that at least one of those physicians identified by the Coni Inquiry had even worked as official team doctor to the British Olympic team. Dr Jimmy Ledingham is an Edinburgh-based GP who in 1980 accompanied the British athletics squad to the Moscow Olympics.

Ledingham first became involved with athletes in 1971, when he was team doctor to Hibernian, the Edinburgh football club. There was so little medical provision for athletes at that time that they would visit the football club's Easter Road ground and seek out Dr Ledingham. The doctor then became involved in the establishment of a sports injury clinic at the Meadowbank stadium.

After nearly ten years of hard work, Dr Ledingham's efforts were recognised when he was recruited as athletics team doctor for the 1980 Moscow Olympics. Because of the political boycott of the Games, Dr Ledingham was very apprehensive about his duties. 'I was a bag of nerves throughout the Olympics, because I did not know what some guys were on. I knew from my involvement in sports medicine for ten years that some of the top people were using steroids, but I didn't know what some of the UK athletes were using, some of whom I'd never clapped eyes on before.'

Dr Ledingham was convinced that if any British athlete failed a dope test, he would be implicated because of his position. 'The first person they would point the finger at was me, the doctor.

'The results took about seven days to come through after the end of the Olympics. I was sitting at home in Edinburgh, terrified that the phone was going to go or there would be a knock at the door.' The doctor need not have worried: there were no positive tests at Moscow. 'That I found to be unbelievable. Even if nobody was taking performance-enhancing substances, you would still expect some people to fail the test. Some banned substances are to be found in normal medication for common complaints. To have no false positives was ludicrous.' Such an absence of positive results also pointed towards one thing: that officials at the very highest levels of the International Amateur Athletic Federation and the International Olympic Committee were involved in a cover-up. Subsequent discoveries show Dr Ledingham's suspicions were well founded.

Dr Ledingham, who was still in general practice in Edinburgh in 1995, has admitted supplying the steroid Stromba to at least half a dozen top internationals, including Drew McMaster, a member of Scotland's gold medal-winning 4x100 metres relay squad at the 1978 Commonwealth Games. 'What I was doing it for was that I knew bloody well that the bloke standing next to you in the blocks was taking the stuff,' the doctor told McMaster.

While individual doctors in Britain took the decision to assist athletes using drugs, elsewhere in the world there was a more systematic use of medical advice. The discovery of the Stasi papers – documents from East

Germany's secret police – showed how the old GDR had employed doctors to dope their top athletes and then make sure that they were 'clear' of banned drugs before the major competitions. In America, Dr Robert Kerr, an adviser to numerous members of the United States' Olympic team, admitted that he had been prescribing performance enhancing drugs to more than 20 medal-winners from the 1984 Los Angeles Games. Dr Kerr rationalised this as a safer, healthier way than allowing the athletes to organise their own dosages with suspect drugs obtained on the black market. He says he gave up the practice in 1985 when, twice in one day, he found that his patients had ignored his advice and taken larger doses than he had prescribed.

Despite uncovering evidence about Dr Ledingham and his steroid-supplying medical colleagues, Peter Coni, after conducting the 1987 British inquiry into drugs in athletics, felt his efforts had been unsatisfactory because he lacked enough powers to call witnesses, while those people who did give evidence were never under oath. When an inquiry into drug use in Australian sport was set up in 1989, however, the Canberra government-backed Black Commission had all the judicial powers which Coni had craved. As a result, some decisive action was taken in Australia, including the banning of a senior official after he admitted he had attempted to interfere with a drug test. The official's admission involved a meeting staged in the United Kingdom. Yet four years after Maurie Plant had been banned from the sport in his own country, he was still active in British athletics, acting as Andy Norman's *de facto* assistant in the organisation of meetings, and in 1995 he was working for BBC television as 'athletes' liaison' at the World Championships in Gothenburg, as the man who grabs competitors as they finish and brings them in front of the cameras for interview.

It was when Plant was Australia's assistant team manager at a Commonwealth Games warm-up meeting in Belfast in June 1986 that he grabbed one of his athletes and asked them to perform something far less innocent than a television interview. Plant admitted to the Black Commission that he had approached heptathlete Jane Flemming and asked her to pee in a drink container in order to help cover up for one of her teammates, Sue Howland.

Howland, a javelin thrower, had just produced her best performance of the year, a 69.80-metre throw, and was then selected for a drugs test. She approached Maurie Plant with a 'problem'. 'As I had not had much experience of this situation, I became rather panicky,' Plant said in evidence to the Commission. 'I had heard rumours surrounding Sue Howland and drugs, I was not sure how to cope with the situation. As a knee-jerk reaction . . . I made a grave error of judgement. I approached the heptathlete Jane Flemming, and asked her to produce for me a urine sample. This was whilst Howland was awaiting her prize money. Flemming, who was rather naïve and very shocked at the suggestion, nevertheless produced a sample for me in a small drink container. My plan was that if there was a problem, then maybe somehow I could switch the sample.'

Plant then told the Commission, 'As I walked across the Mary Peters stadium to meet with Sue and the IAAF delegate . . . I began to think about my actions. Here I was, a person with ambitions and responsibilities in the sport, carrying a receptacle containing someone's urine. The more I thought, the more stupid I felt. Before I joined the athlete and the delegate, I got rid of the urine and . . . totally abandoned any thoughts of interfering with the testing procedure.'

Flemming confirmed to the Commission that she gave Plant a urine sample, while Howland insisted that she provided her own urine sample for the testers. Howland's test eventually came back negative, and she went on to compete at the Edinburgh Commonwealth Games the following month, when she won a bronze medal behind England's Tessa Sanderson and Fatima Whitbread. A year later, though, when Howland returned to compete at Belfast, she was drug tested again, and this time was found positive for steroids. She was banned for two years (the mandatory first offence punishment at that time).

After considering Plant's testimony, the Black Commission was damning in its comments. 'The committee finds it remarkable that the first response of an Australian official on being asked to accompany an athlete to a drug test was to seek a substitute sample. The committee finds it all the more remarkable given that he would have had to consider an attempt to corrupt the IAAF delegate and the whole system would have had to be corrupt if his attempt were to have succeeded.' But would it have been *so* remarkable if doping control procedures in Britain were regularly being flouted with official help?

Certainly, that was what was suspected by one of the world's leading drug testers, Dr David Cowan, now the head of the internationally accredited testing lab at London's King's College. And Dr Cowan's chief suspect was Maurie Plant's close associate, Andy Norman. 'We were very surprised that we didn't find any positives in the samples delivered to us by Andy Norman from the AAA meetings, which we would have expected, given the positives from samples collected in other branches of athletics,' said Dr Cowan, who was the London lab's assistant director at the time.

Dr Cowan was suspicious for a similar reasoning that had made Dr Ledingham describe testing at the Moscow Olympics as 'ludicrous'. 'We weren't even getting ephedrine traces – that is to say, from accidental, over-the-counter remedies,' Dr Cowan said of the samples being delivered to his Chelsea laboratory. 'Either Norman was being super-careful to make sure none of the athletes were taking drugs, or we were not getting genuine samples.' As a result of Dr Cowan's concerns, Norman was relieved of all responsibilities for drug testing at AAA meetings.

The doubts about the sport persisted until the Sports Council, the government agency which funds doping control, was forced to take drug testing out of the hands of British athletics altogether.

In 1987, Sebastian Coe was working together with the Minister for Sport, Colin Moynihan MP, on a report on the misuse of drugs in sport. In the course of their investigations, they did some checks on the drug testing protocol for a meeting at Crystal Palace. Coe and Moynihan were horrified when they discovered that, in the week before the meeting, the testing lab received a list on official, headed notepaper from the athletics governing body, detailing the events and positions that would be subjected to drug testing. When Charlie Francis was at Gateshead in 1979, this information was only being leaked the night before the event. Nearly a decade later, and the organisers were now giving themselves nearly an entire week in which drug users might be warned of what finishing position or what event to avoid if they did not want to be tested.

This was the final straw: the Sports Council could no longer trust British athletics to conduct drug tests in their own sport. Ever since, independent officials selected by the Sports Council have overseen drug tests at British athletics events, and, more recently, in out-of-competition testing. These developments have coincided with a dramatic increase in the number of British athletes being tested positive: in 1994-95, seven British athletes tested positive for banned drugs, virtually doubling the number of captures from the previous 20 years of drug testing.

Yet even when British athletics' responsibilities for drug testing were reduced to the bare minimum, the instinct to deceive and cover-up was still not far away. It was not until 1994 that it was revealed that at least six top British athletes, including 1984 Olympic 100 metres finalist Donovan Reid, had at some point failed drugs tests in Britain and served their suspensions without their transgressions being publicised. All the cases involved the minimum three-month suspensions for stimulant offences, the reason for the official silence being that each case was adjudged to be what is termed an 'inadvertent positive', the result of taking over-the-counter cold cures shortly before a test. Once the Sports Council had reported the positive tests, it was left to the sport whether to publicise the suspensions. British athletics decided to stay silent.

This preference for being economical with the truth is in contrast with the approach Charlie Francis decided to adopt after Ben Johnson was caught at Seoul, and the Canadian government set up its own official investigation into drug use in that country. 'For years I had kept the conspiracy of silence that governs international track, a see-no-evil world where high-minded condemnations of drug use co-exist with the cynical protection of doped-up superstars,' Francis said. 'But silence wouldn't work any more. It was finally time to speak up.' It had taken 12 years to build Johnson into becoming the fastest human ever seen on earth, but once he got into the witness stand in Toronto to swear on oath, it took Francis only four days to unravel a world sporting myth.

Francis was the star witness at the Commission of Inquiry into the Use of Drugs and Banned Practices Intended to Increase Athletic Performance, or the Dubin Commission for short, so called after the presiding judge, Justice Charles Dubin.

The Canadian government, a long-term benefactor to its country's sportsmen and women, had set up the judicial inquiry in January 1989 to investigate the extent to which drugs were being used following the shock of the previous October, when Johnson was sent home in disgrace after testing positive for the banned drug stanozolol after he had been seen by a global television audience of two billion winning the Olympic 100 metres in a world record 9.79 sec in Seoul.

There had been a day of national mourning in Canada when Johnson's 'little secret' was publicised. The shock of this national icon being found out, the man who had beaten the world – and most especially the Americans, led by Carl Lewis – was too much to take in for most sports mad Canadians. Canada had not won an Olympic track gold since 1928, and now the International Olympic Committee was demanding the return of Johnson's medal in the direst of circumstances. 'A moment of great disappointment for all Canadians,' their Prime Minister, Brian Mulroney, was forced to comment. 'From Hero to Zero in 9.79sec' read one headline in Toronto. 'Thanks a Lot, You Bastard' was the *Ottawa Citizen*'s considered comment after the discovery.

It was nearly 20 years earlier that Francis had come to the wretched conclusion that the only way to succeed in international athletics was to cheat, and to cheat big. That meant using drugs. Francis's own Olympic career had been very brief, restricted to the preliminary rounds of the 100 metres at Munich in 1972. All around him, Francis saw other sprinters using drugs to aid their performance. Drugs, in particular anabolic steroids, had been in sporting misuse by competitors in 'power' events – sprints, throws, weightlifting – in America and the eastern bloc since the 1950s.

But what Francis witnessed in 1972 was not against the rules at that time. Tests had been introduced for stimulants in 1968, but the first drug tests to detect steroid use were not introduced in athletics until 1975. As Francis was to discover, the will of many in authority to implement those rules and act on them was often woefully weak.

For example, even as early as 1973, Professor Raymond Brooks, of London's St Thomas's Hospital, the expert who had developed the test for anabolic steroids, told the IAAF that the only effective way of testing for steroid use would be to have out-of-competition tests: steroids were an effective training aid, but they could be cleared out of the body's system by the time of a competition.

It is a simple flaw with in-competition testing: you can see it coming.

Apply the same principle to the drink-driving rules. If the police came into your local pub and announced that next Saturday night they would be parked outside, ready to breathalise anyone driving down the road after closing time, it is likely that business at the bar would be slow that night. Thus drug-using athletes make sure they are not 'over the limit' when they go into the competitive season. Yet it was not until Johnson was caught at the 1988 Olympics, 15 years after Professor Brooks's warning, that moves were made to introduce widespread out-of-competition drug tests internationally.

From his own failure and his rivals' successes in Munich, Francis was to reach a conclusion which was to influence him profoundly as a coach and take him, his athletes and the sport of athletics to a nadir of public disrespect. 'For anyone who continued to compete after 1975, the choice was clear,' Francis said, 'they could either break the rules or they could lose.'

Francis testified to the Dubin Inquiry that in 1981 he discussed steroids with his three best male sprinters, Desai Williams, Tony Sharpe and Johnson, then a gangling 19-year-old with a stutter, who had emigrated to Canada from Jamaica in 1976. For the 100 metres, 'it's pretty clear that steroids are worth approximately a metre at the highest levels', said Francis. 'Johnson could decide to set up his starting blocks at the same line as all the other competitors, or set them up a metre behind them all. And obviously that would be an unacceptable situation for a top-level athlete.'

From 1983, Francis's athletes began having their drug programmes monitored by Dr Jamie Astaphan. Francis said Dr Astaphan administered shots in his office and in late 1985 switched the athletes from one anabolic steroid, stanozolol, to another, Furazabol, which he believed to be a gentler drug. After Astaphan returned to his native Caribbean island of St Kitts in 1986, Williams, Sharpe and Johnson either injected themselves or were injected by Francis in his Toronto apartment. All told, Francis testified that 13 of the men and women he coached used steroids.

According to Francis, Johnson would go to St Kitts whenever he needed treatment for injuries, Astaphan using steroids to aid the recovery. By 1987, Astaphan was giving Johnson a naturally occurring substance, Human Growth Hormone, hGH. This hormone, quite literally, 'builds' the body, but no one has ever failed a drug test, in or out of competition, for hGH. Like several drugs new to use in sport, although hGH is technically banned by the IOC, by the end of 1995, no effective test had been introduced to determine its administration to the body of an athlete. Thus, it could be used with impunity.

The story of the biggest scandal ever to rock the Olympic Movement is revealing of how the drug-testing system can work. Francis was never able to explain satisfactorily why Johnson, who had evaded capture during seven years of drug use at so many previous tests, this time – on the most important occasion of his life – came up positive. One possible scenario was that, after Johnson lost to Carl Lewis in Zurich just before the Seoul Games, the Canadian panicked, and went 'rogue', taking a dose of drugs unsupervised, not mindful of the clearance times.

Once in Seoul, though, the sceptics who had been watching Johnson's rapid progression over the past few years spotted some tell-tale signs. On the training track a few days before the track events began, an American coach saw Johnson and was shocked. 'His eyes were so yellow with his liver working overtime processing steroids that I said he's either crazy or he's protected with an insurance policy."

That was a none-too-oblique reference to the 1987 World Championships staged in Rome. There, Johnson had set the world record of 9.83sec. But he was not caught for using drugs. In fact, there was only one positive test from the Rome championships. These were the same the IAAF-run World Championships where the Italian long jump judges had added a few centimetres to the jump of countryman Giovanni Evangelisti to ensure that he took a bronze medal in front of his home crowd. If that kind of chicanery – carried out in front of a packed stadium – was possible, then why would it not be possible behind the scenes for the results of positive drug tests also to be tampered with, in effect as an 'insurance' against any of the stars of track and field being disgraced and the accompanying negative publicity?

In Seoul, the Games – and the doping control – were under the auspices of the International Olympic Committee. Roughly four hours after the 100 metres final, the urine samples were delivered to the Doping Control Centre less than half a mile away, across the Han River. By 6 a.m. on the morning after the greatest sprint race ever seen, Dr Park Jong Sei, director of the testing centre, learned that a sample he was testing contained stanozolol, a dangerous anabolic steroid that can be taken in tablet form. Even though it was not required under the testing procedures, and although the identity of the source of the sample was completely unknown to him (even to the extent that he did not know from what event the number-coded bottles had been taken from), Dr Park was very aware of the wide-ranging effects the news of a positive test would have on the Games. To be absolutely sure of of his results, he tested the same sample once more. He got the same result. Dr Park then notified the IOC's Medical Commission.

Manfred Donike, the German professor who was then head of the IOC Medical Commission, checked the results and assured Dr Park that no mistake had been made. It was inconsequential if the test revealed a small, medium or large amount of steroids in the urine. 'That doesn't matter, because there's no borderline case in steroids,' Professor Donike said. 'Just like you can't be a little bit pregnant, either it's there or it isn't. In this case, it was not a small amount.'

Yet there were other cases of positive tests which were never acted upon. After the Games, Dr Park told *The New York Times* that as many as

20 other Olympic athletes had tested positive in Seoul, but the IOC's Medical Commission opted not to take any further action, sometimes on split votes, which may suggest that sport's international politics was as much a consideration as any scientific evidence. Indeed, according to Dr Tony Millar, the former chief medical officer of the Commonwealth Games Association, some nations, including Britain, Italy, Germany and the United States, exercise more power in the back-room discussions which determine athletes' fates. 'The people who don't matter are eliminated. If Ben Johnson had come from the USSR, he would have received a negative instead of a positive test in Seoul,' Dr Millar claimed.

The views of Drs Park and Millar seem to have been supported by a conversation which a German sports journalist had shortly after the Games with no less an authority than Professor Donike, in which the German expert suggested that *80 per cent* of male track and field athletes in Seoul had drug tests which indicated previous steroid use. Professor Donike, while disputing the figures when called to give evidence to the Dubin Inquiry, did admit that a number of tests were positive. No action was taken because the athletes' endocrine profiles – analyses of the secretions into the body by glands affected by drug use – were not deemed reliable.

That, at least, was a better excuse for inaction than in 1984, when the confidential documents relating to a dozen positive tests at the Los Angeles Games were shredded, according to IOC officials, by a hotel cleaner, preventing any further action being taken against the cheats. How careless . . .

Even the IAAF's secretary, John Holt, felt prompted by the furore over the Johnson case to suggest that '30 or 40 per cent of the athletes in the leading 20 in the world have at some time been tempted to dabble in drugs'. If Holt's guesstimate was accurate, that would mean that in any final lineup, at the Olympic Games or World Championships, at least three athletes would have got there by using drugs. Even though the first three plus one at random is tested from every such final, the detection rate is nowhere near that level. As Francis observed: 'Taken together, these demonstrate that Ben's case was special only because he got caught.'

Now Holt was a widely respected official, not prone to exaggeration. Indeed, when he made his comments in 1989, he was attempting to emphasise the IAAF's official position that much of the information which was emerging from the Dubin Inquiry was an 'exaggeration' of the extent of the problem in athletics. Yet, in doing so, he provided a rule-of-thumb estimate of drug use – 'Holt's Ratio' – which has since been shown to be quite accurate. Four of the IAAF's own world champions from Tokyo in 1991 were unable to defend their titles in Stuttgart two years later because they were serving doping suspensions. And at those 1993 championships in Germany, another three top performers were caught by the dope tests. At least, it seemed, the authorities were no longer able to turn a blind eye to all the positive findings.

There remain discrepancies in how drug testing is carried out around the world, though. Canada, Australia and Britain have tried to clamp down on drug use in sport, usually at the insistence of their governments. Other countries are less thorough: for instance, American athletes were not subjected to random, out-of-competition tests from their own governing body, US Track & Field, for more than six months in the build-up to the 1995 Gothenburg World Championships, simply because UST&F's doping control administrator quit her job in November 1994 and no system was instituted to replace her until a private company was given the contract, beginning in June 1995.

Johnson's return to the Olympic arena four years after Seoul produced one of those ironies so common in sport. As Johnson was waiting for passport clearance at Barcelona airport, on his way to take part in the Games, also waiting in the departure lounge for his flight home was a young British sprinter, his shaven head bowed in the hope that he might not be spotted by any passing pressmen. For Jason Livingston, his Olympic career was over even before it had begun.

Johnson was a hero to Livingston – who was even dubbed 'Baby Ben' because of the way he had modelled his sprinting style on the Canadian. When Johnson was caught in 1988, the sport of athletics held him up as an example of how they were getting tough with drugs cheats. He would be banned from the Olympics, they said. The Minister for Sport in Canada immediately decreed that Johnson, the one-time national hero, would never compete for his adopted country again.

That Johnson did compete again for Canada, that he raced at the Barcelona Games (he failed to progress beyond the semi-finals), and that he was eventually caught out again using drugs, all went a long way to prove that much of what is said about drug use in sport, and the costly testing campaigns waged against it, is full of cant and hypocrisy.

In 1996, Jason Livingston, his four-year ban over in July, is expected to attempt to make a comeback as an international sprinter. He will be doing so soon after a 12-month period in which Britain banned eight other athletes for doping infractions. He will be doing so within a year of a former British record-holder, Keith Stock, being jailed for seven years after being convicted for the possession and supply of 'hard' drugs, ecstasy and cocaine. And he will be doing so less than two years after another former British international, sprinter Claude Moseley, was left bleeding to death on his own doorstep in west London, the victim of a brutal gangland stabbing because of his involvement in drug dealing.

'Drugs in sport' is clearly no longer distinct from drugs in society. What ought to be of particular concern is how the drugs used in sport are increasingly becoming part of a wider, growing trade for organised crime. With this has come another worrying trend. This can see children, often no more than 13 or 14 years old, obtaining supplies of body-building drugs such as anabolic steroids, sometimes from pushers even operating in their school playgrounds. In 1995, one survey estimated that 100,000 British children aged under 16 were using anabolic steroids.

The children buying steroids do so to try to manufacture bodies like those of their 'role models', whether seen on the athletics track, the football pitch, in the boxing ring or in new 'sports', such as the *Gladiators* television programme. With success, glamour and wealth so easily equated with the use of steroids, it is little wonder that impressionable children might leap to half-baked conclusions. Certainly, some young athletes are quick to reach similar conclusions. But it is important to be realistic about the issue of cheating with drugs. The people who turn to steroids are not evil monsters. They do not *want* to use drugs: they have to, just to keep pace with sport's steroid standards which have been established over the past 30 years or so.

Jason Livingston was one athlete placed in such a quandary. The European Indoor Championships staged at the Kelvin Hall in Glasgow in March 1990 had been the first major international competition for Livingston. Despite his small stature and inexperience, at 18 years of age, Livingston had blistering speed and rapid reactions. Thus over the swift patter of an indoor 60-metre dash, he could beat the world. And he knew it.

That weekend, Livingston surpassed himself, qualifying for the televised championship final against five other seasoned European sprinters. Although the youngster walked off the track disappointed not to have won a medal, he was entitled to expect a hero's welcome when he got home to south London after the weekend, having so ably represented his country in his first senior international championship. Instead, when Livingston turned up for work on the Monday morning, he was given his cards and told to collect his things and leave: he had been fired for taking too much time off work. It was an early, bitter lesson in the cost of commitment for Livingston.

Left with nothing else other than athletics, Livingston gave it his all. Thus it was that two years later, Livingston would again pay the price for wanting to win too much. Just before midnight on Wednesday 29 July, 1992, Livingston, by now 21 and Britain's second fastest man, was just days away from the biggest moment in his sporting career, his first appearance at an Olympic Games. Getting ready for bed in his cramped, shared apartment in the Barcelona Olympic Village, he answered the door when a courier arrived with an urgent letter addressed to him.

'I thought it was going to tell me that someone had died,' was Livingston's only recollection of the moment, a reaction strangely similar to other athletes who have found themselves in such a situation. There had been no deaths, though, just the terminal ending of an elaborate lie. The note inside was clear and unmistakable in its message: Livingston had tested positive for the anabolic steroid, methandianone.

Within a couple of hours, he had packed up all his things and was on his way home. Livingston was caught before the drugs he had been using had helped him win any false fame or fortune, before he had made a name for himself. As Dr Millar had said, 'The people who don't matter are eliminated.'

Another British sprinter, short of stature like Livingston, who enjoyed great success as a junior but who found it more difficult to progress once he moved into his 20s was Jamie Henderson. The Scot, the European Junior 100 metres champion in 1987, eventually reached a different conclusion to Livingston. 'Standards have improved so much that realistically one of two things would have to happen,' Henderson said. 'Either the sport cleans itself up totally, or I need to go on steroids. I am not willing to do the latter, and the former seems highly unlikely. I do not want to train for the next 12 years waiting for it to happen.

'Both the use of steroids and the amount of money available have devalued the sport. My most enjoyable moments in athletics have been at university and club meets, not going down to Crystal Palace on a Friday night to pick up a cheque. We need to get back to the values of when athletics was more fun. Some people will try to win, whatever the cost. I will not. It is unfortunate that my stance means that the odds are reduced for me and other athletes with a similar view.'

The steroid standard: not only do clean athletes struggle to keep up, but they can be excluded from top competitions because they have refused to take drugs. Nearly a decade on from the exposure of Ben Johnson, and the international governing bodies are still using qualifying standards based on previous drug-assisted performances to determine who can compete at forthcoming major championships, such as the Olympic Games. Yet there has been a massive down-turn in performance levels in track and field events since 1988. For instance, in the doping control clampdown that followed the Johnson scandal, there was not one world record set in a women's Olympic event for five years.

A comparison between other world records and the best performances in recent years shows an abrupt halt to what once seemed an unstoppable progression in human achievement. Leroy Burrell is now officially the world's fastest man, with his 9.85sec 100 metres run from 1994. No one has been able to get close to the steroid-boosted 9.79sec it took Ben Johnson to run the same distance in 1988. There are several other marks from 1988 which have continued to defy attack. For example, the men's 400 metres world record was set in 1988 by Butch Reynolds, who subsequently served a (lengthily contested) ban for a positive drug test. No one, not even Michael Johnson, double world champion at 200 and 400 metres in Gothenburg in 1995, has been able to better Reynolds's 43.29sec.

The men's discus world record stands to Jürgen Schult for the 74.08 metres he threw in 1986. According to the Stasi papers, Schult was one of East Germany's élite athletes to be administered drugs. No man has thrown beyond 70 metres in the 1990s: the 1995 world title was won with a throw of just 68.76 metres by Lars Riedel, more than 13 per cent short of the world record performance.

The differentials between world records and present performances in women's events are even wider, and therefore force more stark conclusions. Florence Griffith-Joyner's 100 and 200 metres world records, 10.49 and 21.34sec from 1988, are 0.27 and 0.30sec faster than anything managed by any other woman, ever. The differential over 100 metres equates to about two and a half metres margin on the track, while the gap over 200 metres is wider still: 'Flo-Jo' seems to have left history standing still.

In the javelin, Petra Felke, another East German drug user mentioned in the Stasi files, has held the world record since she threw 80.00 metres in 1988. Seven years later, the world title was won by Natalya Shikolenko. Her 67.56-metre effort in Gothenburg was the shortest winning distance at an Olympics or World or European championships since 1976. Shikolenko is one of only 18 women ever to manage to throw beyond 70 metres. Of the others in the '70-metre club', three have been caught using drugs, neatly fulfilling 'Holt's Ratio'.

Thus, many of today's athletes have their performances devalued – and their earnings diminished – because of comparison with records set under a different, more lax regime. It is a sad reflection on the sport that when Jonathan Edwards lightly skipped across the triple jump runway in Lille, France, in June 1995 to leap 18.43 metres – the furthest triple jump ever seen, unratified for record purposes only because the Gateshead Harrier had too strong a tailwind behind him – the first reaction of some in the stands to the greatest performance of the year was 'What's he been on?'. Even Edwards himself said he might have been prompted to ask a similar question had he witnessed someone else make such a quantum leap. The press might have been half joking, but sadly drugs have often reduced athletics to little more than a joke, thus tarnishing even Beamonesque achievements such as those of Edwards. More than any other factor, drugs has seen the sport's innocence replaced with cynicism.

Twelve

Guilty Until Proven Innocent

ATHLETES who test positive for drugs rarely accept their fate at the hands of the doping control system, but few proceed far beyond the initial denials. In truth, few have any cause to. And fewer still have ever been successful in challenging the edifice that is 'The System'. It may seem, therefore, that doping control, from sample collection to analysis, is beyond reproach.

In fact, the basis on which drug testing's quasi-legal system of appeals works is almost impossible to challenge successfully. For it requires the accused athlete to prove a negative: that it was not their sample that was tested; or that it did not contain traces of the drug which analysis suggested. In fact, far from being beyond reproach, the often flawed international drug testing system is disdainfully impregnable in its own, self-satisfied, self-proving branchline of science.

Butch Reynolds and Katrin Krabbe are the two best-known cases of athletes who fell foul of the drug busters but who fought the ruling through the courts, using the legal systems in the United States, England and Germany. Both athletes had some degree of success initially, Reynolds at one stage even being awarded £18 million damages against the International Amateur Athletic Federation. Yet neither athlete was ever able to walk away from the law courts and just step on to the track: the IAAF saw to it that they both served the full term of their suspensions.

With multi-million dollar track careers at stake, it was perhaps understandable that Reynolds and Krabbe should contest their suspensions. More unusual was the threat of a legal challenge against the doping control system by someone who never even tested positive for drugs, Britain's former javelin world champion, Fatima Whitbread.

It was in March 1990 that Whitbread first wrote a letter of complaint to Sir Arthur Gold, the chairman of British athletics' Drug Advisory Committee. Whitbread was unhappy with her treatment when selected for testing. That August, Whitbread followed up her original letter with solicitors' threats of legal action over two tests, one an out-of-competition test and the other a drug test following what was her final competition, in Cardiff at the 1990 United Kingdom Championships. Whitbread's solicitors, Simon Olswang & Co, also wrote to Marea Hartman, then chairman of the British Amateur Athletic Board, alleging that Whitbread's drug test in Cardiff could have interfered with emergency hospital treatment to the serious shoulder injury Whitbread sustained during competition.

During the winter of 1989-90, the Sports Council's out-of-competition drug testers had had to go to great lengths to test Whitbread. Then, on 3 March 1990, Whitbread was tracked down while she was in the stands at Glasgow's Kelvin Hall for the first day of the European Indoor Championships. There she was approached by two doping control officials. When she was asked to go to the doping control centre behind the stands for an out-of-competition test, there was an argument. With Andy Norman, her fiancé, close by, Whitbread had been watching the athletics as the championships began to get underway. When the doping control officials asked her to be tested, she said that she had a business meeting to attend. She refused to go to the drug test centre, and she also refused to allow a sampling officer to accompany her to her business meeting. She said she would return from the meeting in an hour and a half's time. This she did, and then gave a urine sample, which tested negative for any banned drugs.

More serious were the athlete's solicitors' complaints over the incident in Cardiff three months later. After two years of illness and injury, Whitbread was desperate to resurrect her world-beating career as a javelin thrower, but after recent operations, her right shoulder failed to stand up to the pressure of top-flight competition. Going into the final round of the event, her best effort of 51.50 metres was a long way short of her world record-breaking best, and placed her only third. Her mighty effort with her last throw seemed to have the entire crowd in the new Leckwith Stadium wincing as a sickening crack sound reverberated around the stands. In agony from the pain in her shoulder, Whitbread was rushed to hospital. But as the third placed finisher in the javelin, Whitbread had been nominated for a drug test: a determined doping control steward followed the athlete to the casualty department of the nearby hospital.

According to Whitbread's solicitors, the injury ought to have prevented their client from having to submit to the doping test. The solicitors advised Whitbread that by being confined by the drug tester to a doctor's room at the hospital, she had been subjected to what amounted to false imprisonment. Whitbread's solicitors wanted an apology, explanation and assurances about doping control procedures for injured athletes. At one point, it was even suggested that some form of injunction might be taken out against named Sports Council officials to prevent them from carrying out further tests on Whitbread.

A month after her solicitors' letter was received, Whitbread received an apology on behalf of the British Board from Marea Hartman for the experiences at Cardiff. But when Derek Casey, a Sports Council director, conducted an internal investigation into the allegations against his officers' conduct, he was satisfied that all procedures had been properly implemented. According to Casey, Whitbread had no cause for complaint.

In theory, drug tests are supposed to deter athletes from using performance enhancing drugs. Most athletes have welcomed such tests, since the clampdown against the cheats ought to make for fairer competition. Before 1988, such testing was often ineffective, sometimes deliberately so, and as a result some athletes used drugs with impunity.

Charlie Francis, Ben Johnson's coach, recalled one meeting he had before the Olympics in Seoul in 1988, when 'a well-known western European official approached me . . . and asked if I had anything that might help one of his country's top female athletes'. According to Francis's book, *Speedtrap*, he and Dr Jamie Astaphan met with the official and athlete at the Seoul Hilton. 'The woman told us she'd been stacking Stromba (oral stanozolol), Primobolan (another steroid), and 50-milligram shots of aqueous testosterone daily for several years, in addition to regular doses of amphetamines on competition days.'

When the athlete asked if Francis or Dr Astaphan had any stimulants she could use in competition at the Olympics, even 'Charlie the Chemist' was shocked. 'I asked the woman how she could use amphetamines and still pass her drugs test. She replied that she routinely evaded her home country's random-testing programme by infusing clean urine into her body with the aid of a makeshift catheter – a West German bubble-making toy – and planned to do the same in the Olympics.' Some athletes, it seemed, would go to any lengths to beat the system. Most succeeded.

While Fatima Whitbread may have complained in 1990 about the intrusive nature of doping control, the more stringent measures being used by drug testers at that time were simply the determined reaction to the revelations which followed Ben Johnson's positive test, carried out barely a week after the meeting in the Seoul Hilton which shocked even Charlie Francis.

Six years on from Seoul, and doping control seemed to have become so much more refined that only the completely foolhardy would try to use drugs in competition, especially those banned substances which did not have an immediate effect, but might be used for a longer term, anabolic, body-building use. Yet in the middle of the 1994 track season, that was what Diane Modahl was accused of doing – loading herself up with a massive dose of the body-building hormone testosterone within a couple of hours of a race. The results of the drug test carried out on Modahl after she had raced in Lisbon, Portugal, that June were so incredible that for the next 20 months the British runner and her husband would contest them, winning one of the most celebrated cases to question the authority of the all-powerful drug-testing system. 'As two individuals against whole institutions,' Modahl was to say, 'we've been like a couple of Davids against Goliath.'

It was more than nine weeks after the Lisbon drug test before Modahl was made aware of the result. By that time, she was on the threshold of one of the most important races of her life.

It was before breakfast on a bright, sunny summer's morning in Victoria, on Canada's Pacific coast, and Diane Modahl was jogging easily into the athletes' village after a loosening run. It was 24 August, the day of her 800 metres qualifying round in the Commonwealth Games. A small but strong woman who had managed to ally her 400-metre speed effectively to middle distance stamina, Modahl had won the gold medal in the 800 metres at the previous Commonwealth Games in Auckland, New Zealand, four years before. Now, she was in Canada determined to defend her title. While running through the woods behind the village, Modahl had been rehearsing in her mind that day's race. She was convinced that no one could beat her. She was wrong.

As she eased down on the end of her easy half-hour run, she was startled from her thoughts by her team manager, Sue Deaves, who was waiting outside one of the accommodation blocks to call her to her room.

'Shut the door, Diane,' Deaves said as they entered the small bedroom. 'I think you should sit down. I've got some bad news for you.' As Modahl sat on the edge of the bed, Deaves took the athlete by the hand and looked her in the eyes. After a brief pause, which probably lasted just seconds but which must have seemed like an hour, Deaves said, 'We have had a fax from Peter Radford saying that the drug test carried out in Portugal on 18 June was tested positive for testosterone and another substance.'

Modahl was shocked, unable to take in the enormity of the news. As if trying to cling to some sort of normality, she asked if she could leave to continue to prepare for that afternoon's 800 metres heat. Deaves told the athlete that she was being withdrawn from the competition. Total disbelief washed over Modahl, her knees buckled, and Deaves just stopped her falling to the floor as she fainted. 'Her big brown eyes were very wide open and I thought, "My goodness, she's dead",' Deaves recalls. 'She was extremely distressed, absolutely devastated, and she just kept repeating the same words, "This is terrible, this is terrible".'

Amid the tears, when Modahl came round and composed herself a little, she asked Deaves if she could get her training log, the diary that most athletes keep to record their every training session, their every mood. Modahl wanted to check if she had been tested since Portugal. After all, she thought, she had a race to run in a couple of hours . . . Deaves hurried out of the room, so shaken by the experience that, when she returned home from the

Games a couple of weeks later, she needed professional counselling herself.

Then Roy Axon, the team doctor, arrived in the room with Alan Lindop, the England men's team manager. The doctor decided that Modahl needed a sedative. Then, slightly embarrassed, he asked Modahl whether she had taken any illegal substances. 'Of course not,' came the screamed reply.

Dr Axon had brought with him the fax sheet which carried the news of Modahl's positive drug test. On the headed notepaper of the Portuguese athletics federation, it was originally addressed to Professor Peter Radford of the British Athletic Federation, who had sent it on. The doctor read the fax aloud to Modahl as she read over his shoulder, barely able to believe what she was seeing. The letter said that her drug test at the St Antonio Meeting in Lisbon on 18 June had shown administration of exogenous testosterone through a ratio of testosterone and epitestosterone of more than 42:1. 'I wanted to talk to Vicente, I wanted to talk to the whole world and scream my innocence. I wanted to *scream*,' Modahl was to recall. It was as much as she could do not to faint again.

Just as the race in which she should have been running was starting in the Games stadium, Modahl was instead leaving the village. Her bags had been packed by her room-mate, and with half a tablet of Valium, Modahl was driven to a local hospital to spend the night before flying back to London.

It was not long after Diane had had the news broken to her that the telephone rang at her home in Sale, Cheshire. There, preparing his last lunch at home before setting off halfway around the world to see his wife compete, was Vicente Modahl, Diane's husband. The phone call brought the worst news he had ever heard. For Vicente, it was the beginning of a battle to clear not only his wife's name, but also to restore his own reputation.

The Modahl case was unique because it was never just the athlete, Diane, who stood accused, but Vicente as well. An athletes' manager, he had taken on the task of coaching Diane in late 1992. When news of the drugs positive broke, accusing fingers were soon pointed in his direction, not least by officials from the international governing body, effectively the prosecuting authority in this case. 'Who's been sprinkling the stuff on her cornflakes?' one source mischievously suggested. One IAAF official in Monte Carlo went to some lengths to point out the relationship between Vicente Modahl and Nigerian-born, Norway-based sprinter Ahem Okeke, who failed two drugs tests in 1994 and who had sometimes had races arranged for him by Modahl.

Norwegian-born Vicente is tall, well dressed, a softly spoken polyglot, one of a rapidly growing band of athletes' managers and agents, the middlemen who organise racing deals, sponsorship and endorsement packages for their clients, professional athletes. If Diane Modahl was not cleared, the implications for the family business would not be good. Indeed, after 20 months' struggle and more than £100,000 spent on legal and medical experts to help clear his wife's name, the Modahls were forced to put their family home up for sale. Throughout it all, though, Vicente always maintained 'It will be a crime if Diane is not proved innocent.'

A former junior international steeplechaser, Vicente Modahl settled in Manchester in 1992, shortly before his marriage to Diane. Before that, he had been an assistant meeting director of the Bislett Games in Oslo, one of the top four international meetings in the world. It was through his work at Bislett that Modahl had met Said Aouita, the 1984 Olympic 5,000 metres champion and world record-breaking runner from Morocco. During the mid-1980s, when he was Steve Cram's biggest rival, Aouita was one of the top earners on the lucrative European track circuit, and Modahl was soon organising his racing programme and collecting a percentage of the Moroccan's fees. But Aouita demanded the absolute attention of his manager. 'He didn't want me to have a girlfriend or get married,' Modahl said. 'He gave me an ultimatum and we parted.'

Vicente Modahl's arrival in Britain was not warmly welcomed: the business of managing athletes is very new, the rules virtually non-existent, and the number of athletes likely to be 'valuable' assets to an agent's stable quite limited. When Vicente Modahl quickly snapped up the promising youngsters David Grindley, Steve Smith, Curtis Robb and Guy Bullock, his presence in Britain was resented. 'You'll be rowing your own boat back to Norway in three months,' one rival warned.

Thus it came as a blow for Modahl when, shortly after arranging a £37,000-a-year shoe contract for Curtis Robb, Britain's most promising miler, that Robb decided that his racing arrangements would instead be handled by Andy Norman. Norman at this time was still employed by the British federation as their promotions officer.

There was another instance when one of Modahl's athletes resisted all approaches to use a different manager. One day the athlete received a phone call from a journalist who asked about the drug test which the athlete had just failed. The athlete was dumb-struck. He knew nothing about a failed drug test. Then, shortly after the journalist rang off, the athlete received another phone call. This time from the manager who wanted to sign up this new talent. He wondered if there had been any change of heart.

Despite this apparent intimidation, the athlete, and most others, remained loyal to the Modahls thoughout their struggle against the findings of the drug tests. 'He's the best agent in the world,' Steve Smith, the European high jump silver medal-winner, said. 'He certainly does the business for his athletes,' Chris Butler, coach to Grindley, the British 400 metres record-holder, said. But from August 1994, business often had to take a back seat as Vicente led the struggle to clear his wife's name. Convinced that Diane had never taken any performance enhancing substances, the Modahls sought to fight her ban. For unlike English, Scottish or American Law, where the burden of proof is on the prosecution, under sports' rules against drugs, once the accusation of drug use is made, the authorities can sit back and rely on the evidence of their drug testing system. Effectively, athletes accused like Diane Modahl are guilty until they can prove their innocence. It is a near-impossible task.

In their efforts to win their case, Diane Modahl was taken to a series of Harley Street specialists to try to discover a medical explanation for the extraordinarily high levels of testosterone found in her urine sample taken in Portugal. Modahl's 42:1 ratio would later be described as a 'record level', four times that discovered in Ben Johnson when a second positive drug test saw him banned for life for in March 1993. But the findings in the Modahl case left many incredulous. The androgenic effects of testosterone on women are so well known that the suggestion that Modahl, relatively slight, not particularly muscled, had used massive doses of the hormone led her international team-mate, Tony Jarrett, to scoff at the findings. 'If she'd taken that amount of the stuff,' Jarrett said, 'she'd look like Barry White.'

Because testosterone occurs naturally in everyone, male or female, use of the hormone has always been popular with drugs cheats: after all, how can you test for something that occurs naturally? It was not until the early 1980s that a test for the administration of testosterone was introduced under the International Olympic Committee rules. The test was based on the comparison of the amounts of testosterone with epitestosterone, another related, naturally occurring hormone. Research on thousands of people, mainly in Europe and north America, showed that the two hormones are usually found in equal amounts, expressed as a ratio of 1:1.

There had been a delay in introducing the test because the scientists could not agree between themselves on the level at which they could be certain that testosterone had been administered: the hardliners wanted a low ratio, something like 4:1, while other experts, aware that theirs was a new area of science, were more cautious. Initially, anyone showing a ratio of 6:1 was deemed to have a positive test and was subject to sanction. Yet by the early 1990s, the drug testers were having second thoughts about the T:E ratio test. Further research had shown that some racial groups, such as Asians and Polynesians, did not always fit in to the accepted pattern of the 1:1 ratio. 'It's an analytical emergency in its tenth year,' Dr Don Catlin, the head of the IOC-accredited lab in Los Angeles and one of the foremost world authorities on the subject, told a seminar in London in 1993.

Such were the disagreements between the specialists that the values at which the doping control alarm bells are set off have been changed several times. By the mid-1990s, the threshold ratio which needed to be reached before anyone was deemed to be banned was moved to 10:1. The testers did admit, though, that anyone showing a ratio of 6:1 would be 'target tested' to observe any tell-tale signs of drug use through changes in the individual's ratio.

Nothing in Diane Modahl's doping control history had caused her to be placed on the testers' 'hit list'. The Lisbon result seemed completely out of place. Could the lab have made a mistake? Four years earlier, when another woman distance runner, Jeanne-Marie Pipoz, of Switzerland, was 'caught' by the same Lisbon laboratory, also for excessive levels of testosterone, further medical evidence showed that Pipoz had liver damage, caused by anorexia nervosa, which had distrupted her hormonal balance. Pipoz was cleared to run again.

In another case, Trine Hattestad, the Norwegian who won the 1994 European javelin title, was suspended after a positive 'A' test result after competing in Brussels in 1989. But the result was not confirmed by the 'B' sample analysis. The Utrecht laboratory which conducted the testing subsequently lost its accreditation, and Hattestad was awarded substantial compensation. To err may be human, but in doping control it is also very expensive.

According to Michele Verroken, the head of the Sports Council's Doping Control Unit in London, the problem with the T:E ratio test was not only the inconsistencies between racial groups. The science was not properly understood for more than half the population. 'We have not properly investigated testosterone levels in women,' Verroken said. 'We don't understand its relationship with things such as the contraceptive pill. We must be careful not to label everyone as cheats.'

In Modahl's case, the extensive medical tests might have offered partial explanation. Modahl had a polycystic ovary. Not a seriously health-threatening condition – as proved by the birth of Modahl's first child in October 1995, a daughter, Imani – such ovarian cysts can be common in women, particularly those who exercise regularly and who use the contraceptive pill, as Modahl did. These cysts are known to affect the natural production of testosterone and the feminising hormone oestrogen.

Modahl also had a secondary, and much more rare complaint, a deficiency of the enzyme called 5-alpha-reductase, which helps to convert testosterone into other substances. This condition is more prevalent in people of Afro-Caribbean descent like Modahl. Without the enzyme, Modahl's testosterone levels increased, while her athletic endeavours probably suppressed the usual symptoms observed in women with such an enzyme deficiency. Modahl also had special tests conducted to check for cancer. In 1993, she had found a lump in her breast, though doctors had reassured her it was benign, and after a few months the lump dispersed. Then came the shock of the drug test findings. 'Because I hadn't been taking drugs, I couldn't understand what had caused the urine test to come back positive,' she was to recall. 'That's when I began to think of the lump. Did I have cancerous cells? Was there any connection? Was I seriously ill in some other way that was affecting my system and making it produce testosterone?

'I suppose I was clutching at straws, but I went for another check with the doctor and explained my fears. I was told there was no connection.'

When it came to her hearing before a BAF panel in London in December 1994, Modahl's medical conditions were deemed not to be significant in the dope test findings. Instead, her defence was to depend on criticism of the Lisbon lab's techniques and procedures. When the Portuguese laboratory officials failed to appear for the hearing, a crucial opportunity to cross-examine them was lost.

Following a full day of hearing evidence, on the second day the five-person panel discussed the case for less than an hour. The panel chairman, Dr Martyn Lucking, read a prepared statement outside the entrance of the hotel to announce that the panel had unanimously found against Modahl. She was condemned as the first British woman ever to fail a drugs test, and faced a four-year ban from athletics. The athlete was devastated.

Even the IAAF, which had been expecting a 'home town' verdict in Modahl's favour, expressed surprise at the outcome. Before the hearing, the IAAF had restated its definition of a testosterone positive: 'Testosterone – a sample will be deemed to be positive for Testosterone where either the ratio of Testosterone to Epitestosterone, or concentration of Testosterone in urine, so exceeds the range of values normally found in humans as not to be consistent with normal endogenous production . . . A sample will not be regarded as positive . . . where an athlete proves by clear and convincing evidence that the abnormal ratio or concentration is attributable to a pathological or physiological condition.' As one IAAF official put it, 'Either she's ill or she's guilty.'

But the Modahls' lawyers concentrated their defence on the degradation of the sample, suggesting that by the time the scientists got round to analysing the urine, the sample was so badly decayed that it could not be a reliable test.

Certainly, according to two senior British drug testers, Professor Arnold Beckett, one of the founders of modern doping control, and Dr David Cowan, his successor as head of London's drug testing laboratory at King's College, the sample was not fit to be tested. Both experts had attended the testing of Modahl's 'B' sample analysis in Lisbon on 30 August 1994 – more than two months after the sample had been taken. Failure to properly refrigerate the sample had seen it smell rank by the time the second test was carried out. Dr Cowan would say later that his laboratory would never consider analysing a sample so badly decayed, and therefore unreliable, as that which was used to prosecute Modahl.

Professor Beckett was more outspoken: when he was in Lisbon, he wanted the test abandoned and the Lisbon lab stripped of its accreditation to conduct international drug tests. According to Professor Beckett, who established sport's doping control procedures during a quarter of a century of work with the International Olympic Committee, the case against Diane Modahl was not proven because it has not been satisfactorily established that the tests were actually carried out on Modahl's urine.

'If Cowan and I had not been conned in Portugal,' Beckett said, 'we would not have gone ahead with the "B" sample test, and there would have been no case to answer. But we were given assurances that the full chain of custody documentation would be forthcoming. It never has.'

In order to protect all doping control samples from outside interference, a set of documentation is supposed to accompany the samples throughout the testing process to account for their whereabouts. Although the BAF hearing was 'satisfied that the specimen tested was that of Mrs Modahl', Modahl's lawyers maintained throughout that the contemporaneous chain of custody documents were never produced, as Professor Beckett had been promised by the Lisbon officials. The International Amateur Athletic Federation's legal advisers, however, took a different view, saying that it was the best chain of custody record they had ever seen. One of their firm actually went to Portugal to interview various officials involved in the testing process at the meeting in order to reconstruct the records from scratch.

'It's the only case I've come across where it has proceeded without such evidence. It seems the panel must have disregarded their own expert, Dr Cowan. The case should never have been brought,' Professor Beckett said.

Nearly a year after the original test, the IAAF bowed to pressure from the Modahls by accepting a request for the remnants of the urine sample to be tested for an unprecedented third time. Then, six months later, in January 1996, the officials in Lisbon announced their refusal to conduct a third set of tests. There is no other system of jurisdiction in the world – apart from in countries ruled by dictators – where the accused is refused the right to question and examine the evidence against them.

Following the Portuguese officials' reluctance to attend the London hearing, and their inability to provide the chain of custody documents, some speculated that their refusal to allow a third test of Modahl's sample probably indicated that the remnants of evidence had probably been flushed down a toilet long before. Certainly, when Modahl went before an appeal panel in London in July 1995, they concluded that the case against Modahl could not be proved beyond reasonable doubt.

It took another eight months, though, before the IAAF eventually accepted the same conclusion, firmly pinning any blame on the Lisbon laboratory when it issued a statement that expressed 'serious concern over the way in which this analysis was handled by the laboratory in Lisbon'. After nearly two years, Diane Modahl was at last free to compete internationally again. But the costs of her struggle against the false accusations of drug use saw her begin a £480,000 law suit against the British Athletic Federation, and had left her bitter against the governing bodies in control of her sport. 'The powerful organisations in control of sport can make or break you,' she said after hearing the decision of the IAAF Council meeting in Cape Town on 25 March 1996. 'I believe there were those who wanted to break me.'

Perhaps Modahl had heard how Primo Nebiolo, the head of the international athletics federation, had banged his fists on the table with frustration during a discussion of the Modahl case at an earlier Council meeting as he demanded, 'We must win this one. We cannot have any more mistakes.'

The task of ensuring that there were 'no more mistakes' was given to Professor Manfred Donike, the German doping expert who had been running drug control in international sport for nearly two decades. It was Donike who supervised the accreditation of all the laboratories licensed to conduct drug testing by the International Olympic Committee. And it was Donike who, in the late 1970s, devised the T:E ratio test to detect illicit testosterone use. Modahl's case presented Professor Donike with serious challenges to two key areas of his responsibility. He, like Nebiolo, was determined to 'win this one'.

What Donike was less concerned with defending was the truth of Modahl's case, for the Cologne-based professor had a record of bending the rules to suit his own ends, sometimes warning German sportsmen that they had failed a drugs test, rather than passing on the paperwork to get them banned. And Professor Donike also had a dark doping secret: he had used performance enhancing drugs himself during his own sporting career.

For the man charged with leading the battle for drug-free sport had used drugs himself when a professional cyclist in the early 1960s. 'There were no rules then,' he admitted. 'You could buy amphetamines over the counter. There was no testing then, no bans. There was not the atmosphere that has been created.'

If Professor Donike had lived, there is little doubt that he would have continued a strong, rearguard action against Modahl's acquittal. He, personally, had too much to lose if the British runner was cleared. The IAAF's own estimates indicated that flaws in the doping control system had cost the sport about $25 million between 1992 and 1996 in challenges in the law courts around the world. But when Professor Donike died of a heart attack during a flight to South Africa in August 1995, with him died official opposition to Diane Modahl's reinstatement in international athletics. His passing left a legacy of doubt and distrust in the drug testing system.

The Modahl case highlighted many of the inconsistencies in a sometimes haphazardly administered system of doping control. Gwen Torrence, the 1992 Olympic 200 metres champion, has often spoken of how she feels she has been victimised by what is supposed to be a random testing system. Torrence had made the mistake, as she sees it, of speaking out against drug cheats. 'I get picked for drug tests at every meet I go to,' she said, angrily. 'You take your life in your hands when you hand over your urine sample to these strangers.' So fearful is Torrence of the consequences of the dope control system that she goes to the extraordinary length of splitting her samples into three, retaining one for independent analysis in case of a 'positive' finding.

As Roger Black, Britain's 1986 and 1990 European champion at 400 metres, said: 'The fact that this has happened to Diane is just a coincidence. It could happen to any of us. Athletes around the world will be under a lot of fear as we take our drug tests.'

It is not only the athletes who have a great deal at stake in doping control. So do the 26 laboratories around the world which the International Olympic Committee has empowered to carry out sporting drug tests. The dope testing system now is a multi-million dollar international business for the labs involved. Manfred Donike's Cologne lab is on a £2 million per year budget. London's testing lab receives nearly £1 million of public funding each year to conduct tests, which can cost nearly £100 per analysis. Other IOC-accredited laboratories have similarly large-scale operations. That is a lot of money to spend on peering at people's pee every day. A serious mistake in doping control, as happened with Utrecht in the case of Trine Hattestad, can see the loss of IOC accreditation and therefore a lot of lost business.

Dr Don Catlin is the director of the accredited testing laboratory in Los Angeles. He does not believe that the 90,000 tests each year on a range of sports which he and his colleagues conduct is enough. 'It's not a large number of tests, not enough, really,' Catlin says in his languid, west coast American way. For despite the problems – such as the cost of testing, the constant questioning of laboratories' methods, the challenges in the courts – Catlin remains convinced that drug testing is totally defensible, and very necessary. 'Is it expensive? Not at all, and not when you look at what drugs is doing to sports. If we gave up testing, that would mean that everyone competing would be *forced* to take drugs.'

Dr Catlin is a long-term advocate of a new system of doping control, what he calls 'steroid profiling'. In effect, he wants to build up a library of every competitor's steroid 'fingerprint'. An initial test at the beginning of an international athlete's career would establish a standard based on the testosterone to epitestosterone ratio. Since that ratio is unique to the individual it would only alter if the athlete were ill or taking drugs. By using steroid profiling, the labs would be comparing the athlete's drug test results with their own history of previous tests. Any deviation from the norm would result in immediate further investigation. 'The road to abolishing testosterone abuse is to test athletes over time,' Catlin said. 'All you have to do with testosterone profiling is join the dots.'

Catlin points out that International Olympic Committee rules on doping control already recommend that, in the event of a positive test, all relevant information on the competitor, including previous test results, should be taken into consideration. A move to regular monitoring would only be an extension of that.

Catlin is keen for a hard line to be taken against cheats because he knows that they are using all possible resources to beat the system. His lab at the University of California receives circulars from around the world offering all sorts of anabolic steroids and related products, for sale by mail order, or offering the services of commercial laboratories, which can carry out 'screening' tests. A practice common in the former eastern bloc, athletes' samples are tested privately and then they are advised on how to avoid a positive test at the next major competition.

Catlin is acutely aware that substances, such as Human Growth Hormone and EPO, erythropoietin (the pharmaceutical equivalent of blood doping), are helping some to evade the testers, but not necessarily fate. He is suspicious of the 'epidemic' of sudden deaths among cyclists from Holland and Belgium in the late 1980s and Scandinavian orienteers in the early 1990s, for which there has never been any satisfactory explanation. 'We need to do some pharmacological detective work there,' he said. 'Our problem is that there is virtually no money spent on research and development in drug testing.' He is embarrassed to admit that for two or three years he ignored findings on probencid, a gout remedy which was not banned from use in sport. At first, Catlin thought nothing of the occasional finding of probencid in a sportsman's drug test, but after a time, when the drug cropped up increasingly often in his analyses, he began to wonder why so many ultra-fit athletes were suffering from gout. It was only after the 1988 Olympics that probencid was banned because it could mask the use of steroids.

'Now probencid's role with steroids was only ever recorded, briefly, in an obscure medical paper from 1957,' Catlin recalls. 'Someone out there went to a great deal of trouble to unearth that paper and test its findings before they used it for sports. It all costs money. That gives some idea of what we're up against.'

Thus it is that some sports administrators refer to 'the war on drugs in sport'. Just like any other war, there are sometimes innocent casualties. The sad part is that a system originally introduced 20 years ago to protect athletes from cheating and drug abuse is now the subject of fear by the very people it is supposed to protect.

Thirteen

Totalitarian Commitment

WOLFGANG SCHMIDT never had managed to find an easy way of getting into his car. The gleaming white, Soviet-made Lada 1600 was among his most cherished possessions, but its small size was an obvious drawback for the 6ft 7in, 18st discus world record-holder. But in the East Berlin of the early 1980s, in the then Deutsche Demokratische Republik, such a car was a prize indeed, driven only by top officials of the government, plus a few of the GDR's top sports stars.

East Germany, as a nation state, was unique in the history of mankind because it had the importance of sport written into its constitution. And Schmidt was one of the state's greatest sporting heroes. He was one of their *Botschafter im Trainingsanzug* – ambassadors in tracksuits. Indeed, even among the many young sportsmen and women, who were usually bulging with equal amounts of muscle and socialist self-belief, Schmidt was so important to East Germany that when the Lada was given to him as reward for his athletics achievements, the presentation was made by Erich Mielke himself. Mielke's official title was minister of state security, but everyone in the GDR knew that his most important position was as the head of the *Staatssicherheitsdienst*, the ruthless secret police, more infamously known as the Stasi.

On this summer afternoon in 1982, Schmidt was making a two-mile journey which he had made thousands of times before from his home, to SC Dynamo. This prestigious Berlin sports club boasted Mielke as its president, since it was owned by the police. Schmidt's membership of the club since the age of 19 effectively made him a policeman, too, a salaried officer of the *Volkspolizei*, or VP. Promoted three times, with a monthly pay cheque, after seven years' service, Schmidt had never once walked the beat or done any real policing. For Schmidt had one of the sinecures common for sportsmen and women in the eastern bloc at that time, allowing him to train full time without being declared 'professional'.

On his way to training that day, Schmidt had not driven far when he spotted the dark red VW Golf closely following him. 'I sped up, but the Golf didn't drop back,' Schmidt recalled. 'After a couple of blocks, I swung quickly into a tiny, narrow street with cars parked on both sides. No one would follow there unless they were chasing me.'

The Golf followed Schmidt. The chase was on.

Like something out of a Len Deighton spy thriller, the huge thrower in the tiny car swerved his way around the East Berlin streets, desperately trying to lose his 'tail'. 'I was moving very fast – 120kph – dodging through traffic. The Golf fell back, out of sight. Then a motorcyclist roared up, and I assumed he would pass, but he held his speed at my side and glared furiously at me. I accelerated again, but there were traffic lights and I could not outrun the motorcycle. I slowed. Then I saw a green-and-white police car in the mirror, and I eased off.'

For Schmidt, the reckoning which had been approaching had finally arrived. His athletics career had been thrown into limbo four months earlier, in March 1982, when the DTSB, the *Deutscher Turn und Sportbund*, the East German sports ministry, had declared Schmidt *Sportverbot*. Schmidt was banned from competition, even banned from training. 'The bastards told me I no longer fitted the system,' Schmidt said.

Schmidt was permitted to do only enough training at SC Dynamo to ease down gradually from the levels required of a top, international competitor to a fit, normal individual. 'They let me keep a locker. They let me eat lunch at SC Dynamo. Beyond that, *Sportverbot!* For the world-record holder? I didn't believe it,' Schmidt recalled for the American magazine *Sports Illustrated* a decade later. 'I convinced myself it was a transparent ploy by the DTSB to break my spirit and make me a sheep like all the others in their goddamned pen. I believed it was a trick. How wrong I was . . .'

Schmidt remained in the Lada, and watched as two cars pulled out of a side street and parked nearby. In his rearview mirror, he saw the red Golf and another car roll up behind him. Out of the four plain cars and the police vehicle came three uniformed VPs and about ten Stasi agents. 'They never asked for my papers and they never called me by name, but I knew this was certainly not a case of mistaken identity. I have sometimes wondered what would have happened if I had refused to go, fought them and fled. Possibly I could have got away for a time, but I knew that if the Stasi really wanted me, they would get me sooner or later.'

Schmidt was shoe-horned into the back of the police car, where a young officer, obviously intimidated by the discus thrower's massive size, had to squeeze in next to him. The police drove Schmidt out of Berlin on the autobahn to Motzener See, a lake about 25 miles outside the city. The car turned into some woods, passed through sentried gates and eventually stopped at a dacha on the lake shore. The building resembled most of the other holiday homes which lined the lakeside, except that it was built of concrete blocks and it had iron bars across every window.

Schmidt was ushered up to the first floor and into a room. It appeared comfortable enough, with its homely bedspread and curtains. But the reality was that it was a cell, a reality which was brought home to him when he heard the turn of the keys and the click of the latches on the double doors. Schmidt was denied the use of a phone to let his parents know what had happened. The guards refused to tell him of what he was charged, or how long he was to be held. Wolfgang Schmidt, the discus world record-holder, Olympic silver medallist in 1976, 1978 European champion, twice awarded Order of Merit of the Fatherland and a hero of the state, was now a prisoner of the state.

It was easy for this good-natured, handsome giant to guess what his 'offence' might have been. Schmidt often irritated the Communist Party apparatchiks in charge of the DTSB. For a start, he was far too friendly with the 'enemies of the state' who competed for the 'decadent western nations'. He had even had an affair with a Canadian woman. And Schmidt's conduct in competitions was not all it should have been. The DTSB was badly embarrassed when he had offended the entire Communist world at the Moscow Olympics in 1980. After placing only fourth, Schmidt had rushed across the infield of the massive Lenin Stadium and ostentatiously shaken his fist at the partisan Soviet spectators who had greeted his every throw with catcalls and jeers.

Yet all those offences might have been forgotten had not Schmidt committed the unforgivable mistake of declaring a desire to leave the German Democratic Republic. The young man's fascination with the West had seemed to grow with each trip abroad to represent the Fatherland. Schmidt even discussed life on the other side of The Wall with team-mates and friends. He would still have been at liberty, though, had he not argued over the matter with his own father in his own home.

Ernst Schmidt won a record number of East German championships – ten – at shot, discus and the decathlon in the early 1950s (only Udo Beyer, the shot putter in the 1980s, would break Schmidt senior's record, with 11 national titles). After the war, and the effective division of his country by the occupying Allied forces, the young Ernst had joined the Communist Party and was to become a leading figure in East German sport.

East Germany was recognised as a new nation by the Soviet Union in 1954, though it was another ten years before the International Olympic Committee accepted the GDR as a separate state for sporting purposes. But by the time of the IOC's clearance in 1964, Ernst Schmidt, as chief coach to the national athletics team, had already helped to build the sporting machine which, within barely a decade, was to dominate international track and field, beating the mighty Soviet and American teams, and – perhaps most importantly – the West Germans, despite the new country's small population of just 16 million.

Schmidt senior was a man with a mission, since the German Democratic Republic's constitution demanded that the superiority of its system should be demonstrated through sport. On the basis of their height, weight, limb length and aptitude tests, children of seven and eight years old were selected for particular sports and put into special schools to hone and develop their natural abilities as runners, throwers, swimmers, rowers or weight-lifters. The best became full-time sportsmen or women, with full-time coaches to train them, physiologists to monitor their progress, and doctors to maintain their health. The state paid all the costs of its sports development: as much as £400 million per year by the 1980s. While that was cheaper than being in an arms race, it was still a massive proportion of the small country's meagre wealth.

For the 20 years up to 1982, Ernst Schmidt was East Germany's chief coach of men's throws, and thus supervised his son's rise to the top of the world's discus throwers. Ernst's success as a coach ensured he maintained his position in a system riddled with intrigue. Wolfgang's success in competition was a further guarantee of the Schmidts' status. This status was demonstrated in a number of ways which, perhaps, many westerners might take for granted, but which in the old eastern bloc were precious comforts in an otherwise often bleak life. Wolfgang's Lada was one example. The Schmidts' home on Stahlheimer Strasse was another.

Unusually for East Berliners, the family of four (including Wolfgang's mother and sister) enjoyed a state-owned apartment with four cosy rooms. That was four times as many rooms as any regular East German worker's family might ever hope to call home in this paradise for the people. The Schmidts had turned their home into a virtual shrine to Wolfgang's sporting excellence: shelves lined the walls with the trophies, medals and pictures which their son had collected since he won his first national title at the age of 15.

Yet the Schmidts did not always enjoy domestic bliss. The modern, outward-looking son and his card-carrying Communist father were often at loggerheads over their country's politics. 'Our arguments about socialism went on all our lives,' Wolfgang said. 'Father would give me one of his many slogans: "Jeder ist seines Gluckes Schmied" – "Life is what you make it." And I would scream back, "You know what my slogan is? Better dead than Red! Just give me a hole, and I am gone!".'

What Wolfgang Schmidt objected to most fiercely was also his ultimate downfall: for he was not an individual, but merely another asset of the state, a weapon in their propaganda war against the West. For years, the DTSB had provided Wolfgang with his home, his car, the best coaches, the best food, the best doctors. The price of his disloyalty would be to have his very essence, his discus throwing, denied to him.

Schmidt was detained at the dacha without charge for nearly two weeks, subjected to repetitive interrogation each day, and denied the opportunity to phone his parents or a lawyer. 'On orders of the district attorney,' a stiff-looking Stasi man read to Schmidt in his cell ten days after his arrest, 'a warrant for your arrest has been issued, and preliminary proceedings have been initiated against you on the grounds of the strong suspicion that you have made preparations for illegally crossing the border.'

Schmidt was then taken back to Berlin and the *Untersuchungschaftanstalt* – UHA – a grim Stasi remand prison. He was to be held there for another six weeks. Each day through that time, Schmidt was interrogated, the same questions each day from the same Stasi officer. They were trying to grind him down. Sometimes, once every two weeks or so, a senior Stasi man, who called himself Colonel Wiedemann, would come to question Schmidt. He arranged special meals of steak and asparagus, plus enormous bowls of ice cream, a feast compared to the usual thin rations of sausage and bread with rancid margarine. 'Wiedemann wondered how I planned to live without my sport. I told him I had no intention of living without my sport.'

Soon after arriving at UHA, Schmidt was allowed to write to his parents. He needed a lawyer, he told them. Gretel, his mother, went to the law firm of Wolfgang Vogel, who had been involved in the exchange of the American U-2 pilot, Gary Powers, for two Soviet spies in 1962, and then, 14 years later, had helped arrange the exchange of the Soviet dissident Anatoli Shcharansky. With the help of Vogel's law firm, it was not long before Schmidt was allowed to see his parents. Now allowed to receive four letters each month, Schmidt soon learned that his father was being forced to retire from his job as a coach for the DTSB. The son's disgrace had had wider consequences for his family. Wolfgang Schmidt's trial was set for 12 October, three months after his arrest. It was held in a suburb of Berlin, the courtroom empty, not even Schmidt's family allowed to attend.

The first witness for the prosecution was Jochen Bruggmann. Bruggmann had met Schmidt at a track meeting in the spring of 1981 when he asked the champion for his autograph. He worked his way into Schmidt's life so effectively that he became a frequent guest at the apartment on Stahlheimer Strasse. On the witness stand, Bruggmann, the 'friend', coldly spoke of Schmidt's criticism of East Germany and his desire to leave the country. Wiedemann testified too. The trial took one day. There was little defence that Schmidt could offer. The next day the judge sentenced Schmidt to 18 months in prison. 'When I get out, I'll still be able to throw, and I'll show them!'

Schmidt was transferred to a prison in Frankfurt an der Oder, about 50 miles east of Berlin. When he left the UHA, they gave him the clothes he had been wearing when arrested. His trousers were now far too big around the waist, the shirt was loose and baggy. He tried to settle in and do his 'time'. Sharing a four-room apartment with 20 other inmates, Schmidt knew he had to be careful. 'I didn't complain about the GDR or the sports system. Everybody knew that if he said anything out of line, someone could grass you to the authorities. It could add months to the sentence.'

Schmidt had to work in the prison garage, repairing and cleaning prison vehicles. He watched television with his cellmates and was allowed to do some training, lifting weights and doing some running around the prison yard. He was still interrogated at least once a month by Wiedemann. Schmidt dubbed him 'My brainwasher'.

'I looked forward to the steak and the ice cream, but I did not like what he said,' Schmidt remembers. 'He kept asking, "What do you want to do with yourself when you get out of jail?" I never varied my answer: "I would like to become a world-class competitor in the discus again." And he would shake his head: "Not possible anymore. Not possible ever".'

As the months passed, Schmidt became more frustrated. He asked another inmate if there was anything he could try to get an early release. He was told to make a formal application to Weidemann for an exit visa. On 6 April 1983, Schmidt did exactly that. The Stasi colonel seemed surprised, but he offered Schmidt his own ballpoint pen to write the request. 'I only wish I had known what trouble it would cause.'

He had no reaction from the authorities for about eight weeks. Then one morning, the warden and two guards bundled him out of his work area and into a 10ftx10ft solitary cell. Ten days passed, and he was moved again, this time back to a normal cell. After a brief bout of questioning from the warden, Schmidt lost his temper. The guards were ordered to return Schmidt to solitary, and on the threshold of his dank, dark cell, Schmidt lost his nerve. He could not face another second inside the stinking cubicle. He fought. The guards beat Schmidt into the cell with their truncheons, hitting him across his back time and time again. 'Their eyes were popping and they were grunting with every blow. They pounded harder, harder on my back and shoulders. I gave up. I might beat these two, but there were dozens of guards.

'Sometime around the seventh day of my second ten days in solitary, Wiedemann came from Berlin. I was summonsed to an office downstairs. "Have you gone mad?" he asked. "Do you want to add two years to your sentence? I suggest you withdraw the exit visa request".'

Schmidt did not withdraw his application. After his second ten days in solitary, he was returned to his usual duties. His once mighty frame was now badly bruised and sore from the beating, and from trying to sleep on the slatted wooden bed in the solitary cell. Schmidt had lost a stone in weight in little more than a week. He got little sympathy from his fellow inmates – they resented his fame and former privileges, they felt he was only getting what he deserved – but at least one of them warned him. The word on the block was that the guards had decided to break Schmidt unless he withdrew his exit visa application.

Schmidt could not face another spell in solitary, and was frightened at the prospect that there might be other punishments for him. The next time he visited, Schmidt told Wiedemann that he had changed his mind about leaving East Germany. The Stasi man dictated as Schmidt hurriedly scrawled the withdrawal: 'Herewith I withdraw my application for an exit visa. It is my wish to work in the GDR as a coach in the throwing events or as the caretaker of a fitness club.' The colonel paused for thought, then insisted that Schmidt add another line: 'My decision is voluntary.'

Five weeks later, on 14 October 1983, Schmidt was released from prison, ten weeks ahead of time. 'That was all it took – telling them a couple of lies they wanted to hear.'

The warden who had flung Schmidt into solitary had tears in his eyes when the prisoner was about to leave, and would not let him go without having a picture taken together with the former inmate of his jail. Wiedemann was waiting outside the prison gate, and took Schmidt to a waiting car for the journey to SC Dynamo, Schmidt's old club.

Waiting for Schmidt there was Major General Heinz Pommer, vice-president of SC Dynamo, whose rank was held in the Stasi itself, and Manfred Ewald. Ewald's presence in this little reception committee would have been an honour under any other circumstances. A close personal friend of Erich Honecker, the GDR President, Ewald, as the president of the DTSB, was the mastermind behind the East German sporting machine. 'They asked about my plans for the future,' Schmidt recalled. '"I would like to compete again,"' I said.

'Ewald said, "Oh, please, Wolfgang, do go ahead and try. We are behind you".' It was not long before Schmidt had his Lada 1600 returned, washed and polished, and he was also told that the house in the country which he and his father had been working on before the incarceration had been completed and furnished, under Stasi orders. But the assurances and benefits were just another twist in the systematic, psychological torture to break the man's will. Wolfgang Schmidt was never again to compete for East Germany, nor was he permitted to rejoin the international training programme. Instead, he was effectively sentenced to another four years, this time doing time while trapped in East Berlin, coaching the children of army officers. He was still *Sportverbot.*

Several times, Schmidt got involved in plots to escape, all failed. The Stasi uncovered his final attempt through a bugging device built into his country house. The secret police even warned Schmidt against illegal escape attempts and told him to make another application for an exit visa instead.

A year later, on 2 November 1987, Schmidt finally was allowed to leave the German Democratic Republic. He stayed with some relatives in Hamburg, and started training immediately. A Stuttgart sports club offered him good facilities, a small stipend for food, a free apartment and an £8,000-a-year job with Mercedes-Benz that allowed him time to train whenever he wished.

Six years with no competition, though, has its effect. The lack of training had taken its toll, too. It takes many years to make a champion, and Schmidt soon found that it can take almost as long to remake a champion. At 34, time was not on his side, either, although discus throwers do like to say that they, like good wine, mature with age.

After having to watch the Seoul Olympic Games from the stands – the International Olympic Committee insists that athletes who change citizenship must hold their new passport for at least one year before being allowed to compete at the Games – in 1989, aged 35, Schmidt was once again ranked as the world's Number One, spinning the discus out to 70.92 metres, the best throw in the world that year and his best throw since he had set his world record of 71.16 metres 11 years before. To add to the five East German records he had set between 1975 and 1978, Wolfgang Schmidt set three West German records in 1988 and 1989.

The following year, 1990, in Split, amid an intranational tension which was soon to become the Yugoslavian civil war, Wolfgang Schmidt returned to championship competition for the first time since he had made his angry gesture to the crowd at the 1980 Olympics. He had been European champion in 1978 when wearing the blue vest of the GDR. At 36, 12 years on from his last appearance in these championships, Schmidt, now wearing the white and red vest of West Germany, took the European bronze medal in the discus. Schmidt had gone into the sixth and final round of the discus final in second place, only for his successor as East German champion, Jürgen Schult, to relegate him to third by heaving the discus a championship-winning 64.58 metres.

As they had always done from the Olympic Games in 1964, East German athletes were to the fore, winning 34 medals. But Split was to be the last time that Germany would have two teams competing internationally. Politically, the world had changed dramatically after Schmidt had managed to leave East Berlin. Two years after he had crossed the border, the Berlin Wall came down. The Stasi men who had kept Schmidt and thousands of others penned behind the Iron Curtain now found themselves running for their lives.

Schmidt, despite all his efforts, never did get another chance of the ultimate sporting glory, to win an Olympic gold medal. Robbed of too many years of his peak by a political system, it was a sporting mundanity – injury – which prevented him representing the reunited Germany in Barcelona in 1992. At 38, his throwing career was over.

But it was only in 1992 that the tensions between the two German sporting systems began to be revealed. As the old East German regime was dismantled, so more of its secrets came out into the open. Not only had Schmidt been watched and listened to by Stasi officers. He had been training and competing alongside Stasi officers, too.

It was perhaps the ultimate irony that the Stasi, which had the job of suppressing internal unrest and discontent in the old GDR, would ultimately provide the wider world with the deepest insight into sporting life in the old East Germany. For in keeping tabs on everyone with an obsessional detail, the Stasi, with its plain clothes army of 90,000 officers and 170,000 snoops and collaborators, seemed to have recorded every semi-official meeting, every conversation, every hiccup during the GDR's brief existence. When the Wall finally came down and Stasi offices were opened up by western officials, there was more than 50 miles of files to be examined.

Among the western officials given the task of combing through the GDR's bureaucratic remnants was Professor Werner Franke. A prominent biochemist and chairman of the science council of the German Cancer Research Centre in Heidelberg, Professor Franke had more than a passing interest in East Germany's sports science, since his wife, Brigitte Berendonk, had competed in the pentathlon for East Germany before fleeing to the West in time to make the Olympic discus finals at the 1968 and 1972 Games for West Germany.

Acting on a tip-off from a former East German hammer coach, and making the most of the confusion that reigned in the handover between the two authorities during 1989 and 1990, Franke and Berendonk unearthed evidence of something which had long been suspected, but never proven: widespread, systematic drug use by East German sportsmen and women.

'We were very scared,' said Professor Franke, 'because many things still had not changed in the East. Even at that time, some people who had released to the public secrets of the old regime just disappeared. Two were found dead.'

Franke got access to the files held at a military hospital at Bad Saarow. 'They had destroyed most copies of reports in the shredder, but I knew I had to get into the military academy because nothing gets destroyed there without an order.' Using a small 'spy' camera, Franke obtained document after document, until eventually he uncovered files which came from the very heart of the GDR system – the Stasi.

The paperwork showed that at centres in Jena, Leipzig and Berlin organised medically supervised doping of sportsmen and women was conducted. The most important was the *Forschungsingstitut fur Koerperkultur und Sport* (FKS) in Leipzig, founded in 1970, and with more than 400 doctors and academics on the staff dedicated to training, psychology and development of sports. The collected know-how of the FKS was considered so important by politicians that they decided to preserve it for the common German future. The continuation of the institute was expressly written into the unification treaty – a unique privilege among research institutes of the former GDR.

In the Stasi files which recorded the progress of athletes, the athletes' names were in code. But through meticulous research, comparing competition results on the files against the known performances in championships, Berendonk and Franke were able to identify several of East Germany's leading competitors. These included Heike Drechsler, the 1983 world champion at long jump, Marita Koch, who still holds the women's 400 metres world record, and Jürgen Schult, who succeeded Schmidt as the GDR's top discus thrower.

In 1971, the year before the Munich Olympics, the Stasi took control of East Germany's sport system. Anabolic substances were developed in Leipzig's sports institute and then manufactured in Jena. The Stasi controlled everything, including drug use and monitoring, and athletes' foreign travel.

According to Professor Franke, the Stasi documents 'proved without doubt that every single East German world class athlete was doped'.

'In just one sports club,' Berendonk said, 'the University Club of Leipzig, we discovered not only that Thomas Munkelt, the 1980 Olympic sprint hurdles champion, was a member of the Leipzig "steroids" club, but that whole teams of women track and field athletes were given these drugs.'

The drugs included anabolic steroids such as oral turinabol, the hormone testosterone, and another steroid drug, STS 646, which had never been passed by the drug control authority for human use. Girls and boys as young as 14 were administered the drugs, often secreted among mineral tablets or in vitamin drinks, but rarely with the knowledge of the child or its parents.

The files confirmed that East Germany had begun a systematic use of performance enhancing drugs in the early 1960s. Similar drugs were also being used in the West, but never in such an organised or supervised manner. Drugs were not outlawed until the Mexico City Olympics of 1968, and even then there was no effective test for steroids until 1973. This test was not generally adopted until 1975.

By then the scientifically thorough East Germans had prepared themselves. They did this by testing the testers – sending over a group of scientists to London to learn all they could about the new testing procedures being developed at St Thomas's Hospital by Professor Raymond Brooks.

The most incriminating records discovered after the Berlin Wall came down were the minutes of top-level meetings which included Manfred Ewald, the powerful head of the DTSB, his internal memos and the frequent reports of a sports doctor code-named IMV Technik. In the minutes of one of the earliest meetings, held in 1975, it is recorded that: 'Manfred Ewald stressed that, in order to win, everything possible must be done, and that *Sportmedizin* had its part to play.'

Ewald was convinced of the effectiveness of a drugs regime for success in sport, but was equally convinced that the GDR could not afford to have any bad publicity from positive drugs tests. In 1978, at another of the meetings minuted in the Stasi files, Ewald proposed that if there were no positive tests at the Moscow Olympics in 1980, the lab staff at Kreischa should be decorated.

It was clear to Professor Brooks quite what the East Germans experts had been about when they came to his laboratory in London in the early 1970s. 'The East Germans dedicated their centralised scientific effort to beating the system,' Professor Brooks said. 'They were able to use their laboratory at Kreischa, accredited to conduct international testing by the IOC, to monitor their own athletes and so were able to take them off drugs at the last possible moment. They wouldn't let their athletes leave the country unless they were clear.'

Ewald also realised, though, that some westerners such as Professor Brooks were wondering if the East German performances were too good to be believed. Sooner or later, Ewald told one meeting, people were going to start asking awkward questions. He then discussed the possibility of 'sacrificing' an older athlete, nearing the end of his career, to illustrate to the rest of the world the GDR's apparent no-nonsense, tough stand against drugs cheats.

But by eliminating the results they did not want – positive drug tests – the East Germans got exactly the results that they really wanted: 30 Olympic medals in 1968; 80 at Munich in 1972; 109 in 1976; 149 in 1980; and 127 in 1988.

Despite such dramatic improvement in East German results, and the suspicions of many, no action was taken by the international sporting community to investigate. In fact, in the often cosy world of international sports politics, Ewald and the GDR were honoured. As a respected member of the world sporting community, Ewald was awarded the Olympic Order, a prestigious award in the gift of the International Olympic Committee. In 1985, he and his country were also honoured by holding a session of the IOC in Berlin. There, in front of IOC President Juan Antonio Samaranch, Ewald even had the gall to announce that, 'The GDR closely identifies itself with the humanistic content of the Olympic ideal.'

Yet the perversion of the Olympic ideals went even deeper in East Germany's all-conquering sporting system. The researchers delving into the Stasi records eventually indentified the mysteriously code-named 'Technik' as Dr Manfred Hoppner, the head of the IOC-accredited testing laboratory at Kreischa, and for many years a member of the International Olympic Committee's influential medical committee.

Hoppner was never really working for the greater ideals of the Olympic movement: he was working for the Stasi, right from the time he filed his first report in August 1973. His 16 years' worth of records are possibly the most complete work of research into the effects of performance enhancing drugs on athletes.

As befits a 'secret agent', the reports from 'Technik' are shrouded in code. Steroids are never openly referred to – instead, they are described as *unterstutzende Mittel* ('additional means'). Of course, drugs were not the only reason East German athletes won so many golds. The early identification of talent, the nurturing of that talent, and a lot of extremely hard work all played a role. Not all East German sportsmen and women took drugs – there are recorded examples, such as the case of top marathon runner Uta Pippig, which show that the drugs had no discernible effect on their performances and therefore the dosages were stopped. But drugs certainly played an important role in the rise of East German sport. The example of one of the first East German sporting 'experiments', Margitta Gummel, illustrates why the GDR put such an emphasis on the role of drugs. Gummel's use of turinabol was reported to a secret meeting of coaches and doctors in 1973. Reviewing their team's achievements in 1972, Gummel's shot putting was shown to have improved dramatically.

Without drugs, Gummel was fifth in the shot at the 1964 Olympics, throwing 16.91 metres. Over the next four years, she improved by sheer hard work to 17.86 metres. Then, recorded as having been given 5mg a day of turinabol from 28 July 1968 to one week before the Olympic final on 20 October that year, Gummel managed to improve by nearly two metres to a world record and gold medal-winning 19.61 metres. Four years later, by now on dosages of 10mg a day, Gummel took silver at the Munich Olympics when she threw 20.43 metres. Despite the Stasi records, Gummel has always denied using steroids. In 1992, Gummel was a member of the German Olympic Committee. It may be that, like many former East German sporting stars, she did not know what she was being given among her 'food supplements'. But even in 1995, turinabol was still showing up in positive drug tests on German athletes.

When Susen Tiedtke – a product of the East German system who won the long jump bronze medal for the now united Germany at the 1995 World Indoor Championships – tested positive in an out-of-competition test in Berlin in March, the drug discovered was turinabol, described by leading drug expert, Professor Manfred Donike, as 'the drug of choice for East Germans'.

Whatever East German athletes were using, the Stasi were undoubtedly watching them, just as they watched Wolfgang Schmidt and every other privileged member of East Germany's sporting elite. For the Stasi even had spies within the sport stars' ranks.

Among the documents uncovered by Berendonk and Franke, and published in their 1992 book, *Doping Dokumente*, were reports of meetings with Heike Drechsler. Drechsler, a world champion at 17 years of age, was a model sportswoman of the GDR: a Communist Party member, and a member of the *Volkskammer* (people's parliament), the meetings between the Stasi and the long jumper established her in a long-term, secret career as an informer. In the meeting reports, Drechsler, codenamed 'Jump', gave details of the behaviour of other top performers, such as Marlies Göhr. A team-mate of Drechsler's at Jena, Göhr is referred to in the reports as 'my enemy'. Gohr's coach was called 'an alcoholic' by Drechsler.

Doping Dokumente further revealed that Drechsler had been administered drugs between 1982 and 1984, allegations which the athlete unwisely decried as lies at a press conference after she had won the Olympic gold at the Barcelona Games of 1992. 'It's a lie,' Drechsler told the assembled journalists, 'I never took steroids. I am a big talent. I don't need them.' But at the end of 1994, Drechsler lost the ensuing libel case brought by Berendonk, and was ordered to pay around £7,500 costs and give a formal apology.

There were other nasty shocks for the former darlings of the East German system, though, as the sports machine was dismantled, more slowly but just as thoroughly as the Berlin Wall which had come to symbolise the old GDR's separateness from the rest of Germany. East Germany's immense sporting infrastructure, once abandoned, left many people out of work. There was no way, for instance, among all the other costs of reconstruction and unification, that the West German government was going to pick up the tab to maintain the many élite sports centres in the old East, or to pay the salaries of the coaches and scientists who were employed there. In 1989, East Germany employed an estimated 4,500 full-time sports coaches. By 1992, the new Germany hired just a few hundred coaches. The rest, and their sporting charges, had to make a living in some other way. There were new priorities, a whole new system. Market forces had taken over. According to Volker Frischke, a top swimming coach at SC Berlin who guided Franziska van Almsick to international domination, 'In the past, you were given money before you were good. Now, you only get money when you have good results.'

Some coaches managed to find money through sponsorship deals with clubs. Others looked to other countries to sell their expertise. Technically, East German coaches were among the best trained, most experienced and most successful in the world. But it was not long after the fall of the Berlin Wall before it became evident that it was not only curious German scientists and journalists who had obtained the secrets of the Stasi's files on drug use in the old GDR.

Reports from further east suggested that several East German coaches had started to work in the world's last remaining Communist totalitarian superpower, China. It seemed that the fall of the Berlin Wall may not have only marked the ending of one sporting era, but also the beginning of another.

Fourteen

Out of Africa

IT WAS ONE of those days native Oregonians call 'as grey as a big dog'. The clouds had scudded in off the cold north-west Pacific and made the streets of Portland slick with rain. By the time the cars turning into the PacWest Center had descended into the skyscraper's underground car park, their windscreens were covered with an oily, urban, grimy grit. There, buried below the ground in the Third Basement Level, a smiling attendant with 'Henry' on his name tag happily polished the dirty windscreens until they gleamed again. When Henry Rono was earning more than £100,000 a year as one of the greatest distance runners the world has ever seen, he used to take equally good care of his own cars.

Rono these days works from 7.30 in the morning sometimes until 9.30 at night. Where he works is a cold, dark echo chamber, full of petrol fumes and carbon monoxide. He tries not to breathe in the choking smog too deeply. It is a long time since he last smelt air as clean and light as he remembers from his home in the Nandi Hills of Kenya's Rift Valley. 'When I go back, I want to go back as a hero, as a winner,' he says. It is a long time since Henry Rono won something. At least now he thinks he is winning his battle with the bottle.

Rono was last in Kenya in 1987. For nine years he did not see his wife, Jennifer, and missed his son and daughter growing up. The farm which Rono once bought with his earnings from running has been closed and demolished, and he ekes a living as a car park attendant, looking forward to the day when he hopes to race again. 'I need to resolve my problems through running,' he says. For running is what caused Henry Rono's problems. Like many Kenyan children, the young Kipwambok Rono used to run up to 12 miles each day, across country in the thin air one finds at high altitude, 7,000ft above sea level. Rono ran not because he was entered into a world-beating training regime, and certainly not because he wanted to. To the children of Kenya, running comes as naturally as the dawn. Young Rono ran simply out of necessity. It was the only way for him to get to school.

Not all Kenyans are born to be great runners. Kenya is a multi-ethnic nation of 23 million people, drawn from 41 different tribal groups. Born in the Kilibwoni area, Henry Rono's birthright was to be born into the running tribe of Africa. Only 300,000 Kenyans are like Rono, of the Kalenjin, which comprises 16 sub-tribes, including the Nandi, herdsmen who centuries ago emigrated south from the Sudanese Nile until they reached the high savanna of the Rift Valley, where they settled near the shores of Lake Turkana.

The Nandi have developed a rugged, innate ability to deal with pain and to run at pace over long distances. As Josh Kimeto, one of Kenya's legion of world-class runners, once observed when one of his American college team-mates was complaining of a twinge in his knee, 'Pain? Pain is when you're 12 years old and they take you out into the bush, cut off your foreskin and beat you for three days. That is pain.'

For food, young Nandi would go as a group into the bush hunting antelope, chasing after their quarry, relentlessly jogging and sprinting, sprinting and striding, sometimes for hours, until their prey was forced to stop through exhaustion. In the early years of this century, the trait was modernised somewhat, making the Nandi notorious with neighbouring tribes because of their cattle-rustling raids. Significantly, the local colonial authorities decided to direct Nandis' energies into more 'positive' pastimes, such as sport.

Since the 1964 Olympics, the world has been witness to the outcome of that policy. These tough, hard-working Kenyans have won 32 Olympic medals, including eight at the Barcelona Games in 1992, a tally which placed them fourth in the athletics medal table behind the United States, the former Soviet states and Germany. And this by a nation whose team ignores esoteric field events, instead concentrating on running races of one lap of the track or more.

Kenya's hall of fame might have been greater were it not for politically inspired boycotts of the 1976 and 1980 Olympics, which denied one of their greatest runners his chance of Games glory. Henry Rono's home region had already produced Kip Keino, winner of Olympic golds in 1968 and 1972. It was similar medal-winning potential that saw Rono recruited into the American collegiate sports system in 1976. Washington State University, WSU, offered Rono, aged 24, an athletics scholarship to attend the university tucked away in America's top left-hand corner. It was while at WSU that Rono's talent blossomed. 'What we are witnessing is not taught and is not learned. It is a mysterious gift and we have never seen a man more blessed with it than this one,' said Bill Exum, the United States' track team manager, after seeing Rono destroy a world-class field at Hayward Field in Eugene, Oregon, during the Kenyan's first summer in America.

Kenya's Olympic boycotts hurt Rono – 'It made me cry, when I saw my friend Steve Ovett there and I was not there, winning medals'. Nevertheless, there were compensations. Although athletics was, supposedly, strictly amateur then, Rono's paid performances at European invitation meetings quickly made him a rich man, especially by the standards of his home country, where even today the average annual salary is just 1,000 shillings, or about £20. To a Kenyan, mere selection to run in a race abroad is akin to getting all six numbers on the National Lottery.

In 81 days in 1978, Rono broke four world records, from 3,000 to 10,000 metres, and the steeplechase, too. As his fame grew, so did his wealth. From the $1,500 fee he got for his first world record, over 10,000 metres in Vienna in 1977, Rono was soon able to demand $6,000 per race. By 1980, shoe manufacturers Nike made Rono their highest paid athlete when they put him on an annual contract worth $150,000.

But outside his running, Rono had little to occupy himself beyond the company of friends, and he found plenty of friends in city bars when he was buying the round. 'It was beer, beer, beer all the time. Anyone who was my friend would sit and drink with me,' Rono remembers. After a while, he began to do more drinking than running. For a time, he still managed to turn in the performances, such as in 1982 when he ran a 10,000 metres race at Hayward Field despite being more than a stone over his racing weight. Somehow Rono managed to win a relentless duel against Alberto Salazar, the record-breaking American marathon runner.

A decade later, while the Nike corporation has named one of its gleaming buildings in its headquarters complex after Salazar, on the other side of the same Oregon state Rono works a 14-hour day in the bowels of a different building. In the end, the drink beat the runner. 'All those years you are drinking,' he says, 'you're training in a different manner.'

No one, probably least of all Rono himself, knows the real reason for his drinking. The loneliness of this long-distance runner must have been one factor. The manner in which he had greatness, and great wealth, thrust upon him was probably another. Perhaps the acute disappointments of missing two Olympics also made him ponder the pointlessness of all the hours during the bleak winter months which he had spent, with his head bent into the wind and rain, running repetition quarter miles against the stopwatch.

What Rono will never blame is himself. He lays some of the blame for his plight at the door of John Chaplin, his coach while at WSU. Described as a combative man who in his spare time bred fighting cocks, Chaplin's control over the Kenyan was absolute. One day, when Rono was racing in the steeplechase at Hayward Field, it was clear as the early laps clicked past that the Kenyan was on world record schedule. Chaplin stepped on to the side of the track and waved at his charge with his raincoat, telling him to slow down. 'You don't break a record in a place where they don't like foreigners,' Chaplin told Rono. Turning to amazed reporters, Chaplin said, 'We'll save the record for Seattle.' Four weeks later, just as Chaplin commanded, Rono turned on the magic once more and broke the steeple-chase world record by three seconds.

'He had a leash on me,' Rono says today. 'I didn't know it was a free world. It was like being in jail.' There were other factors in the demise of Rono, too. Although WSU offered him the chance of a degree education, with the prospect of employment after his running career was over, Rono spent little time in lectures. He preferred to run alone through the forests and along the trail that swoops down a canyon 2,000ft to the Snake River. Even for runners of Rono's ability, though, there are few openings for graduates in running 100 miles per week.

Rono and money never went together too happily, either. Wherever Rono travelled when he was on the athletics circuit, he carried with him an expensive-looking, Italian-made leather briefcase. It rarely left his side, because it contained his appearance fees, cash paid for running in races, which in those days of 'shamateurism' would have been large wads of untraceable used notes. Rono says that he sometimes had as much as $100,000 stuffed inside the case.

The British world record-breaker, Steve Ovett, tells a story about the time he, Rono and the Kenyan's famous briefcase shared a flight to Tokyo for an end-of-season all-star meeting. On the plane, Rono decided that he wanted to sleep. First, he tried to curl up under a blanket, clutching his briefcase to his chest. When he found that position impossibly uncomfortable, he asked Ovett to hold on to his cherished case for him.

As the hours crept past, Ovett's curiosity got the better of him. Could he crack the combination? As Ovett recalled, 'What sort of number would Henry pick? My fingers rolled the lock – zero, zero, zero – and I touched the catch and the case sprang open. As the locks sprang up so did the blanket beside me and two arms reached out and grabbed the case. Henry was not so much cross as puzzled. "How did you know the combination?"'

After Ovett explained that Rono could have changed the combination after he bought the case, the Kenyan's innocence of the ways of the western world was made plain. 'I thought they were all different,' he said.

So it is that while Ovett lives now in a castle on the Scottish borders which he bought with the proceeds of his golden athletics career, Rono works like some latterday troglodyte in an underground car park in Portland, scraping muck off windscreens for $5.75 an hour.

When his racing career eventually staggered to its drunken end, Rono decided to shun running altogether. He put on a lot of weight, drifting from small town and small job to small town and small job. 'There was a time when I didn't have running in my heart any more,' he says. 'It was my experiences in the sport that did that to me.' Then he found he was shunned by his own country. When he turned to the Kenyan embassy for help, 'They told me I was a disgraced man in my own country. Then they gave me five dollars to go away.'

Rono is angry at the way he has been treated by Kenya, and by those in authority within the athletics governing body, the Kenya Amateur Athletic Association, or KAAA. 'The people who were around me, they were embezzling my money,' Rono claims today. 'I was surrounded by fear. When you come from nothing, you cannot trust anyone. But some Kenyan officials would say to me, "Henry, you cannot carry thousands of dollars around with you. Give us that money, the Kenya AAA needs it, we will look after it for you." There was a lot of manipulation going on. I never saw the money after that.'

Rono as victim. There are other versions of how he came to lose so much money: he had a house built in Nairobi, where his wife still lives, but a farming venture was less successful. Bizarrely, there is also the suggestion that, wherever Rono went in Europe, he would open a new bank account for the cash that he had just received. The only problem was that, like his briefcase's combination lock, he never bothered to learn the new numbers. But what is known is that, as an American-based runner at a time when payments in athletics were not legitimate, there was never any need for Rono to make formal cash transfers to the Kenya AAA.

It took nearly a decade before the allegations Rono made about corruption within the the Kenya AAA were acted upon. In that time, many more runners came forward with similar accusations. Athletes such as Moses Tanui, who was to become 1991 world champion at 10,000 metres. In 1988, Tanui ran in a race in Spain, and the organiser sent the $3,000 fee to Nairobi. Eventually, Tanui was paid $10 by the Kenya AAA for his efforts. When this happened again, Tanui became so incensed that he eventually moved to Italy, so that Kenyan officials could never again get their hands on his money.

By 1988, the whispers of back-handers and financial malpractice against the all-powerful honorary secretary-general of the Kenya AAA, Robert Ouko, had become so loud that the Kenyan government felt bound to investigate. Ouko was suspended, together with the association's treasurer and his deputy. The trio were never returned to office.

Ouko had been a great runner in his own right, winning the 1970 Commonwealth Games 800 metres title and an Olympic gold in the 4x400 metres relay at the 1972 Munich Games. Once he was elected to the all-powerful position in the Kenya AAA in 1984, though, 'he acted more like an old-style colonial ruler than an ex-athlete', according to one Kenyan runner.

Ouko had total control over where and when Kenya's top athletes might race. When a foreign promoter wanted a Kenyan athlete to compete at his meeting, he would send the invitation to Ouko at the Kenya AAA offices. Ouko then dispensed the invitations to the runners of his choosing. He even kept individual athletes' passports in his desk drawer to control their travelling. Rarely would the athletes discover what fees might be due to them.

As amateurism was dispensed with in 1985, Ouko should have established special trust funds for the runners' legitimate earnings. The Kenya AAA would have been entitled to deduct an administration fee, but the money would have been clearly earmarked for the athletes. No such trusts were ever set up by Ouko, however, and consequently athletes' money disappeared forever into the morass of the KAAA's general finances. In the meantime, Ouko, despite spending so much time working, officially in an unpaid capacity for the KAAA, had managed to privately acquire property and expensive foreign cars.

Ouko was exposed in early 1988 after two of Kenya's greatest ever runners, John Ngugi and Paul Kipkoech, had between them won nearly £30,000 by placing first and second in the world's richest road race on the paradise Pacific island of Bali. The race organiser was aware of the difficulties Ngugi and Kipkoech were having over their payments, and sent the athletes' cheque for $58,000 directly to the International Amateur Athletic Federation, by-passing Nairobi. The international federation refused to send the money on to the Kenya AAA until they had been sent proper proof that the runners had trust funds.

All further investigations into Ouko's activities proved inconclusive, however. An official KAAA report, published in 1989, estimated that at least £30,000 in appearance fees earned overseas by Kenyan athletes in 1987-88 had disappeared, its whereabouts described as 'a mystery'. But no criminal proceedings were recommended.

The financial accounts of the KAAA were in such a mess, with no bank statements nor audited accounts for nearly five years, that none of the specific allegations against Ouko or the association treasurer could ever be checked. 'Ouko's response to our questions was highly deficient,' the then IAAF secretary, John Holt, said at the time. Yet in one of the administrative ambivalences seemingly common to athletics, Ouko has retained a position on the IAAF's influential technical committee, his latest nomination in October 1994 being made by the African confederation.

That nomination was hardly likely to come from Kenya. Ouko was ousted eventually from the Kenya AAA in 1988 because he allowed one of Kenya's top runners to race in South Africa, before the post-apartheid Republic was welcomed back into the world's sporting community. But his reputation still dogged Ouko when, three years later, he tried to organise a Kenyan junior team for a meeting in Japan. Kenya's ambassador to Tokyo raised the alarm when he noticed that all the competitors were from Ouko's own sub-tribe, that two of them were over-age for the competition, and that the meeting organisers had been requested to pay the whole of the team's expenses and fees into a private bank account rather than to the Kenya AAA.

Even with Ouko gone, the Kenya AAA still fought to maintain control of the runners, and their earnings. In 1990, when a Kenyan sports journalist, Charles Ouko – no relation of Robert – tried to act as an agent of some runners at a meeting in India, he was confronted by KAAA officials at both Nairobi and Delhi airports. Yet it was the athletes on the official KAAA team who ultimately rebelled. It did not take them long in the gossip-filled changing-rooms at Delhi's Nehru Stadium to discover that, while the KAAA was keeping their appearance fees and prize-money, their compatriots managed by Charles Ouko had received relatively handsome payments.

It was all symptomatic of what one African magazine has described as 'the confusion, power struggles and sheer ineptitude characteristic of athletics management in Kenya'. The greatest shame which tarnishes the reputation of Kenyan athletics, though, lies in the story of Paul Kipkoech, one of the athletes most badly out-of-pocket when the cash 'mysteriously' went missing from his national federation's offices. At his peak, the 10,000 metres world champion of 1987 could command appearance fees in the dollar equivalent to his best racing distance. Yet when Kipkoech died in March 1995, aged just 33, he was penniless, leaving a widow and three children in penury.

Part of the reason for Kipkoech's death was that, despite a successful career as a professional athlete in the late 1980s, he was unable to afford proper medical treatment for his condition, which the autopsy described as cerebral malaria. No one knows exactly how all Kipkoech's wealth came to be frittered away. He bought cars, he drank heavily. Certainly, he was short-changed by his federation. For example, from four races between November and January in the 1987-88 cross-country season, the runner banked barely one-quarter of the total £10,000 that was due to him. The monies were all forwarded by the promoters in Spain, France and Britain to Nairobi, but most of it never got past the Kenya AAA.

During his final days, Kipkoech, his muscular frame wasted away to nothing, languished in a dirty, ill-equipped bush hospital. It is suggested that his illness may also have been complicated by alcohol. 'Paul liked beer, too,' Rono, a friend of Kipkoech, remembers.

Rono, Kipkoech: for every Kenyan story with a happy ending, such as Kip Keino, there seems to be another tale with a darker, more twisted conclusion. Richard Chelimo, who at the age of 20 won an Olympic 10,000 metres silver medal at Barcelona in 1992, was described three years later as 'a short fat man who cannot run any more' according to one African observer. A serious car accident in 1995 left Chelimo badly injured. A familiar tale of money spent on cars and beer, a talent nearly lost.

Some people blame the Kenya AAA for their failure to look after the interests of their athletes. Even the International Amateur Athletic Federation, an organisation not known for its decisive action against its member federations, criticised the KAAA early in 1995 for its mishandling of the doping case involving John Ngugi, the 1988 Olympic 5,000 metres gold medallist who was suspended for two years.

The general store at Nyahururu, which Ngugi had bought with his earnings as the greatest cross-country runner the world has ever seen, is 200 miles north-west of Nairobi, nearly a day's bumpy, dusty jeep ride out into the bush, but even that is no longer beyond the reach of the world's sporting drug testers. It was February 1993 when the two 'flying squad' doping control officers, sent from London, arrived at Ngugi's home. They were there as part of a new, get-tough testing policy designed to catch steroid cheats. The only problem was that, while the Kenyan authorities knew about the new out-of-competition tests, they never told their athletes, nor did they update their rules. So when Ngugi, whose English is not very fluent, was approached at his home by an unknown, unannounced and unaccompanied official, he was suspicious and wary. Without realising that he would be subject to an automatic four-year suspension, he refused to submit to the test.

Ngugi's British-based agent, John Bicourt, enlisted the legal help of the Princess of Wales's firm of solicitors and a legal battle ensued which ended in May 1995 when the IAAF decided, 'Ngugi had suffered enough', while politely censuring the Kenyan authorities for their poor administration and lack of consistency in their approach to the case.

Ngugi – so scared of unwelcome visits from strangers that he began employing a bodyguard full time – was less polite about his governing body. 'The Kenya AAA was never on my side during the time of tribulation. This was a very simple case but, because the KAAA refused to co-operate, it went on and on. Some of the officials were too jealous. They wanted kickbacks from athletes. Some wonder why we own big cars. They forget that talent is God-given which they cannot take away from us. Some officials were happy about my predicament. Only my fellow athletes fought for me.'

The Kenya AAA, according to Joseph Baldwin, a writer on athletics for *The Daily Nation*, the Nairobi newspaper, 'are world champions at bungling'. At the World Championships in Gothenburg in 1995, it took KAAA officials more than 24 hours to lodge a complaint when one of their athletes was disqualified in a preliminary round. By the time the organising committee received the KAAA complaint, it was too late to reinstate the runner because the next round of the competition had already been staged.

In the final event of the World Championships, the eighth lane in the men's 4x400 metres relay final was left empty because three of the Kenyan team, despite having a chance of a medal, refused to race. They objected to the way their team management had tried to impose on them a (slower) favoured athlete, at the expense of one of the runners who the day before had seen them win their heat so convincingly. The Kenya AAA chairman,

Isaiah Kiplagat, refused calls for him to resign over the team's disappointing performances in Gothenburg. Apart from briefly banning the relay quartet, no other action was taken. 'Performances for all countries go up and down. Once in a while you perform badly,' Kiplagat said, '1995 was a bad year for us.' Kiplagat explained that, after talking to the top athletes, KAAA wants to work with the athletes, to help them. 'But there are problems,' he added, exasperation in his voice. 'The agents . . .'

The foreign agents: the other half of an international tug-of-war for control over Kenya's talented runners. While the KAAA can offer glory at the Games, the agents offer the athletes hard cash. The two are not always compatible. In 1994, Kenya fielded a much weakened team at the Commonwealth Games in Victoria, Canada, with potentially title-winning runners such as Moses Kiptanui, William Sigei and Benson Koech absent, preferring to run for cash in Europe.

Some of the agents have proved to be unscrupulous. Raymond de Vries, a Dutch agent, was banned from athletics for life in 1993 after pocketing an estimated £25,000 of appearance fees that should have gone to athletes, many of them Kenyans. In America, another manager faced criminal prosecution after he was caught altering the names on cheques from a shoe company made out to Kenyan athletes, making himself the payee on the pretext that the runners had no bank account.

Of course, foreign agents also cut the best deals for Kenyan athletes. After he had retained the steeplechase world title for the second time in Gothenburg in 1995, Moses Kiptanui's manager, Kim McDonald, organised a world record attempt for him at Zurich in which the Kenyan, by becoming the first man to break the eight-minute mark for the 'chase, collected about £130,000.

Not all Kenyan runners are as athletically gifted, nor as financially astute, as Kiptanui though. For many of the middle-ranking Kenyan runners, who enjoy perhaps one or two brief summers of fleeting glory as the journeymen and pacemakers of the European track circuit, there is a less certain future. 'These agents, they can make Kenyans rich men overnight,' says *The Daily Nation*'s athletics correspondent, Peter Njenga. 'But the runners are often young and naïve. Their managers fix their races for them, but they do not guide them. After one summer season, perhaps they drop out of school, do not get an education, or they might leave the army, their steady job. When they come back from Europe, they languish.'

Former 10,000 metres world record-holder Yobes Ondieki believes the KAAA should take more responsibility and develop the sport in Kenya. 'There's a lot of money coming into Kenya from sponsorship, from athletes, but we don't see where that money is going. What is the federation doing to develop the sport in Kenya? The KAAA now has a big contract with Nike. We are not saying: "Pay that Nike money to us". We are saying that the money should be allocated to develop the sport, and that we should see how it is allocated. Now top Kenyan athletes like myself are fighting against the federation. We want to disband it. It is useless. The officials should all be thrown out.'

Ondieki's athletic militancy has come at least a decade too late for Henry Rono. Rono is well into the veterans' age groups for running, the bigger prizes of Olympic gold or Grand Prix cash beyond him now. In any case, Rono is certain that the solution to his problems lies in his own hands. Rono does not drink any more. 'For ten years, I tried to control it. It did not work. The only way is to quit altogether.'

Instead, he gets himself up at 4 a.m. every day to go for a training run of up to ten miles. He is well aware that Britons such as Hugh Jones, who won the masters' (over-40s) category at the 1995 New York City Marathon, and Nick Rose, winner of the same race the year before, are successful veteran athletes, and make a tidy sum from age group prizes in America. 'And I used to beat Nick when we raced years ago. Now, I must just run each day and I must make sure my weight is OK, it must be what it was when I used to race. It's not good my going to a big marathon and dropping out at five miles. I want to go home a winner.' Henry Rono makes it sound as if he is on the last lap of the long, lonely road home.

Fifteen

That's Shoe Business

INSIDERS CALL it 'The Swoosh' – one of the world's most familiar pieces of branding, which appears on all Nike products. Over the past 20 years, anyone following athletics could not have escaped noticing the very best athletes swathed in the tick-mark symbol: Steve Ovett, Sebastian Coe and Steve Cram all bestrode the world in Nike gear; Joan Benoit carried The Swoosh to golden distinction in the first women's Olympic Marathon; and in the 1990s, Michael Johnson and Sergei Bubka, recipients of hefty Nike endorsement deals, have been the flag-bearers. All have seemed to exemplify the Nike slogan: 'Just Do It'.

Nike's carbo-loaded marketing machine has turned a modest little operation begun in the out-of-the-way north-west American state of Oregon two decades ago into one of the biggest movers and shakers in world business. Using a formula of identifying stars early, embracing controversial figures, and designing products and advertising campaigns around them, Nike has pulled away from its sportswear competitors, leaving rivals such as Adidas and Reebok gasping.

Success in the highly competitive running shoe market is not just about the quality of the product. It is also about the quality of the sports stars who are wearing the shoes. That is why the major sportswear companies go to such great lengths to secure the services of the top performers. 'It was a holy mission, to Swoosh the world,' Nike's first employee, Jeff Johnson, remembers, 'to get Swooshes on everybody's feet.'

Steve Prefontaine was Nike's first sponsored athlete in 1972, although advertising and endorsement deals contravened the strict amateur rules of the time. Prefontaine held every American record, from 3,000 to 10,000 metres. He was charismatic and handsome, his longish, blond hair flowing behind as, inevitably, he would surge to the front of the pack in races. Prefontaine's death, at 24 in 1975, in a car crash after a night of partying and drinking, made him the James Dean of American track and field. At Nike's modern headquarters complex at Beaverton, Oregon, the new glass and steel buildings are named after the well-known sportsmen who have been sponsored by the company: Michael Jordan, Andre Agassi, *et al*. Only Prefontaine has a statue as well as a building.

'We owe so much to him,' Geoff Hollister, a former team-mate of 'Pre', and now a Nike executive, says. 'Athletes had a lot of restrictions placed on them and Steve felt the rules were unfair. He would step out of line and take a risk of getting banned. At that time, it was a lonely road.

'Because we were a young company, we were restricted, and Steve was a guy we could identify with. He was in our backyard, he had this exceptional talent but, beyond that, he packed the house. He was a real showman. But he was taking a risk by associating himself with Nike. By his actions, "Pre" was a pioneer of the sports marketing phenomenon of today.'

Prefontaine was not the first athlete to receive money to wear a particular brand of shoes, just the first to admit to it. Money for shoes had started at the 1960 Olympic Games in Rome, when Puma made an under-the-table payment to German sprinter, Armin Hary. Up to that point, Hary had been wearing the shoes of Puma's great German rivals, Adidas. Hary went to Adidas and asked if they could match the £1,000 offer from Puma. When they declined, Hary won the Olympic 100 metres gold wearing Puma spikes. Once Hary got away with it, few other athletes were prepared to wear a company's shoes for free. The opening shot in the shoe wars had been fired.

Now each summer's athletics season is followed by an autumn 'hunting' season, where the trophies being sought are athletes' signatures on contracts to wear a particular brand of sportswear the following year. The pool of top-class athletes is small, so when someone talented and marketable comes along, the leading sportswear companies have no hesitation in getting their cheque books out. In a manner similar to the football transfer market, athletes now switch between shoe companies for handsome fees.

Britain's most successful male athletes, Linford Christie and Colin Jackson, receive £120,000 and £100,000 as annual retainers from Puma. Catapulted to the top of the earning tree by his triple jump feats in 1995, Jonathan Edwards was able to secure a £500,000 three-year deal from the same shoe company, made up of a £100,000 annual retainer, plus possible, if unlikely, bonuses for becoming the first man to triple jump 19 metres (Edwards's best jump before 1996, with wind assistance, was 18.43 metres), or for breaking Lynn Davies's British long jump record, which has stood since 1968. Sally Gunnell, meanwhile, as the top woman, makes £80,000 a year from Japanese firm Mizuno. Liz McColgan is signed to another Japanese manufacturer, Asics, who pay the marathon runner £50,000. Elsewhere, middle distance runner Curtis Robb receives £37,000 from Nike, while Roger Black gets £35,000 from Reebok.

In this fitness conscious era, the shoe companies have realised the value of being associated with leading competitors. These athletes receive coverage in newspapers, magazines and (most coveted of all) on television. And that coverage translates into shoe sales on the high street, where during the 1980s and 1990s, the training shoe became the *de rigeur* youth fashion item. The landmark of the first £100 pair of training shoes was reached in British sports shops in 1985.

As television coverage of athletes has grown, so the commercial possibilities have multiplied beyond recognition. But athletics is still a relatively small pond of sports endorsements when compared to the sports popular with the American public – gridiron football, basketball, tennis. Michael Jordan, the Chicago Bulls basketball star, is estimated to have made £250 million during his ten-year contract with Nike – who even launched the Air Jordan brand of shoes around their main man – while in 1994, tennis player Andre Agassi finalised a £75 million ten-year deal with the same company.

It is unlikely that athletics will ever move into that sort of league, though the basic annual retainers are only part of the equation. Success pays, with top athletes perhaps doubling the basic value of their contract with performance bonuses (which the company will have insured against). McColgan, for example, might expect to receive an extra £5,000 for a British record, £10,000 for a world record, while an Olympic gold medal might be worth £50,000.

The logic of endorsements is simple. It combines an attempt to advertise the brand with a more subtle effort (depending on the athlete) to add credibility to the company's products. If an athlete is the best in the world, goes the argument, then the product they use must also be the best in the world. That is the theory. Whether the public buys it, literally, no one really knows. For despite the sophistication of the marketing approach, while the shoe companies know if a product is selling, they can very rarely tell *why* the product is selling.

'Adidas tried to assess its athletes by adding up how many minutes of television coverage or column inches in the print media they received,' says Paul Atherton, who looked after Jackson and Black when they were signed to Adidas. 'But putting an objective value on a particular athlete is impossible.'

Tim Hutchings, 5,000 metres bronze medallist at the 1986 European Championships, now works for Reebok. He says: 'You have to have a balanced strategy. Athletes alone will not sell shoes. You need to have the right products first, and then back that up with advertising and promotions.'

Finding the right athletes can also be a problem: success alone is not necessarily the best guide to marketability. Carl Lewis (Nike) and Ben Johnson (Diadora) fought out a sprinting duel in the late 1980s, but even before Johnson was exposed as a drugs cheat, Nike had their part of the contest won, pitching college educated, articulate Lewis against the stammering, self-conscious Canadian.

Then there are the German marathon runners, Katrin Dorre and Uta Pippig. Both are from the old East Germany, blonde and successful, but there the similarity ends. Pippig is the fastest marathon runner of recent years, Dorre the most consistent. Dorre is withdrawn, private, almost introspective, while Pippig made a point of learning English, is charismatic, photographs well and is, in short, a marketing man's dream. Their shoe contracts reflect this. Dorre earns the lion's share of her income from racing, while Pippig, who in 1994 signed a £150,000-a-year deal with Nike, gets most of hers from endorsements. What Nike have invested in is not Pippig's running speed, but her personality. The company hopes she will one day become the woman athlete who transcends her sporting arena, in the manner that Grete Waitz once did.

That is why Adidas were prepared to pay way over the odds for the signature of the young British 400 metres runner, Du'aine Ladejo, after he won the European title in 1994. Adidas reportedly did a £70,000-a-year deal to keep him out of the clutches of Reebok or Asics, who were both keen to have him on the books. For Adidas, Ladejo, with his larger-than-life personality, could be a new Daley Thompson, a national hero who appears regularly on television, and is always seen wearing their three stripes brandmark. 'He's young, fit, vibrant – everything we want so say about Adidas,' the company's Paul Magner says of Ladejo. 'When choosing our athletes, we're looking at more than just their personal bests. We want people who can make a good job of promoting the brand for us.'

In its heyday under the leadership of Horst Dassler, Adidas was by far and away the world's most powerful sporting goods company. At the Mexico Olympics in 1968, it was estimated that 83 per cent of all competitors wore Adidas shoes. As one envious rival put it: 'Those damned three stripes stand out on a track like a Rolls-Royce in a second-hand car lot.' But Adidas was much more than a hugely successful commercial giant. Through his network of contacts, Dassler acquired a vast political influence in the sporting world. He helped to shape world football and was the brains behind the marketing of the Olympic Games, turning the near-bankrupt sports festival into the money-making extravaganza it is today. Horst Dassler made sure that Adidas's three stripes were interwoven into the five rings of Olympism.

Since Dassler's sudden death in 1987, at the age of 51, Adidas has been in decline, even if its shoes are still on the feet of more Olympic champions than any rivals. At first, control of the company passed to Dassler's three sisters, who lacked their brother's flair and dynamism. And, although sales remained remarkably steady at £1 billion per year, Adidas's profits collapsed. In 1990, the company was actually losing money, while Reebok, the market leader in the UK, and Nike, the biggest selling sportshoe brand in the world, pulled away.

Throughout the 1980s, Nike had blazed – or should that be swooshed? – an extraordinary marketing trail, thanks to a stable of world-beating athletes and creative advertising campaigns. The company was conceived by Phil Knight, a one-time distance runner at the University of Oregon, when he wrote a term paper at Stanford Business School on the subject of starting a small business. He received an 'A' for suggesting that athletics shoes could be designed in the United States, manufactured at low cost in Asia, then imported into America and sold at prices lower than those of the most popular brands of the time, Adidas and Puma. History does not record whether the person marking Knight's paper put a swoosh-like tick by the grade, but the business plan for what was to become Nike had been written.

Knight went to Japan, hiked up Mount Fuji – a trek the Japanese believe gives the climber wisdom – and visited the Onitsuka shoe factory in Kobe, where trainers were made. In February 1964, Knight took his first delivery of Tiger running shoes, which proved popular with dedicated distance runners. His new company, Blue Ribbon Sports, did $20,000-worth of business that first year, turning in a $3,240 profit. The corporate nerve centre was based in Knight's mother's laundry room, as the young entrepreneur sold shoes out of the back of a station-wagon at track meetings. Knight was the best salesman Tiger ever had, and in 1969 he finally quit his day job as a university lecturer. But in 1971, with business booming, the partnership was dissolved. Knight was forced to create a new shoe brand, and he named it after the winged Greek goddess of victory. From such humble beginnings, Nike's annual sales now approach $4.5 billion.

Bill Bowerman was the revered track coach at the University of Oregon, where Knight toiled on the athletics team but discovered that his 4 min 10 sec mile was not good enough to make much of an impression. Bowerman was the co-founder of Nike. They had shaken hands on the deal and each chipped in $500 for that first shipment of 1,000 Tiger shoes. Nike's address today is One Bowerman Drive.

During the late 1970s, Nike established a training organisation called Athletics West. Based in Eugene, Oregon, it served as a refuge for Olympic contenders and athletes who had graduated from college and needed some support to continue training. Likewise, Nike's classy, stylised advertisements in athletics and running magazines have long been acknowledged to be as much a way to support the sports' means of communications as to sell gear – the retailing of specialised track spikes has become so nominal in the company's vast business empire as to represent nothing more than a nod of respect to Nike's roots.

The company has always cultivated the idea that it is run by athletes for athletes, always stressing that what drives Nike is its investment in sports technology. Yet even Nike is never overly sentimental about the athletes it sponsors. In 1984, Sebastian Coe had just become the only man ever to retain the Olympic 1,500 metres title, amid a welter of coverage, while wearing a pair of state-of-the-art spikes embellished, suitably, with a golden Swoosh. Coe had been on Nike's books for virtually his whole, record-breaking career. Yet after his Los Angeles triumph the company offered him a reduced deal. The market was growing, but it was changing. Nike was looking at other ways of selling 'product': the clean-cut image of Coe was less valuable to them now than the more controversial profile of John McEnroe, who, perhaps significantly, played a sport to which Phil Knight had recently taken a liking. Rock star Bruce Springsteen, who sang *Born To Run*, was to become a Nike-sponsored performer, ahead of real runners.

The sponsoring of athletes has to be a hard business decision. Brooks pulled off a coup in 1983 when they signed up a major deal with Zola Budd, a runner famous for *not* wearing running shoes. Many good intentions during the boom days of the mid-1980s have long since been forgotten. In 1995, Ruth Wysocki, at the age of 38, made a return to the American team for the World Championships, seven years after her last appearance at a major international championship. She was one of very few top-level athletes competing in Gothenburg who had no sponsorship deal at all. 'In 1984, Brooks said they would look after me for life,' Wysocki says. 'I guess I must have died in 1988.'

What is dubbed in America 'the sports jock culture' still pervades the custom-built offices of Nike, to an almost ridiculous extent. Business meetings are as likely to take place on the in-house running track or basketball court as in the boardroom. If the company is driven by sports equipment technology – from the waffle sole to the air sole, Nike has led the way with innovation – then advertising maintains the all-important image. Yet despite their ad successes, Nike may be best remembered for the 1992 campaign that their rivals dubbed: 'Just Blew It'.

Nike had always had a penchant for understatement, but bigger understatement than anyone else. Thus, when 'little Joanie' Benoit ran away from the field in the 1984 women's Olympic Marathon, she did so against the backdrop of huge images of herself painted on the sides of buildings in downtown Los Angeles, with the Swoosh logo tucked in a corner where millions of TV viewers would notice it, at least subliminally.

In the run-up to the Barcelona Games eight years later, Nike built an even bigger advertising campaign around four of its sponsored athletes who were to compete in the Olympics. Giant posters began appearing, not just in Barcelona, but in every major city around the world, forewarning the public of how successful Nike's athletes would be. The trouble was, only one of the quartet won gold.

Michael Johnson was the firmest of favourites for the 200 metres in Barcelona. He appeared on giant placards which congratulated the reader for doing what none of his rivals would do in the Olympic stadium: passing Johnson. Four athletes passed Johnson in his semi-final, and he did not even qualify for the final.

As Olympic champion and world record-holder, Sergei Bubka of the Ukraine was a sure-fire certainty for the pole vault gold in Barcelona. His Nike posters proclaimed: 'Spanish air traffic control has been notified'. Come the event, and Bubka never took off. He had three failures and did not register a height.

Surely Noureddine Morceli, the 1,500 metres world champion from Algeria, would save Nike's blushes? The Morceli poster slogan read: 'Ever heard the Algerian national anthem? You will'. Indeed, we did, but not for Morceli. Hassiba Boulmerka won the women's Olympic 1,500 metres and stood atop the victory podium in tears, listening to the Algerian anthem, her kit emblazoned with the logo of Italian sportswear manufacturer Diadora. Nike's Morceli, meanwhile, finished only seventh in the men's final.

Thus the company who had created a style of advertising renowned for saying next to nothing was hoist with its own petard when it tried to say too much. Fortunately for Nike, their fourth 'sure thing' was Michael Jordan, and he had the rest of the United States' 'Dream Team' alongside him as they comfortably fulfilled expectations to win basketball gold.

Despite the embarrassments, Nike's image continued to score a slam dunk with consumers. More than one in every three pairs of sports shoes sold around the world today will bear the company's Swoosh logo. And in the shoe wars, those are the figures that really count.

Sixteen

The World's Up and Running

MICHEL BRÉAL'S name will probably not strike a note with many marathon runners. It should: he is the man they have to thank for the pain and agony they have suffered down the years in the name of sport. It was Monsieur Bréal, a historian at the Sorbonne in Paris, who first suggested to Baron Pierre de Coubertin, the founder of the modern Olympic movement, that when he staged the first modern Games in Athens in 1896, he should try to include two events which reflected the glories of ancient Greece.

One event Bréal suggested was the discus throw, the other an endurance foot race to commemorate a run supposed to have been made by a Greek messenger named Pheidippides in 490BC. The legend of Pheidippides has it that he was sent to Sparta to get help against an attack by the Persians. Pheidippides, a trained runner, covered the 136 miles between the cities in a couple of days. The Spartans declined to fight, so he returned home and joined the battle against the Persians at Marathon. There, the Athenians won a great victory against superior forces, and Pheidippides was given the task of racing the 25 miles along dusty tracks back to the city to announce the news. This, the exhausted Pheidippides did, gasping 'Rejoice, we conquer', before promptly falling down dead.

Bréal's ideas were accepted and the first competitive endurance race of its kind, from the battle site at Marathon to Athens, and thus dubbed 'the Marathon', became one of the highlights of the 1896 Games. The Greeks embraced the idea of the race with patriotic fervour as the one truly local discipline of the Games. The official programme stated that the marathon was 'evidence of the Greek dedication to freedom as a nation, and the sacrifice of the individual to maintain that freedom'.

When the runners set off on the 25-mile route from Marathon in the last event of the Games, Greece had won no events. Its last hopes rested on the dozen locals – selected from two specially staged selection events – among the 16 starters. In retrospect, not only was this the first marathon, it was the also the original big city race, since there were generous prizes on offer to the winner. With Greek national pride at stake, George Averoff, the businessman who was the main benefactor of the Games, offered his daughter's hand in marriage and one million drachma to any Greek winner.

The race lived up to the Victorian-style hype. Two of the four foreign entrants were forced to retire before the finish with cramp and exhaustion. A third started hallucinating and fell into a ditch. This left the Greek shepherd Spyridon Louis in the lead. Increasing his pace as he closed on the white marbled Pananthenaic stadium, the crowd was in tumult at the news that Louis, a Greek, was in front. Jewellery was thrown at his feet by women admirers, and two of Greece's crown princes ran with him in the stadium to the finishing line, which he crossed 2 hours 58 minutes 50 seconds after the race start.

Louis, already married, did not accept a second bride, but in addition to his winner's diploma and silver medal, he also collected a voucher for 365 free restaurant meals, shoe polishing for life and a piece of land. When asked what gift he would like from the King of Greece, Louis requested a horse and cart so that he might transport water from a well to his village.

The marathon was established. The Olympic races of 1900 and 1904 were also run over distances of approximately 25 miles, as was the British trial race for the 1908 Olympics, to be staged in London. It was then that royalty took a hand in shaping sporting history. The Princess of Wales, knowing that her parents-in-law, King Edward VII and Queen Alexandra, would be at the finish of the marathon in the White City stadium, thought it would be pleasant if the royal children could watch the start. Thus it was that the start, scheduled to be in Eton High Street, 25 miles west of the London stadium, was moved across the Thames, up the hill, around Windsor Castle and on to the east lawn. This extra section made the total race distance 26 miles 385 yards. That extra mile and a quarter would make all the difference.

The first man into the stadium was a 23-year-old Italian pastry cook, Dorando Pietri. But utterly exhausted, he set off the wrong way around the track before officials re-directed him. He fell. The crowd was urging him to finish, and surrounded by police and officials – including Sir Arthur Conan Doyle, the creator of Sherlock Holmes – Pietri clambered to his feet. He was to fall another three times, the final occasion within yards of the finishing tape. Then another runner entered the stadium. It was the American, Johnny Hayes, and he was still running briskly. With Hayes barely 100 yards away, Dorando fell once again, but was caught by the track officials and supported over the finish.

The Americans protested that Dorando had received unfair assistance. The Italian was disqualified, but he had already found a place in the hearts of all those in the stadium that day, and etched his place in sport's hall of fame. So taken with his courage and ill fortune was Queen Alexandra that she presented Pietri with a special gold cup when she gave the medals to the first three runners. To this day, little Dorando remains one of the most famous Olympians, embodying the spirit of the Games – someone who did not win, but who took part; someone who did not conquer, but who fought well. And the images of his collapse, and later scenes like them, from marathons throughout this century, of thousands of runners exhausted by that last, telling, extra mile and a quarter, would capture the imaginations of millions and make this unique event the stuff of sporting legends.

In the years that followed, great Olympic Marathon champions such as Zatopek and Bikila, have become universal heroes. But outside the Olympic Games, marathon running remained a true minority sport, with marathon runners regarded as oddballs even by fellow athletes. They were the loners. In the early 1970s, Frank Shorter was often stopped by puzzled motorists curious as to what he was doing, running along the roads of Florida. 'Training for a marathon,' he would inform them. Most would shake their heads and drive on, convinced that they had encountered a nut-case. Shorter showed the world that he was not a madman when, one August evening in 1972, he pattered into the impressive stadium at Munich to become Olympic Marathon champion. Although he did not realise it, as Shorter crossed the finishing line and threw up his arms in triumph, he was beckoning in the running boom.

'Everyone saw Frank's victory in the Olympics on TV and that got the ball rolling,' said Bill Rodgers, Shorter's great American marathon-running rival. 'That's when America discovered the marathon. Maybe a lot of people didn't understand it – they could not comprehend anyone running 26 miles – but they were talking about it.'

It was around that time that Americans' attitude to health and fitness was changing. Heart disease had reached epidemic proportions. Running, doctors claimed, was good for you. In one three-year period in the 1970s, the number of American runners swelled from six million to 20 million. At first, there were few opportunities for the new, health-obsessed runners, or 'joggers' as they became known, to compete in marathon races. New York City had had an annual marathon, comprising four loops of Central Park, since September 1970. The first time it was staged, only 126 runners started, and only 55 of them finished. The winner was Gary Muhrcke, a New York fireman who had to finish a night shift on duty before running the race. Even in 1975, when 534 ran in New York, the event was only kept afloat by the donations of 160 supporters.

At that time, the only marathon in the United States with any status athletically was Boston. For that was the race that had always been there, right back to 1897, when some locals, inspired by tales of derring-do at the Athens Olympics the year before, had staged their own long-distance foot race in Massachusetts. Boston was the oldest annual marathon in the world, but to enter this prestigious event, runners needed to attain tough qualifying times, which were often beyond the ability of most of the new breed of jogger.

Then, in 1975, Fred Lebow, the president of the New York Road Runners Club, the organisers of the Central Park race, was approached about staging a marathon through New York's five boroughs. Lebow, an ex-patriot Romanian Jew, had escaped Nazi-occupied Europe as a young boy and then, as a teenager, had 'to live on my wits' to survive on his own. He worked for a gang, smuggling diamonds from Belgium to England, and knocked around the continent until 1951, when he crossed the Atlantic. He moved to New York in the early 1960s, setting up his own clothing business. Lebow played tennis, but as he got older, he was no longer getting around the court as quickly as he would like. So, in 1969, he started running. It was not long before he was hooked. He joined NYRRC, where he developed a reputation as a man who could get things done. But even Lebow thought that taking the marathon out on to the streets of the city that never sleeps was madness. 'It was already difficult enough to put on a marathon in Central Park,' he recalled.

Some of the running club's members pressured Lebow into attending a meeting with the Manhattan borough president, Percy Sutton. Lebow went into the meeting determined to present what he believed were impossible terms: the full co-operation of the city, and a $20,000 budget. Sutton agreed. He thought it would be a nice way to celebrate America's bicentennial. Lebow was stunned. Now he would have to organise the city-wide race.

More than 2,000 entered that first five-borough race in 1976. The organisers were wary of the logistical problems and the increased costs. Thanks, however, to sponsorship from the Rudin family, who paid $25,000, bankers Manufacturers Hanover, $8,500, and *New York* magazine, $5,000, Lebow even had a budget to fly in top distance runners from overseas. But the athlete who received the biggest payment was Bill Rodgers, who got $2,000 as an under-the-table appearance fee, but no prize money, for beating Frank Shorter in the first of four New York victories in 2 hr 10 min 10 sec.

The race received nationwide coverage in the United States, and sent even more Americans reaching for their sneakers and training sweats. In 1979, the New York City Marathon had more than 10,000 runners for the first time. Among the entrants was one former Olympic champion whose presence escaped the notice of most spectators. But then it was more than 20 years since Christopher Brasher had won steeplechase gold in Melbourne, and this balding, middle-aged journalist from England was only taking part in the event as a running tourist, with a group from Britain curious to be part of this new running sensation.

Brasher is a buccaneer of the second Elizabethan age. A reserve for Sir John Hunt's mountaineering team which conquered Everest, he was pace-maker in Bannister's first sub-four-minute mile, then an unexpected Olympic champion who became a journalist and award-winning television producer. Brasher might have invented the phrase 'been there, done that, got the T-shirt', but even he was overwhelmed by his experience in the New York City Marathon.

When he returned home, he sat at his desk, whisky to hand, and hammered out a column for the following Sunday's *Observer*, and out of the night came an inspired and inspiring article which began: 'To believe this story you must believe that the human race can be one joyous family, working together, laughing together, achieving the impossible. Last Sunday, in one of the most violent, trouble-stricken cities in the world, 11,532 men and women, from 40 countries in the world, assisted by more than a million black, white and yellow people, laughed and cheered and suffered during the greatest folk festival the world has seen . . .'

Brasher concluded the article: 'I wonder whether London could stage such a festival? We have the course, a magnificent course . . . but do we have the heart and hospitality to welcome the world?' Brasher had thrown down the challenge, and when no one picked up the gauntlet he, typically, decided to do something about it himself. The London Marathon was born.

In early 1980, meetings were arranged with his editor at *The Observer*, Donald Trelford, and with the relevant authorities – the Greater London Council, the Metropolitan Police and the athletics governing bodies. Independently that August, on a quiet Sunday morning, Avon, the cosmetics company, sponsored a small international women's race staged in the capital, 200 runners starting in Battersea Park, heading east through the City, running around the Isle of Dogs, and returning westwards to a finish outside the Guildhall. The race was won by New Zealander Lorraine Moller, in 2hr 35min 11sec with a little-known American, Joan Benoit, placed fourth. Britain's first finisher was seventh placed Joyce Smith, a 42-year-old mother of two. It proved the idea of a London marathon *was* possible to realise.

Brasher prepared his budget for the first London Marathon, showing an expected expenditure of £75,000. With the help of agents, he found a sponsor, Gillette, prepared to put up £50,000. In November, at a second meeting with the great and the good, Brasher was given a final go-ahead from the GLC leader, Sir Horace Cutler, with the proviso, 'You never ask the ratepayers to bail you out. Not a penny from the ratepayers.'

Five months later, on Sunday 29 March 1981, the first Gillette London Marathon was staged. There were 7,055 entrants that first year, although more than 20,000 applied to run. The American, Dick Beardsley, crossed the finishing line on a rain-swept Constitution Hill hand-in-hand with Inge Simonsen, of Norway, as joint winners. The gesture encapsulated the spirit of the day, while the sight of Joyce Smith galloping to a British record to win the women's race inspired mothers and the middle-aged across the country. But no one could have expected the explosion of interest that followed during the next 12 months.

Brasher decided that for 1982 they would select runners on the basis of the postmarks on the envelopes bearing the entry forms after a given date. Those with the earliest postmarks would be the ones selected to run. Thus it was that in the midst of the bleak winter, queues of hundreds of people formed outside post offices around the country, people hopeful that they could get a postmark that would guarantee them an entry to the following spring's London Marathon. In all, Brasher's mailbag contained more than 93,000 applications. Only 16,350 would be accepted to run, and when 15,758 finished, London was catapulted above New York as the world's biggest marathon.

Every city, and every town, wanted to stage its own marathon. In 1982, there were 115 26.2-mile road races staged throughout the United Kingdom. The event which had once been the preserve of loners and eccentrics was now something which even people who had not run for a bus since leaving school would 'go in for'. Marathons seemed to touch the lives of everyone: if you were not training to run in a marathon, you would probably be approached by someone who wanted you to sponsor them for a specific charity. Cities which did not have marathons, such as Newcastle, staged half-marathons. At times, it seemed, the whole country was on the run.

The marathon phenomenon was also experienced around the world. Where marathons were already established, such as Paris and San Francisco, the organisers followed the example of New York and moved the race out on to the city's streets. The zenith of running popularity was reached on 25 May 1986 when, encouraged by the charities Band Aid and Sport Aid to raise money for the starving in the Ethiopian famine, 30 million people went out and ran in ten-kilometre races, simultaneously staged around the globe. The whole world was up and running.

But as with any boom, there followed a period of bust. In England, Birmingham, from having two marathons staged in the city in 1982, soon had none. The Glasgow Marathon, founded in the boom times of 1982, attracted 20,062 entries by 1985. Three years later, the race lost its sponsor and ceased to exist. Traditional events, such as the Polytechnic Marathon, first run in 1909 over much of the 1908 Olympic course from Windsor to west London, could not cope with the sudden popularity of its branch of the sport. By the 1980s, heavy traffic had seen 'the Poly' confined to roads within Windsor Great Park. With no television coverage, little sponsorship and attractive only to club runners with a strong sense of history, the

Polytechnic Marathon even ceased to be staged at all before the decade was over.

What the events in Glasgow and Birmingham failed to grasp was the importance of a broad public interest in their event. The first law of sponsorship is simple: the greater the media exposure generated by an event, the greater its value to a sponsor. While in the pre-boom days marathon running remained a minority sport, media coverage was usually limited to local newspapers, radio and television. But hours of extensive television coverage of the London Marathon stimulated public interest – could they spot their neighbour or workmate on the telly? – and national newspapers began to devote acres of of coverage to the race and its personalities. Importantly, the move on to streets presented events on a more dramatic stage, drawing attention not just to the runners, but to the city as well.

As race organisers scrambled to create an identity for their events, and competed to attract runners, both the swift and the slow, it seemed for a time that the biggest loser would be the Boston Marathon. Boston had survived two world wars and the economic depression of the 1930s, but could it survive the marathon boom? For it was money that nearly did for Boston, the money being paid out as prizes by other big city international marathons to the elite competitors, while Boston, too aware of its tradition, too conservative to change, clung to its status as a strictly amateur event.

Road running had been the first branch of athletics to openly pay prize-money. The watershed was in 1981 on the eve of a race in Portland, Oregon, called the Cascade Run Off, when several leading runners, including Bill Rodgers and Lorraine Moller, had challenged the United States governing body, then known as TAC, or The Athletics Congress, to allow money to be paid openly and honestly. After first threatening to ban the agitators, TAC eventually backed down and, with the approval of the International Amateur Athletic Federation, set up trust funds for athletes. The runners were able to draw on the funds for living expenses. It was the forerunner of the scheme proposed for track and field the following year.

But Boston set its face against such crass commercialisation. The organisers at the Boston Athletic Association, whose members had won six out of 12 events at the first Olympic Games in 1896, wanted to stay true to de Coubertin's Olympic ideals of amateurism, and seemed destined to stand by and watch as races in New York, London, Chicago, Berlin and Rotterdam established themselves as the world's biggest, fastest and best marathons. As the other races grabbed the headlines with thrilling races, world record times and street-filling fields, Boston floundered. The past did little to attract the world's finest marathon runners. The race was on its knees.

For nearly a century, Boston's prestige alone had been enough, but in 1984, only Britain's Geoff Smith turned up in Boston, beating a field of unknowns by the best part of five minutes. The following year Smith, a former Liverpool fireman, turned up again, ran out alone, blew up, staggered, and ended up walking across the line, shrugging his shoulders as if to ask: 'Where is everyone?' He had failed to beat the relatively modest time of 2hr 14min, yet he still finished a mile ahead of the runner-up.

The quality of the field in 1985 was so poor that the Boston mayor, Ray Flynn, a four-hour marathoner, stated that he was in danger of winning. After a brief dalliance with selling the rights in the event to one entrepreneur, the Boston Marathon was saved when the John Hancock Corporation stepped in. An insurance company with its roots in New England, John Hancock put up a $1.9 million-a-year sponsorship deal which continues until 2003. The transformation in Boston's fortunes was immediate.

In 1986, Rob de Castella, one of history's best ever marathon runners, won Boston in 2hr 7min 51sec. He took home to Australia $30,000 for first place and $25,000 for his course record. In 1996, the men's and women's winners of the 100th Boston Marathon each claimed $75,000, from a total prize purse of $500,000, exclusive of time bonuses and any appearance fees. Boston is now the biggest road racing pay day in the world.

Besides providing money, Hancock emphasises first-class treatment for élite runners, who get chauffeurs, special ethnic meals, top accommodation and massage, among other services. 'Runners are like artists: most believe in karma, environment,' said David D'Alesandro, Hancock's executive vice-chairman. 'Putting them in a position so they don't have to think about anything but running is a good thing.'

At the same time that it signed with Boston, Hancock also agreed deals with the marathons in Los Angeles and New York. The tactic was to tie up athletes, using an attractive bonus system that committed them to a series of races, rather than just Boston. Hancock's investment pushed the price of recruiting athletes through the roof. In 1988, the London Marathon's élite co-ordinator David Bedford offered Britain's Steve Jones a deal worth $200,000 and Gelindo Bordin, of Italy, the European champion, $150,000. They turned him down because Boston had made them better offers.

In 1992, Bedford thought he had finally outwitted Hancock with a spectacular coup. After watching her win her first two marathons in New York and Tokyo, Bedford struck the richest marathon deal ever to sign up Liz McColgan. At that time, McColgan was Britain's most popular sportswoman after a courageous victory over 10,000 metres at the 1991 World Championships in Tokyo. A novice at the marathon, there was no knowing what she might achieve. Bedford agreed a deal worth £450,000 in appearance fees alone for three races over a four-year period. But the gamble backfired: McColgan's career was put on hold as a series of career threatening injuries saw her lose form and even face retirement. Only dogged persistence saw her return to racing at something like world class in 1995 and manage victory in London in 1996.

A marathon runner's career is something like the life of a mayfly: a flourish which can end suddenly, unexpectedly, and all too briefly. It is not necessarily the considerable stress of racing for more than 26 miles – although most top-class runners restrict themselves to no more than two marathons a year to allow for a full recovery from their racing exertions – but the strain of training for such an event which extracts an enormous price on the body. Some say 120 miles a week is enough, others 140, but some of the world's best marathon runners have been known to clock up 200 training miles in a week – at least 28 miles of running every day, day-in, day-out, often for months at a time.

Alberto Salazar lasted just three years at the top of the marathon rankings after bursting on to the scene by winning New York in 1980. Unlike a golfer, whose career may last 20 years, or the footballer, with the opportunity for big signing-on fees, the marathon runner has to grab at the financial chances whenever he can. While sprinters may race two, even three times in a week, the dedicated marathon runner might race only twice a year, and if the runner is good enough, one of those races is 'for free', representing their country in an Olympic Games or championship race where there is no appearance fee or prize-money. The need for a big earning event elsewhere is paramount.

The marathon is fickle: you can toe the starting line as fit as you have ever been, in shape to beat the world, but something, however minor, can make everything go wrong. A grain of sand forms a blister under the ball of your foot, a rain shower chills your leg muscles into cramp, a missed cup at a feeding station breaks concentration or causes a fall. In 26 miles, there's endless scope for something to wreck every best-laid plan and reduce you to a stumbling wreck who fails to finish. All top runners, therefore, want some guarantee that they will get some reward for their efforts.

Payments are usually made to runners in three ways. The very best receive sums just for turning up: Belayneh Densimo, the world record-holder from Ethiopia, was given $100,000 by London in 1990 even though he did not even get to the halfway point in the race. But the majority rely on a combination of appearance money, prize-money and bonuses. In the 1996 London Marathon, for example, the men's and women's winners received $55,000 prizes. But there was also bonuses of $100,000 and $25,000 for world record or course record. Further down the field, time incentives would top up the pay cheques: $10,000 extra would go to each runner finishing inside 2 hours 10 minutes, irrespective of where they placed in the race.

In 1991, however, fed up with paying top dollar to big-name runners who failed to produce fast times, New York started to shift its payment schemes more towards time bonuses than prize-money. Fifth place, which in 1990 had been worth a $12,000 prize, was slashed to $2,500 for 1991. The race got what it wanted. The winning times of Slavador Garcia and Liz McColgan were the fastest for several years, but the race organisers' new tactic was condemned by a number of leading athletes. 'You just can't keep chasing times each time you go out,' said the American, Ken Martin. 'The weather, the competition, everything varies. All those things come together and maybe you'll run fast that day. They're wanting world records, but you're not going to get one every marathon.'

The search for the holy grail of a marathon world record – or 'world best' as it is called, because of the variation in the nature of marathon courses – is common to all of the five big-money marathons (Boston, London, Berlin, New York and Tokyo), with their combined race budgets of $25 million. Marathon records are rare. The men's best time stood for twelve years until Salazar's great run in New York in 1981 – only for the Big Apple course to be discovered to be short of the full 26 miles 385 yards. Densimo's record of 2hr 6min 50sec was set in 1988. But the race organisers desperately need records to create television interest, and pull in sponsors. In 1995, even the London Marathon founder, Chris Brasher, was forced to admit, 'We could do with a world record for the prestige of the event.'

The boom years may have long gone, but London still attracts more than 70,000 applicants every year. Barely half are accepted to run, and only a small proportion of these might regard themselves as 'athletes'. Yet the London Marathon is going through a difficult period. Under siege from rival races, 26,000 runners pounding through the capital's streets no longer guarantees rapt attention of the public or the media.

When Flora signed on as new sponsors for the 1996 race, therefore, it was decided to use their £6 million investment to promote the event through television advertising, rather than as a lure to the world's fleetest racers. It is the same the world over. New York, which no longer receives coast-to-coast network television coverage, has resorted to offering a $1 million bonus to the first runner to break two hours for the race, and $100,000 to the first 100-year-old finisher.

It is usually a clear sign of desperation when a road race starts offering silly money for unattainable goals in order to attract attention to itself. But there is an exception to every rule. The annual Bob Hasan ten-kilometres race in Indonesia was one such exception. Mohamad 'Bob' Hasan is a millionaire industrialist who exports the finest Indonesia timber around the world. He is said to be a confidant of President Suharto, the dictator who has been running the country since 1968. Hasan is the head of Indonesia's athletics federation, and a member of the International Amateur Athletic Federation's inner council. A distance runner himself, Hasan was disappointed when his own country seemed to be by-passed by the running boom. He took matters into his own hands, and staged a world-class road race in his back yard. He wanted to promote tourism and encourage Indonesians into taking up running. To ensure a world-class field, as well as paying $150,000 in prize-money, Hasan made his race the million-dollar challenge: there would be a $500,000 bonus to the man or woman who broke the world best.

In 1993, after several near-misses by other runners, Addis Abebe, a 22-year-old Ethiopian army private, scooped the pool in the race on Java. Despite almost being blown over by the down-draught from a helicopter filming the race, or knocked over by the motorcycle escorts, with a desperate lunge for the line, Abebe improved the seven-year-old world best of Arturo Barrios by a single second, recording 27 minutes 40 seconds. Abebe had been so confident of winning the money that he had travelled across the world with an empty suitcase to put his cash in. He left Indonesia disappointed: the organisers insisted on paying the money into his trust fund in the official manner.

The ten-kilometre race distance – just over six miles – proved to be hugely popular with Indonesian runners, just as it had with runners in the United States and Europe. The jogger who joined the marathon mania of the 1980s had mellowed in the 1990s. No longer does he feel that he has to run a marathon to be a 'real' runner. Shorter events offer more variety, more attainable goals, and more chances to race, without the stresses and strain of training for months at a time with only a single goal, the marathon, beckoning.

In the same year as the first London Marathon, another massive running event was inaugurated on Tyneside. Called the Great North Run, the half-marathon was the brainchild of the local running hero, Brendan Foster, the 1976 Olympic 10,000 metres bronze medallist. Starting just outside Newcastle and running through the city centre to the coast at South Shields, the event was soon matching London in terms of support and participation, with 35,000 now taking part annually.

How different to when Foster used to run in local road races in the 1970s. Then, organising a road race was a simple, low-budget affair. Entry fees were 25p, and fields were often no larger than two dozen. The runners who turned up expected to receive nothing more than their number, four pins, and a result sheet. And at the end of the day, if the organiser had managed to salt away a couple of quid for the club kitty, everyone was happy.

The London Marathon and Great North Run are now huge money-making events. Their success led to other events springing up across Britain to challenge the long-established, low-key races. The new races would offer T-shirts and medals to all finishers, a goody bag and other paraphernalia which the new-breed runner expected. The entry fees were accordingly higher, too, sometimes as much as £10. But it was all in a good cause, with the organiser able to donate several thousand pounds to charity, or, sometimes, to his own back pocket. In 1980, there had been just 300 road races in the UK; by 1986, there were more than 2,000; in 1996, the official listing has just over 1,000 events registered. It is a similar story of consolidation in the United States.

Bill Rodgers, the original professional road runner, who was even nick-named 'Dollar Bill' because he always insisted on being paid top whack to compete, welcomes the shift. We should not fear for the marathon, he says. 'The marathon is a fascinating race,' says Rodgers. 'That fascination will never die. You'll always find a few people wanting to test themselves over 26 miles. I think we'll be running marathons for a long time.'

Seventeen

The Rings of Gold

AS RECENTLY as 1978, with the event plagued by politics, boycotts and terrorism, and with Montreal's multi-million dollar loss from staging the Games, no one wanted to touch the Olympics with a spent match, let alone a lighted flame. Yet when the words 'Let the Games begin' are uttered on 19 July, at the opening ceremony of the 1996 Centennial Olympics, in front of 85,000 people in the brand new Atlanta Olympic Stadium, and watched by an estimated global television audience of 3.5 billion, it will bring to a climax a remarkable chapter in the history of the Olympic Movement.

As recently as 1989, the very thought of Atlanta hosting the Games could have been dismissed as preposterous. Athens, the venue for the first modern Olympic Games in 1896, was the overwhelming sentimental favourite to stage the Games in 1996 as a celebration of the Olympic centenary. But whatever gifts the Greeks were bearing, they were no match for Billy Payne. In September 1990, when the International Olympic Committee met in the New Takanawa Prince Hotel in Tokyo, Athens was so confident – or arrogant – about being awarded the Games that the whole of their final presentation to the IOC was made in Greek. By the time they realised the threat that Payne and Atlanta posed to their candidacy, it was too late.

After the maximum of five rounds of secret balloting, the challenges of Toronto, Melbourne, Belgrade and Manchester were all discarded together with that of Athens, as the Games were awarded to Atlanta. Payne, a former real estate lawyer from Atlanta, had almost single-handedly turned the improbable quest of taking the Games to the southern state of Georgia into reality.

When all the arguments were unravelled from the illogicality of the Olympic bidding process, you were left with one indisputable fact: Atlanta's bid was best. Athens was strong on tradition, but weak on economic and organisational ability. Atlanta would build the necessary facilities and promised that after the Olympic flame had been extinguished, there would be a profit to show for the whole exercise. Besides, with American television paying so much of the IOC's income, to stage the Games in the United States for the second time in just 12 years was hardly a great sacrifice. For while to many people, the Olympics may seem to be about the ideals of sportsmanship, the reality at the end of the 20th century is that the Olympics are very much about money. Dr Alan Tomlinson, a lecturer in the social history of sport at the University of Brighton, argues that the Olympics have always been influenced by the nature of the times. The ancient Greek Games were 'rooted in ruthless patriarchy', while the early Games of the modern era were closely linked to trade fairs and the development of new commercial markets. In the age of the 'Global Village', it therefore follows that television can turn the Olympics into a vast sales pitch, with the sport used as a vehicle to sell soft drinks, photographic film and credit card services.

'The notion of wonderful sportsmanship has been grossly over-idealised,' Dr Tomlinson says. 'We should not be too pious about the Olympics – they are almost inevitably involved with markets and power.'

One thing is certain: it is more than just a love of sport which persuades cities to battle for the right to stage the Games. 'We want to put Atlanta on the map,' was Billy Payne's reasoning, and in that aim he will probably be successful. Helsinki in 1952 established Finland firmly as an independent state; Melbourne showed the world that fine cities existed in the southern hemisphere; Rome in 1960, Tokyo in 1964 and Munich in 1972 helped to rehabilitate Italy, Japan and Germany after the Second World War; Mexico was showcased in 1968 and South Korea in 1988 as developing nations; Montreal got French Canada noticed in 1976, while Barcelona was the Catalans' Games in 1992. Only in Moscow in 1980 were the darkest undertones of Olympic history, from the Berlin Games of 1936, recalled, with a political philosophy, as much as the venue, being put on display to the world.

The Soviet Union, though, might have learned the lessons from the 1936 Olympics. A study carried out in America during the late 1970s showed that rather than proving to the world what a wonderful system National Socialism was, by trying to put the Olympics in jackboots, Adolf Hitler actually began the process of turning public opinion against him around the world. He was reluctantly forced to accept Jewish participants at the Berlin Games; the star performer was Jesse Owens, a black American, which somewhat undermined Hitler's theories of a master race; and the machine-like precision of the German organisation at the Olympic ceremonies merely emphasised the dehumanising nature of the Nazis.

It was the free enterprise Games in Los Angeles in 1984 which changed the nature of staging the Olympics once and for all. The Olympics were in peril, since the increasingly expensive infrastructure required to play host to the world for three weeks was becoming so costly that no one wanted to take the risk. It seemed that only massive state investment, as in Moscow, or ever-lasting debt – Montreal's local tax-payers will still be footing the bill for the 1976 Games well into the 21st century – could allow a city to stage the Olympics.

Thus it was that, when the IOC met in Athens in 1978 to decide on the venue for the 1984 Games, there was only one candidate: Los Angeles. For the IOC, it was very much a case of 'take it or leave it'. The LA Games bid offered, for the first time since 1896, an Olympics without any central government funding. It offered the IOC a $225 million television deal for US rights; and the Los Angeles bid offered an unashamedly commercial Olympics. For it was not the city of Los Angeles which put forward the bid at all. The state of California, under Governor Ronald Reagan, at that time was undergoing massive cut backs in public expenditure. The LA bid was therefore tendered by a group of local enthusiasts who recalled that when the city last staged the Games, it made a useful surplus of nearly $1 million. They were sure that this success could be achieved again, provided the IOC allowed a degree of leeway over the manner in which they arranged the Games. Faced with no alternatives, the IOC agreed. The 1984 Los Angeles Games went on to be a great success and they made a massive profit of $200 million for the city.

Thereafter, the race by other cities to grab a slice of the Games money-making action was as fierce as anything seen in an Olympic 100 metres final. By the time the votes had been cast to select the host city for the 1996 Games, the six bidding cities had spent an estimated £75 million to promote themselves to the IOC's 91 members. In the process, each of the bidding cities had made sure that the self-electing members of the self-perpetuating IOC were wined and dined, fêted with presents and lavished with free travel to luxurious hotels around the world, all in the cause of selecting a host city.

For Atlanta, the lucky winner, it was just the down payment when compared to the £750 million which it had to spend to build the Olympic facilities, or the hoped-for £5 billion in long-term business and trade the Games could generate. Atlanta is betting its future on the Olympics. The city which was razed to the ground by the Union's General Sherman during the American Civil War has only recently emerged as a bustling metropolis for the United States' poorest region. The challenges Atlanta faces in staging the Olympics are enormous. Atlanta expects more than two million visitors in a 17-day period. From complaints about accommodation for the visitors expected in the city during the Games, to fears of massive traffic jams and

worries over racial sensitivities, the city seemed to be suffering the hang-
over headache even before the big party began.

The total number of tickets on sale for Olympic events – 11 million –
eclipses those of the 1984 and 1992 Games combined. More than 10,000
competitors from a record 197 countries will take part, including 3,779
women (a 32 per cent increase on any previous Olympics). They will be
housed in eight Athletes' Villages (until 1984, the IOC used to insist on a
single Olympic village), with the bulk of them accommodated a mile north
of the city centre on the 330-acre site of Georgia Tech, mercifully, considering Atlanta's sub-tropical climate, the first Athletes' Village to be
air-conditioned. Los Angeles is a city five times the size of Atlanta;
Atlanta's Games are twice the size of those in Los Angeles.

But while Los Angeles operated on a 'make do and mend' policy for
Olympic facilities by updating and upgrading existing venues, such as the
Coliseum stadium, originally built for the 1932 Games, Atlanta had under-
taken to privately finance a $500 million building project which was to
strain its planning and budgets almost to breaking point. There are the sta-
diums: three new arenas and the expansion of a fourth, at a total cost of
$230 million. More than three-quarters of that is going on the new Olympic
stadium, which will be used for just four athletics meetings – including the
Olympics itself – before the track is ripped up to make way for the new
home of the Atlanta Braves baseball team. Meanwhile, down the road at the
Braves' 30-year-old Fulton County stadium, where Hank Aaron broke Babe
Ruth's home run record in 1975, the Olympic baseball tournament will be
staged before the stadium is torn down to make way for a car park.

Atlanta has, in turns, been envied, admired and derided for landing the
Centennial Games. Only the Olympics themselves will show whether this
city of the Deep South has got itself in too deep. The city which was home
to both Margaret Mitchell, author of *Gone With The Wind*, and slain civil
rights leader Dr Martin Luther King Jr, now touts itself as *the* place to do
business. The local Chamber of Commerce boasts that while other cities
have culture and beauty, 'Atlanta has commerce at its heart'. In trying to
raise Atlanta out of the ashes of the Civil War, the city elders are keen to
disprove Colonel Stephen H. Long, who in 1837 gave the place its beginnings as a railroad terminus before declaring that Atlanta 'will be a good
location for one tavern, a blacksmith shop, a grocery store and nothing
else'. Today, Atlanta is home to the global Coca-Cola empire – the first
glass of Coca-Cola was served in Atlanta in 1886 – as well as Delta
Airlines, Ted Turner's Cable News Network media concerns, Holiday Inn
and United Parcel Service.

But beyond big business, and Atlanta has some severe social problems.
Despite its slogan of 'The City Too Busy to Hate', Atlanta is the most violent big city in the United States, with about 200 murders each year. The
poverty of its residents ranks Atlanta as the fifth poorest inner city area in

the United States. In 1993, when it tried to come up with a new, more appropriate slogan, the Manhattan advertising executives on Madison Avenue ridiculed the Southerners by suggesting: 'Atlanta: The City Too Dumb to Be Ashamed'.

With the huge infrastructure bills and no government aid, even in the final months before the Games, Atlanta organisers were searching everywhere for corporate sponsors to meet its $1.58 billion budget. Some of the deals have made the purists cringe: 'Wheel of Fortune' and 'Jeopardy' have been nominated as 'the official television game shows of the 1996 Atlanta Olympic Games'. The Atlanta organising committee has put an 'official' stamp on everything, from jet planes to pistachio nuts to a 1,996-foot-long hot dog.

Even the age of corporate hospitality has touched the Atlanta Games. Twelve-seater hospitality boxes in the Olympic stadium can be hired for the Opening Ceremony, Closing Ceremony and nine days of athletics action, for a bargain $500,000. Despite such efforts, Atlanta looked as if it would fall a long way short of the fabulous riches which Los Angeles was able to generate for its citizens. This in spite of the Olympic merchandising deals – which are forecast to generate retail sales of $2 billion for the backers of Atlanta – and the 30 sponsors, led by Coca-Cola, who are pumping $100 million to froth up the Games.

Coca-Cola is a long-standing Olympic sponsor, and with good reason. In 1992, half-a-million Coke drinkers in the United Kingdom sent in ring-pulls from cans in order to obtain Olympic merchandise bearing the cherished five-ring symbol. Research carried out for the IOC in 1995 suggested that the Olympic rings are the world's most recognised corporate logo. 'The Olympic Games are the ultimate image-transfer device,' says Michael Payne in the curious sales-speak one might expect of the IOC's marketing director, the man responsible for selling the Games. Nevertheless, even in Coca-Cola's home town, no branding opportunity has been allowed to be missed: Coke rented a church in downtown Atlanta for the six months leading up to the Games, so that they might plaster their own logo in a suitably visible location.

Visa is another global sponsor which has experienced the success of marketing its brand through the Olympics. They doubled the number of credit cards they issued in Norway after the 1994 Lillehammer Winter Games. When Fuji became the official film sponsors of the 1984 Games, their market share in the United States grew from two per cent to ten per cent, despite a huge advertising campaign mounted against them by Kodak. In Atlanta, Kodak will be among the main Olympic sponsors.

The Olympics are the greatest symbol of universally admired values such as success and excellence. As the amounts of corporate cash in the Olympics has increased, so too has the financial success of those competitors renowned for their excellence. The amateur creed has disappeared, allowing some athletes to cash in on their Olympic golds and become millionaires. There is no reason why not: when de Coubertin (a French baron, remember) founded the modern Olympics, he insisted that they should be amateur because he felt that that would be the best guarantee of the highest standards of gentlemanly fair play. In effect, he wanted to keep the 'riff raff' out: when the rules on amateurism were being drafted by the eminent Victorians who founded the Amateur Athletic Association in England, they did so deliberately to exclude artisans and labourers. Such working men (there was no women's athletics at the time) could not afford to train and compete for nothing, so by making their sport strictly amateur, the governing bodies reinforced class divisions through sport.

There was no historical basis for amateurism, since the ancient Greek Games on which de Coubertin modelled his Olympics were very much professional. But this amateur ethos became ingrained into the concept of the modern Olympics. The leisured rich did not want to compete with workingclass athletes, whose muscles had been hardened and toned by manual labour. As the Establishment reinforced the idea that accepting money for competing was beneath the dignity of a true Olympian, the amateur rules were applied to ensure that competitors were banned from receiving their regular job's salary while they were training, and that they never received a penny profit off the track for the fame that they had won on the track.

The rules on amateurism were applied so strictly that disgrace awaited anyone who transgressed. The most famous, and saddest, case is that of Jim Thorpe, the American who was possibly the finest all-round athlete of the first half of the 20th century. Thorpe was stripped of the gold medals he won for the decathlon and pentathlon at the 1912 Stockholm Games when it was discovered that he had received $25 per week for playing baseball during the summers of 1909 and 1910. It was not until Thorpe had been dead for 30 years, in 1983, that the medals were restored to his family.

Sixth in the decathlon behind Thorpe in Stockholm had been another American, Avery Brundage. Brundage had no sympathy for his team-mate. 'The Olympic Games are a devotion to cause and not reward,' he said. But then he could afford to, since unlike part-Indian Thorpe, Brundage became a millionaire through his Chicago building interests. Brundage was to be president of the US Olympic Committee from 1929 to 1953, and held the most powerful position in the Olympic Movement, president of the IOC, for 20 years, until 1972.

During his time in charge, Brundage ruled the Games 'with despotic firmness', according to one insider. One of his last acts was to ban the Austrian skier, Karl Schranz, for taking money for wearing a particular brand of skis at the 1972 Winter Olympics. Yet when Schranz returned to Vienna, far from finding himself in disgrace for taking the filthy lucre, he was met at the airport by a crowd of 100,000 people demanding his reinstatement. Brundage refused to budge. 'The devotion of the true amateur athlete is the same devotion that makes an artist starve in his garret rather than commercialise his work,' said the IOC president.

After Brundage stood down following the Munich Games, the irresistible tide of professionalism began to flow into the Olympics. A year after Brundage's death, at the Montreal Olympics of 1976, his own event and that of Jim Thorpe, the decathlon, was won by another American, Bruce Jenner. After the Games, Jenner cashed in on his Olympic gold, making $3 million by appearing on everything from Wheaties boxes to television shows such as *CHiPS*. It was in 1987 that the IOC finally struck the word 'amateur' from its charter, allowing the individual governing bodies to determine their own rules on eligibility.

By 1992, when Linford Christie won the 100 metres title in Barcelona, almost anything went. Overnight, Christie's Olympic victory catapulted him on to millionaires' row. Instead of being able to get perhaps £15,000 per race in appearance fees from European meeting promoters, Christie was able to demand £25,000 a race. He received a gold medal bonus of £50,000 from his kit sponsors Puma, and had his retainer increased to £120,000 per year when he renegotiated his contract. It was not as if Christie was not already acknowledged as one of the best sprinters in the world. The difference was the Olympics: everyone in the world watches the Olympics.

'The Olympics are a tremendous focus for world attention,' David Hemery, a gold medallist at 400 metres hurdles in 1968, says. 'Everyone is watching the Olympics. They offer a great chance to influence the way people think.'

Not even athletics's own World Championships can compete with the Olympics. After Donovan Bailey won the 100 metres at the 1995 World Championships in Gothenburg, he expected a hero's welcome in Canada. He could not have been more wrong. One evening at home in Toronto after the season had finished, he was showing a couple of friends around town and took them to a nightclub. On the strength of his Gothenburg gold, he thought he might be able to persuade the doorman to waive the $5 admission charge. The bouncer was nonplussed. 'But I'm Donovan Bailey.'

'Who?' the bouncer replied.

'The world 100 metres champion,' Bailey said.

'It's *still* $5.'

It is hard to believe that Bailey would have received the same treatment had he been able to say that he was the *Olympic* 100 metres champion.

One thing which the Olympics did seem to stand for, though, was that winning was not everything. In July 1908, while in London for the IV Olympic Games, Baron de Coubertin attended a special service in Westminster Abbey in which the Bishop of Pennsylvania preached a sermon which was to influence him profoundly. De Coubertin adopted the sermon for a speech he was to make a few days later and which has been used at every Games Opening Ceremony since:

'The most important thing in the Olympic Games is not to win but to take part, just as the most important thing in life is not the triumph but the struggle. The essential thing is not to have conquered but to have fought well.' But try telling that to Mike McLeod.

Mike McLeod would probably not have the admission charge waived for him, even in a nightclub in his native Elswick, in north-east England. Yet in the early 1980s, McLeod was one of the world's finest distance runners. His career reached its pinnacle in 1984, when he finished third in the Olympic 10,000 metres final in Los Angeles. To McLeod, this was reward aplenty for 20 years of pounding the roads and tracks around Tyneside, since his athletic ability was first spotted when he won the Newcastle Schools' cross-country wearing a pair of two-shilling Woolworth plimsolls.

By rights, though, instead of being on the third rung of the presentation podium when the medals were handed out in the LA Coliseum, Mike McLeod should have stood on the top of the rostrum and collected gold. Yet like so many Olympic competitors, McLeod was denied his greatest moment by runners for whom the only important thing was success at any cost.

Two days after the presentation ceremony, silver medal-winner Marti Vainio made history when it was announced that he was the first athletics medallist at the Games to fail a drugs test. The 33-year-old Finn was warming up for the heats of the 5,000 metres when he was pulled off the track and given the news that traces of the muscle-building steroid Promobolin had been found in his urine sample. Despite protesting his innocence, Vainio was disqualified. It was only much later that it was revealed that Vainio should never have been allowed to even toe the start line in the Olympic Games. Earlier in 1984, Vainio had raced in the Rotterdam Marathon and had failed a drugs test then, but the outcome had been hushed up by the Finnish federation to allow their man to compete at the Olympics. The national coach, Antii Lanamaki, resigned after admitting to the cover-up, and Vainio was banned for life by the International Amateur Athletic Federation.

McLeod was officially promoted to second place in the Olympic 10,000 metres, but because Vainio refused to surrender his ill-gotten silver medal, it was not until the spring of 1985 that McLeod was finally presented with the second place prize – a new one had had to be struck.

Although the 10,000 metres had long been one of Britain's strongest events, no British athletes had ever finished higher than third in an Olympic final. McLeod's feat was not acknowledged in front of nearly 100,000 cheering spectators in the Olympic Stadium, though: instead, McLeod received his Olympic silver medal in London's Battersea Park on a chill, damp April day, prior to the AAA 10-kilometre road race championship, witnessed by just a handful of athletics die-hards and a few bemused dog-walkers.

Yet today, of the three men who stood on the medal rostrum in Los

Angeles, only McLeod's athletics reputation remains untarnished. For Alberto Cova, the Italian who took gold ahead of the Briton and Vainio, has even admitted to using a technique which was to be banned straight after the Games.

The sudden rise of Italian distance runners in the 1980s reached a pinnacle at the 1986 European Championships when Stefano Mai, Cova and Salvatore Antibo enjoyed a clean sweep of the medals in the 10,000 metres. Such domination created much suspicion, and within weeks of their triumph the runners' achievements had created a national scandal in Italy. Romano Tardelli, for more than 15 years responsible for middle distance running with the Italian athletics federation, FIDAL, openly accused his bosses of buying drugs, supplying them to athletes, and of organising blood doping. Without naming athletes, Tardelli said: 'The practice of doping by anabolic steroids and blood transfusions by FIDAL and other sports federations has now reached such a serious level as to create the real assumption that punishable crimes are being committed against the community and athletes subjected to the treatment,' he said.

The banned practice of blood doping involves the withdrawal and storage of an athlete's red blood cells, the reinfusion of which, prior to competition, helps to increase the oxygen carrying capacity of the blood. It is estimated that the practice can improve performances by five per cent. Blood doping was banned immediately after the Los Angeles Games, though there has never been a satisfactory test developed to determine whether an athlete has been 'boosted' with his or her own blood.

It was against this unsavoury backdrop that Mike McLeod had been trying for years to make an honest impression on the running scene. Despite evidence that Marti Vainio had tested positive for drugs in Rotterdam and Los Angeles, his life ban was dropped by the IAAF in February 1986. Less than two months later, he was back in international competition, lining up alongside McLeod and Cova in Neuchâtel, Switzerland, for the World Cross-country Championships.

'Once caught, they should be banned for life,' McLeod said. 'That is the most sickening thing of all – especially to those who train hard without breaking the rules.'

Today, despite Tardelli's allegations and Cova's own admissions of using blood doping, the 1984 Olympic 10,000 metres gold medallist is an Italian national hero, and a member of his country's parliament. Meanwhile, Mike McLeod runs a modest printing business in the shadow of the Gateshead International stadium, where he used to thrill thousands of Geordies who came to watch him run. How many more might have come to see him race had he not been denied that Olympic gold medal?

McLeod is still an active athlete, regularly competing on the veterans' circuit, but he remains embittered that he was effectively cheated out of what was rightfully his in Los Angeles. 'Part of the problem is that there is too much money in athletics these days and politics is taking a hold,' he says sadly. 'The rewards on offer are so big that some people are tempted to cheat – tempted to the point where they will put their lives at risk.'

Considering that one Olympic champion has gone on record to deride de Coubertin's Olympic motto – 'Whoever said "It's not the winning that matters but the taking part" was a loser' – it is little wonder that athletics has lost its innocence, and that so many athletes are now running scared.